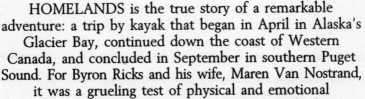

"Soon the entrance w.....
the moment when we leave.....
like generations of pa.....
creatures of the .....

HOMELANDS is the true story of a remarkable
adventure: a trip by kayak that began in April in Alaska's
Glacier Bay, continued down the coast of Western
Canada, and concluded in September in southern Puget
Sound. For Byron Ricks and his wife, Maren Van Nostrand,
it was a grueling test of physical and emotional
endurance: five months spent riding a breathtaking
waterway, exploring the beauty, wonders, and perils of an
enduring but fragile wilderness. Their journey took them
through magnificent fiords and among islands broken by
wind and weather—around capes and across sounds aptly
named "Caution" and "Desolation"—and carried them
into the extraordinary lives and stories of courageous free
spirits and Native inhabitants; those who willingly chose a
more isolated existence and those tied to it by culture,
history, and a tenacious love of these harsh, yet magical
northern lands.

With enthralling, evocative prose, Ricks transports the
reader along with him and Maren on every leg of their
incomparable expedition—sharing awe-inspiring
encounters with bear, wolf and orca, and uncommon
experiences with unique individuals who inhabit and
revere the lonely, endangered places. Their journey is one
that will not be soon forgotten—for it is one that draws
the reader deeper and deeper into a magnificent
wilderness, and ever-closer to that province the heart and
the spirit know as "home."

HOMELANDS
KAYAKING THE INSIDE PASSAGE

BYRON RICKS

With Illustrations by Maren Van Nostrand

AN AVON BOOK

AVON BOOKS, INC.
1350 Avenue of the Americas
New York, New York 10019

Text copyright © 1999 by Byron Martin Ricks
Illustrations and map copyright © 1999 by Maren Thyra Van Nostrand
Inside back cover author photograph by Stacy and Todd Powell
Interior design by Kellan Peck
Published by arrangement with the author
ISBN: 0-380-80918-4
www.avonbooks.com/bard

Library of Congress Cataloging in Publication Data:

Ricks, Byron.
    Homelands : Kayaking the Inside Passage / Byron Ricks.
        p.   cm.
    Includes bibliographical references.
    1. Kayaking—Inside Passage Guidebooks.   2. Ricks, Byron—
Journeys—Inside Passage Guidebooks.   3. Van Nostrand, Maren—
Journeys—Inside Passage Guidebooks.   4. Inside Passage Guidebooks.
I. Title.
GV776.I49R53   1999   99-25357
917.98'2—dc21   CIP

First Bard Printing: July 1999

BARD TRADEMARK REG. U.S. PAT. OFF. AND IN OTHER COUNTRIES, MARCA REGISTRADA, HECHO
EN U.S.A.

Printed in the U.S.A.

OPM   10   9   8   7   6   5   4   3   2

For my grandparents and parents,
for my sister,
for Maren

Each day is a journey and the journey itself, home.

MATSUO BASHŌ, *1689*

AUTHOR'S NOTE

There can never be a single, definitive book written about this complex coast. I am deliberately elusive to guard the places we found to camp and the sites where traditional peoples dwell and visit. When we left shore each morning, we never knew where we would find shelter, and discovering for ourselves these nightly homes was as much adventure as feats of knowledge, planning, and faith. This was part of the contemporary journey as well as the way the coast has been long known—by experience. To name particular places so that readers would be able to unfailingly plot our nightly stops would be to dismantle the spirit of our journey and affront those who have long paddled those waters.

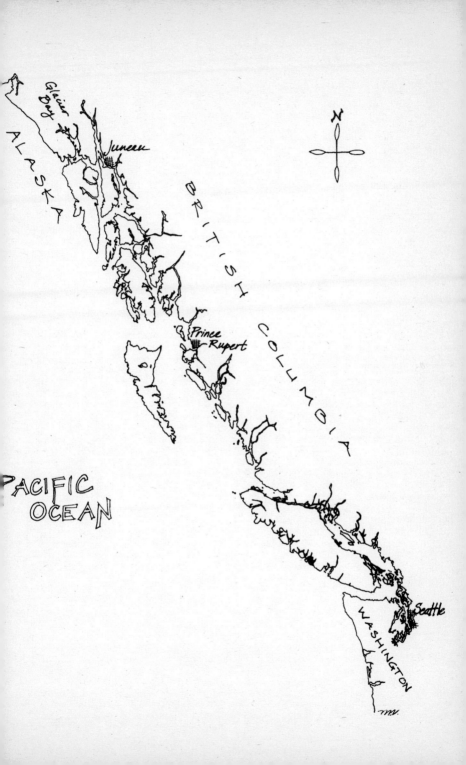

CONTENTS

The Passage North

For five months in the spring and summer of 1996, Maren and I traveled the Inside Passage, an expedition of two, husband and wife, voyaging from our Puget Sound home to Juneau by ferry, then from Juneau to Glacier Bay by small boat. When the motors at last stopped at Sebree Island, dissolving into the great hollow of Glacier Bay, we began to paddle home.

It was a long and beautiful journey, a season of bright sun and dark cloud, above-average rainfall, and broad shoulders; a first for us in sheer length—a human-powered trip that could be measured on the globe. In portions, we navigated the Alaska Marine Highway, where freeway speeds average some fifteen knots. By kayak, our average velocity was three knots, often two. In five months, we spent a single day in shorts and T-shirts. Every day we learned to read the sea. We had no set schedules, and itineraries depended more on tides, winds, weather, and our endurance than any advanced scheming. It was a homecoming of sorts as well as a getting away, a deliberate change of pace from one set by punchcards to one set by paddles. As Maren has so often said, it was a gradual adventure.

It was a time before home ownership, before children—an open window, and all we had to do was leap through. And we did. We could list dozens of journeys—warm ones, dry ones, or trips that involved something more familiar than kayaking. Although we had both developed outdoor skills through other travels together—bicycling, climbing, canoeing, and countless backpacking excursions—kayaking the Inside Passage would require commitments of learning new skills, new equipment. And the uneasiness that came with this uncharted territory soon became part of the adventure. But we had a feeling this coast was in flux, that there would be things to see that in only a few years would be scarce or gone—its vast unlogged sections, its small communities not yet given to mass tourism, other pockets that perhaps no one had visited in more than a century. And unlike other journeys we could have chosen, this one was connected to our lives. Paddling from the glaciers, we would conclude where we had left off—in the city—and that took on a significance all its own. The very name, Inside Passage, carried an intimacy, a knowing. It would be a personal voyage. As much as anything, it would be a journey home.

The Northwest Coast, from Kodiak Island in Alaska to the redwoods of the central California coast, is a temperate region that spans extremes. At its northern reaches it mingles with subarctic environs, while its southern end brushes a desert. It is a middle ground, a distinct ecological unit, a bioregion bound on the west by the Pacific Ocean and on the east by high coastal mountains. The rain forest here is the largest of its kind, carrying one of the greatest sheer masses of life of any ecosystem. Just inland, over the Coast Range, the world changes within a few miles of the mountain crests. Rainfall diminishes, summers are hot, winters frigid. But north to south along the coast such changes are subtle; the weather, wet and mild, the skies mostly gray.

At its midsection the coast is broken into islands that seem to drift from the mainland like freshly calved bergs. Among these islands is a labyrinth of waterways, a thousand miles of flooded glacial troughs that extend from Cross Sound and the upper reaches of Lynn Canal and Glacier Bay in southeast Alaska to the tidal flats of southern Puget Sound, the stretch of sheltered waters known as the Inside Passage.

But "inside" is somewhat a misnomer. South of the Alexander Archipelago, a broad band of nearly 1,100 islands that constitute most of southeast Alaska, the islands part at Dixon Entrance, exposing the mainland to the open Pacific before islands resume along the northern British Columbia coast in an interplay of small sounds and narrow channels. These islands, too, eventually conclude in the expanse of Queen Charlotte Sound. Once behind the shield of Vancouver Island, the waters funnel and race along the mainland in a series of straits and tidal rapids which continue as the Gulf Islands trickle into the San Juan Islands and the gentle shores of Puget Sound.

By the time the Russians and Europeans arrived in these "inside" waters in the mid to late 1700s, searching for sea otter pelts and the fabled Northwest Passage of trade, more than thirty Native groups had developed. They were people of the sea, whose life rhythm was of the tides, whose ways had evolved as the ice withdrew. From north to south along the passage, they are the Tlingit, Nisga'a, Tsimshian, Haida, Haisla, Heiltsuk, Nuxalk, Kwakwaka'wakw, and Coast Salish. Each cultural group embodies numerous tribes and nations, dialects and languages. When the first billowing sails came over the horizon, the Northwest coast was, after California, the second most linguistically diverse area of North America, an established waterway teeming with salmon and flotillas of cedar canoes.

Unlike these Native peoples, who had often paddled the entire length of the passage as polished merchants, warriors, or potlatch guests, we would have no one along who had paddled the coast before us, no uncles, aunts, fathers, mothers, brothers, or sisters who carried the map within. Our mentors would be those whom we met, pallid nautical charts, and a few guidebooks: a thick tide table, *Coast Pilot*, for Alaska and two volumes of *Sailing Directions* for British Columbia. It was a small library, guidance made of paper and vulnerable to the sea itself, and to the extent that this knowledge was not written for paddlers, it was excess baggage, more ballast than benefit. Unlike larger craft confined to midchannel navigational lanes, we could hug the shores, the knobs of headland, the deep coves, and land on beaches as wide as our hips.

We spent the winter in the snowless lowlands of Seattle, shopping and gathering at a wholesale food warehouse by the Duwamish River, preparing for the trip. Food dehydrators hummed through the nights, two cylindrical towering infernos reeking of garlic and herbs de Provence. Maren's home-cooked split-pea, red-rice, and lentil soups were dried and pulverized in the blender to a powder as fine as glacial silt. Sixty-one meals of dried spaghetti sauce emerged as hubcap-sized leather disks, tasty and translucent, so that when held to the light, they resembled stained glass. It was our equivalent to smoking and drying salmon for a long journey. By mid-February we had six months of double-bagged dehydrated meals, and in every spare moment we centered on the sea.

We paddled at every chance. On Wednesdays and Saturdays we would lug the kayaks to a local swimming pool, mastering braces, rolls, and various rescues while kids waited in the locker room to do cannonballs off the diving board. They would laugh at me in my neoprene socks, and when I paddled a kayak around the deep end, they would point and snicker and shout, "Roll it!"

In mid-March the comet Hyakutake swept across the sky, and we spilled out into the yard to see it, stark and visible through the haze of city light. It had last come thousands of years before and shone over the shrinking Pleistocene ice. Its tail swept across the Big Dipper, and we read every foreboding sign into it that we could think of. By early April we had moved out of our apartment and dispersed cats, furniture, and miscellaneous oddities to friends. And in the nights before we left, Maren sealed six boxes of dried food for mailing, while I gathered equipment and trimmed borders off nautical charts so they would fit into waterproof cases. We were ready.

On the morning of April 5, friends drove us north to Bellingham, where we boarded the Alaska State Ferry *Columbia* and bivouacked between seats in the TV lounge—steerage. Then we went to the railing and waved good-bye to the friends who would manage our urban affairs in the months to come, mail our food boxes, pay our bills. With a snort of diesel, the ferry pulled from these known faces. The land fell away, blurred, and the ferry carved a neat white arc and slipped into the northern darkness.

That first night, a bearded man who had been shouting in the café about Jesus and jail stood calmly against the stern railing. The lights of distant towns were as frail as candlelight, and the nebulous haze of Vancouver was fading to twinkling buoys. We stood silently for a time, watching the scene as if watching Earth itself shrink from view. "Lord willing, we'll be away from that city soon," he said. "The money thing. The problems. I can't wait until the sky gets black."

Maren and I went to sleep in known waters and awoke to a new world. I climbed to the high deck that first morning and stared some sixty feet down at the plane of water sweeping by. We glided from clear-cut to forest. Rivers belched ruddy outflows from their eroded drainages. Fragments of floating trees collided with the hull in thunks and scrapes. Logging camps and small towns enshrouded in plumes of blue smoke grew, then shrank from view. We had no clue about the tides.

This early-season ferry was a ship of working people and occasional tourists, and we spent the days hobnobbing among the varied passengers. Conversations sparked easily, and a shipwide camaraderie soon developed, seeming to echo the Klondike Gold Rush days of one hundred years ago as we held in common the exhilarating dreams, the grand tradition of heading north, of going to Alaska. We met rural doctors, foresters, backpackers, helicopter pilots, clergy, stock brokers, restaurant workers, realtors, and folk singers—modern counterparts to the prospectors, scientists, missionaries, traders, and tourists who had once packed Inside Passage steamers. And as we talked and laughed and sang, the islands swept past, the ferry listing to port and then to starboard as it snaked through silver channels, along precipitous shores. In Queen

Charlotte Sound, swells atomized on islets that were no more than rocks, then dissipated once we reached the cover of larger islands. The ferry ride was expedient by our standards as kayakers. In three days we would travel what it would take us months to paddle. It was the brief introduction of our lives to come.

The second night, as we crossed the open waters of Dixon Entrance, a man began to scream in his sleep. I lay bolt awake for some time listening to him, feeling the rising and falling ship, the sheer power of the sea. What were we about to do? I thought about how spare our lives had become. The last night in our apartment, we had slept in two sleeping bags beneath the northern and southern maps of the Inside Passage. Nothing else had been left in the place. The maps had scrolled down the wall, the miles of water and forest trailing to our slumbering bodies. Now we were sailing on it, the real passage, and we were vulnerable to all the forces that had shaped it. The next morning, while strolling along deck, we found dried vomit clinging to the railings. "My god," Maren said, "I want to go back."

The next evening was windless. I found Maren in the café singing harmony on "The Water is Wide" with a wood carver and an Episcopal archbishop. As I listened, a small girl unrolled a sketch that she had made of mountains and water, a solitary canoe tethered to a stump by a cabin. "This is paradise," she said. It was drawn wonderfully, her dream in pencil. When the singers disbanded, Maren and I strolled to the solarium deck and saw the comet brushed into a feathery trail by the solar wind. Venus shone above the western mountains and across the water. We paused. Planet shine.

On April 8, at 5:15 A.M., we arrived at Auke Bay. The peaks to the west were dazzling in the early sun, a snowy blanket simplifying and smoothing their forms. We were gaining seven and a half minutes of daylight each day, and as I scribbled a checklist, my pen's shadow already equaled its length.

We spent the rest of that gloriously sunny week in Juneau, ascending its curving streets and mountain valleys, exploring outdoor shops, buying extra bootlaces and another fuel bottle, asking for advice, watching the tides rise and fall in Gastineau Channel, waiting for our ride, waiting for rain. On Saturday, April 13, as a high plane of clouds marbled the sky, we set out for Glacier Bay.

ARCHIPELAGO

To Glacier Bay

At 7 A.M. Maren and I join Peter, our skipper, and David, a photographer and avid paddler. We heave equipment into a stubby boat, untie the dock lines, and motor from shore. It is calm and smooth in Auke Bay, and we are reeling with the first moments of adventure. But gradually, as the water opens to Lynn Canal, the waves come and, within ten minutes, explode over the bow.

"Lynn Canal can sure scream," Peter says, gripping the wheel.

Boosh. Boosh. Boosh. Maren and I hold on to the superstructure for balance, bending our knees with the dips and rises as if riding horses. I scan the shore, looking for campsites.

Seeing these expanses, the vast stretch of Lynn Canal and Chatham Strait opening to a continuous wind tunnel from Skagway to the open Pacific, we hurl questions at ourselves. Again we mistrust the two-dimensional fantasy of maps, see fiction in the notion that the Inside Passage is a tranquil waterway. It is the paradoxical horror of not knowing exactly what we have gotten into yet knowing exactly. Despite our winter of training, we feel a lacking, an ineptitude as abysmal as the

11

Chatham Strait Fault below us. A crest of salt water beats on the plastic windows, and I jerk away.

"When you leave Glacier Bay, I would think about getting a ride across Icy Strait," Peter says. "Someday, somebody is going to die there."

My knees nearly buckle as the boat plows into a wave.

A humpback whale breaches in a smooth arc of splash water. "Humpsterdumpster!" Peter shouts.

"Getting ready for the tourists," laughs David.

Visitor season is waxing in southeast Alaska, and we have the first charter of the year to Glacier Bay, speeding toward the peaks of the Fairweather Range. Once we round the Mansfield Peninsula, the waves reach from behind, and the engine gurgles as if drowning, then surges as the propeller is lifted free of the water. At last, as we turn westward into Icy Strait and the lee of the northwesterly, the waters flatten, and the boat seems to leap into high gear.

"Spirit Walker, Spirit Walker . . ." Peter radios.

Static.

"Spirit Walker, Spirit Walker . . ."

This is someone I would like to meet about now. But by the time start to I ask who this Spirit Walker is, Peter is on the radio again, hailing Glacier Bay headquarters to announce our arrival.

Our kayaks are strapped to the back deck, hulls to the sky as if capsized. Last night I discovered a moon-shaped dent in my kayak's hull. Oil-canned. I felt weak. We had planned for everything—but not this. After retracing the journey north, I concluded that when the ferry passed through the swells in Queen Charlotte Sound, my kayak had shifted, coming to rest on a piece of plywood. I thought nothing of it at the time, but we were over the engine room. The deck was warm, the kayak heavy, and together, the heat softened the fiberglass resin and the force reformed the hull. During a phone call last evening, the manufacturer prescribed a series of boat bakes, which will take place over campfires with crude drift-wood braces punching out the shallow dish. For now, though,

I do not know how the kayak will perform, and the very problem magnifies other worries tenfold.

We throttle wide around Pleasant Island Reef, around the low knobs of Pleasant Island, named in 1879 by W. H. Dall of the U.S. Coast and Geodetic Survey for its gentle shores—a name that stuck from a first impression. British Captain George Vancouver, who explored and charted this coast between 1792 and 1794, searching for the Northwest Passage, left a much greater legacy all along the Inside Passage in a blanket of place names that often recall the extreme gloom and peril, elation and pleasantry, of his person and his voyage. From an instructive angle, these names impart the moods, incidents, and mistakes of a traveler to this coast and in this way announce what may lie ahead for us: Point Carolus. Point Retreat. Cape Caution. Rather than Icy, I would name this strait "Apprehension" or, if conditions worsen, "Out of our Gourds."

Slowly the mouth of Glacier Bay opens. When Vancouver and his survey crews were here, Glacier Bay was little more than an indentation. The Neoglacial, or Little Ice Age, glaciers, had only begun to retract. Since that time, the glaciers have withdrawn rapidly nearly one hundred miles to the upper reaches of the inlets, where we will find them, leaving a broad bay of shieldlike islands ice free. Past the town of Gustavus, we make the big bend north into Glacier Bay, into the wind, into the waves, on the trail of retreating ice.

At Bartlett Cove, we stop to check in with Randy King, chief ranger, who spreads the large nautical chart across the floor. "You have bear canisters?" he asks. "It's required in the park."

"Six." Maren says.

"Firearms?"

"No," she says, her face falling. And the whole bear question rushes in again, dark thoughts, the stuff of nightmares. "Just bear spray. Repellent."

"Seasoning," someone says. "Shake 'n Bake."

"No firearms are allowed in the park," Randy continues. "Just don't keep food in your tent. Cook in the tide lines."

As we talk, Randy's wife, Sally, brings a tray of hot drinks, and we cup the warm stoneware. Everyone talks about the joys of kayaking, the serenity the trip will bring, and Maren and I laugh and nod as best we can. Then we slurp the chocolate syrup from the base of the mugs, say our farewells, and speed north from Bartlett Cove's old forest of Sitka spruce to the lesser forest on Sebree Island in midbay, where the fifteen-mile-wide face of the Grand Pacific Glacier had last been in 1860.

Coasting toward shore, Maren and I leap from the small boat into the shallows and begin unloading gear and kayaks onto the cobbles. The afternoon has cleared, with a brisk northwesterly gathering among the upper inlets of ice and snow and bellowing across the expanse of the lower bay. We wince in the lunar glare of the beach and fumble to find sunglasses. Accounting for every bag, then leaning against the aluminum hull, I sign a check for the ride, shake hands, and put my checkbook away. It is the moment that we knew would come, when at last the motors have stopped. As the boat pulls away, a picture is taken. And we give a final wave.

For some time Maren and I stare after the craft that has brought us here, an aberration on the landscape, slowly retreating toward the distant western shore, its silver hull becoming gray, then absent.

"Well," I say.

"Well," Maren says. "We are here."

The quiet is uncomfortable and new, and so we began to sing to the bears. "Hello, bears." *Clap. Clap.* "Hey-ho." *Clap. Clap.* Searching for our first campsite among the Sitka spruce and shoreline alder, Maren summons a majestic theme from Hovhaness. I sing the Ramones. No bears. But we carry canisters of bear repellent like ready pistols, a chain of dry bags draped over each shoulder, and go wobbling into the dark forest in search of level ground.

In Glacier Bay

APRIL 14

We are here and alone.

The sky surges with storm, and when it brightens, a distant sun stares through racing cloud. Lenticulars, roaring with wind, truncate the Fairweather Range to the west, and south, to Icy Strait and Chichagof Island, the mouth of Glacier Bay is blue with squalls. By midmorning, the first rain spits against the tarp. On this date eighty-four years ago the *Titanic* struck an iceberg and began to sink. We will not paddle today.

Our world has been distilled into mounds of equipment, the stuff of survival piled about like strange precipitate: parachute flares, a month of food crammed into the bear canisters, an extra tent, extra tarps, a stove, stainless pots, five fuel bottles, extra paddles, AA batteries for the radio, dry suits, dry boxes, a water filter, a bow saw, two headlamps, a bulk of winter clothes, rescue beacons, six candles . . . All in bags. Mostly sausagelike. Mostly waterproof. Mostly yellow and blue. Bags heaped in the vestibule and around the tent. We believe the weight of Earth may only differ by a factor of four. As I reach for the bag I believe holds my hat, the screech of nylon wakes Maren. She smiles and resumes her dream.

We've counted more than a decade together. We have routines for cooking and camp. Trust. Things will fall into place.

I am sometimes amazed that she agreed to come on this journey. It has taken her from her career as an environmental planner, her singing. She carries a natural grace and rhythm with her life that grew from early years spent in Minnesota's quiet lakes with the paddle. She is muscular, even powerful, sleek and fit, a veteran canoeist with lean canoeist's arms. We met on a canoeing trip in college, and journeys into the wilds have been as much a part of our time together as central heating and cats. She is equally at home camping as singing with a symphony. From silence she will burst into song, joyful songs, sung in precise rhythms, exactly on key. She also can read the rhythms of herself, of our dynamics together, and I know this will save us from recklessness, somewhere down passage.

As she rises, the weather has changed little. On clear days the wind generally blows from the northwest. On days of storm it blows from the southeast. But today the wind is shifty. We are between seasons, and the two atmospheric powers that dominate this coast muscle for position overhead. The North Pacific High that hovers off Northern California all winter is pressing northward into its summer range, deflecting the Aleutian Low, rerouting its parade of cyclonic storms and prevailing southerly winds toward the Bering Sea. In late spring, when the transition is complete, when the seasons truly change here, storms will soften and the North Pacific High will bring northwesterly winds to the coast: tailwinds. For now, though, we are early, and no one we have talked with seems certain that winter is over. In Cross Sound, north of Chichagof Island, where the Inside Passage becomes outside coast, seas still build to twenty-five feet, and nearly everyone has a story about some legendary April storm that blew like the depths of winter.

By midday we amble onto the beach. The wind has backed to the southwest, and the crash of waves resonates through the forest. I try to get the weather. Our radio, a portable marine VHF, crackles with static—a radio-dead area. It is a morning that rustles with doubt, inklings that we have unnecessarily disrupted our lives. And I sit, consumed with the why of adventure. Later I catch the glint of Peter's boat speeding past Willoughby Island and out of the bay.

Gradually, almost imperceptibly, time unravels. I find myself spending hours poring over charts, then watch the water bottles drip full of snowmelt. While Maren repacks the bear canisters, I dance to higher ground with a pot of bubbling shrimp Creole, the spidery stove burning like a blowtorch as the waves advance.

After eating, squatting beside dirty pots as the tide sinks away, I pick among the small stones. On beaches, my father is always stooped, fooling with rocks, occasionally lifting one to examine in the sunlight, mesmerized, contemplating the depths of quartz and the moons of Jupiter. He has passed along this tendency to me, and I discover this Sebree Island beach is mostly gray granite and sedimentaries, pebbles and cobbles, broken and smoothed first by ice, now by water. The moon: waning to new. Snow is fresh on the high peaks, and spring is nearly a month old.

It is already tempting to respond to this land with words such as "untouched" and "pristine," in much the same way John Muir did when he first ventured here from Fort Wrangell in the fall of 1879 by Tlingit-guided and Tlingit-powered cedar canoe. And feeling the great alone of today, this conjecture is most easy to believe. But I know that it is not true. It will not be true for the length of this coast where names show the advance and retreat of cultures—Native, Russian, French, Spanish, British, American, corporate—as clearly as striations evidence the advance and retreat of ice. Contemporary placenames tell the story: Hoonah, Baranof, La Perouse, Prince of Wales, Bella Bella, God's Pocket, Fort Rupert, Vancouver, Victoria, San Juan, Swinomish, Seattle, Ideal Bay, Federal Way. And here in Glacier Bay, place names flow across my chart—Muir Glacier, Muir Inlet, Muir Point, Hunter Cove, Mount Cooper, Carroll Glacier—testament that others have been here, explorers, scientists, and sightseers, and not so long ago. With few exceptions, these printed names mask the names that came before, the names known by oral tradition, the Tlingit names, as if a glacier had scoured them away.

Changes came rapidly to these waters. In 1880 when the first steamer, the *Favorite*, arrived to survey the area, its commander, Lester Anthony Beardslee, added the name "Glacier Bay" to the chart. And Muir's talks and tales of Alaska helped bring more steamers—the *Queen, Idaho, Ancon, George W. Elder,* and *City of Topeka*—enterprising captains, and tourists, so that in a decade the Inside Passage and Glacier Bay were quite different than when Muir had first come by paddle.

But the Tlingit, who have long lived, hunted and fished here, had also known the glaciers well. The Tlingit of the Tcukanadi clan own a story, one handed down from mother to daughter, that tells of when an ancestral village was destroyed by advancing ice and the Tlingit clans were driven from the bay, dispersing across Icy Strait, eventually to settle in Hoonah on Chichagof Island.

Most powerfully for me, this Glacier Bay story is an enduring cultural memory of a natural event. I know of no such enduring memory of the inundation of Puget Sound by glaciers, no cultural reminders beyond science that it has been overrun by ice. Too often I see a division between past and present, understand history as a course rather than the stories of ancestors, my own or another's. This beach, once buried by the Grand Pacific Glacier, now represents that nexus of human and natural histories, where a glacial advance was indelibly impressed upon the human mind, upon the heart of a culture. It is the way people first saw much of this coast— the Inside Passage—nearly within reach of ice. This is how we, too, will begin to see it.

In early evening the sky clears. After mending a grommet, we paddle the short distance to Tlingit Point, the center divide of Glacier Bay. We carry the kayaks to the water, one at a time, Maren cradling the bow, me cradling the stern, balancing as we step across the shifting cobbles. Then, like two davits lowering a lifeboat, we place each kayak in the water parallel to the shore and begin the awkward, crablike maneuver of getting in. I step in, one foot at a time, sensing the uneasiness of my weight in water. In heavy surf you paddle straight into the breakers, taking them unabashedly, riding up and over their foamy crests. But along the inside waters it is mostly taken from the side, like stepping across a crevasse, pausing at midstride to peer down into the blue.

As I hang over the shallows, bracing with my paddle, waves surge and slip back. The kayaks, afloat, suddenly fall onto the rocks, as what was just flooded sucks dry. Half piked, I slip in and stab at the water in short, inefficient strokes, finally freeing myself from the rocks. Soon the entrance will become routine, the moment when we leave the land and become, like generations of paddlers before us, creatures of the sea.

Past an offshore rock, a creek fans into the bay, its outflow nudging the kayak. Surf scoters venture near but keep their distance at the threshold of assured escape. A large black stone stands on Tlingit Point, bent and twisted with lines of metamorphosed rock, the inarticulate scrawl of geology.

Bobbing off Tlingit Point, we decide to head up the east arm, an intimate fiord, following the retreating Muir Glacier. It is shorter than the west arm—appealing, for we must paddle far south. It is the first of many such route decisions we must make. And after looking long hours at the charts, tracing fiords, reaches, and inlets that encircle islands and lance the mainland, it is already clear that the Inside Passage is not one passage but many.

At Tlingit Point we are at a confluence, the mixing of currents, the division of arms. We clasp hands. To the south the flat outwash plain that is Gustavus and Bartlett Cove is as faint as a streak of charcoal. There are no roads now except the sea, and the sea is nothing like a road.

The kayaks are unloaded and light and quick to respond. We are excited, smiling at each other, laughing even, paddling back to camp, to the dripping spruce, the cobbled beach, to the curtains of mist that come softly to land like feathers drawn across the forehead.

APRIL 15

The morning is inefficient and frustrating as we break camp and load kayaks, making countless trips with bags to and from the water. Maren crams the cylindrical bear canisters into her kayak. Mine looks like a hay wagon, stacked high with a deckload of motley items. Making a conservative placement of the kayaks halfway up the one-hundred-yard beach, we hope that by high tide we will be able to float effortlessly into the water. But as the waves lap at the kayaks, the beach is still strewn with bags, and we must sling everything up five feet and resume loading. Unlike packing a canoe, which easily accommodates a pile of duffels, kayaks accept their load of oblong bags exactly one way, with little margin for error. The water advances again, and once again we lift and toss.

After three hours we are afloat, and everything is easy and smooth. Maren says it must be how sea lions feel when entering the water after wallowing on the rocks. But now the extra loading time has wrecked the day's schedule. The flood current that was to help carry us north has slackened, and soon the ebb waters will flow from the Muir Inlet back to the mouth of Glacier Bay, to Icy Strait and the Pacific.

Paddling a half hour, savoring the first giddy strokes and gliding past the striated rocks of Sebree's eastern shore, we stop at a steep beach, the continuation of the beach that connects Sebree to the mainland of Tlingit Point, to rebalance the kayaks and repack. Awkward again. We have only gone around the island. Wind howls through the trees. Once we are paddling again, rounding even this small point becomes arduous, fighting a northerly wind and an increasing current, the bows slapping the water. We see a cove and call it off. Paddling day one: two miles.

The cove is fingerlike and ringed with downed spruces. A high tide allows us to land on the beach near the trees. Tomorrow's new moon will bring spring tides, and already the tidal difference is more than seventeen feet. Will camp be high enough? And where are the bears? When the tide drops as we make camp, the inlet drains like a swimming pool, exposing steep sides of cobbles and mud and a garden of seaweed at the bottom. In partial shelter from the rain, we cook beneath an immense coil of spruce roots, the tree probably toppled during a winter storm. We hang bags and towels on the root nubs as if hooking them on the many fingers of Shiva, then cook and eat among the intertidal rocks. Any bear-enticing scraps that are left will be flushed away by the sea.

We are taking so much in that our output is minimal, and conversation is reduced to "neat log" or "tide's out" or "it's in the tent." The land is plush moss, a platform growing on little more than glacial rubble, and I sink into it up to my ankles. For the first time the high peaks are visible, and bars of sun sweep their summits and high snow fields. The intermittent clearings in the clouds soon close as quickly as they opened. "Sucker patches," Maren says. Across the inlet avalanche chutes trail down from the snowy tops and fan out in alluvium as the flanks ease and flatten before the shore. Where they meet the water, currents have smoothed them into broad beaches, places we can land. Long clouds snag among trees. We make a tarp to catch rainwater, but the rain ceases immediately. Early tomorrow, we will paddle north with the flood tide.

APRIL 16

Rain. The tide is low, and the finger cove is dry, with only a shallow tidal stream emptying it in a broad curve of rapids to the bay. So we load from the opposite beach, a long walk down the littoral zone on barnacles, blue bay mussels, and seaweed. Steps are careful. It is impossible to get to the water without tramping over colonies of mussels. I cringe at the thought of a fall and the inevitable burning lacerations. The trip could be finished. Last night I barked my shins on a drift log. It seems time on land may be more perilous than time at sea.

Today we time the tides well, and the water meets the

kayaks as we shove off. Traveling north, we paddle together, rarely more than a few boat lengths apart, riding the morning flood current in the main channel until the ebb begins around 1:30 P.M. Working the tides here is like working a train schedule of northbound and southbound traffic, only more predictable. But tidal currents are vexing and complex as they surge across the ocean floor. Although we will surely see many swifter waters, most currents rarely exceed three knots, not intimidating by terrestrial standards, but in a kayak we cannot oppose a three-knot current and make much progress. Timing becomes crucial. But there are tricks: Against a current, we paddle near shore in the eddies where the current slows or even reverses. The northerly wind lifts and steepens the waves. We are edgy, not quite knowing what the water will do. By Adams Inlet, Maren hears the rustling water, the mixing currents producing a small tide rip, pointed waves that stand up and chatter like a brook.

Last night we were under conifers—old spruces—but today spruce has given way to alder and willow. Soon vegetation will be reduced to horsetail and fireweed, then a crust of lichen on glacial stones, then to rock and ice. It is like retreating in time, and every cove now brings a diminished forest cover. The ice receded so quickly here that the entire bay graphically shows forest regeneration after the glaciers. Not long after Muir's first visits, scientists flocked to the Muir Glacier, which soon became the most accessible tidewater glacier in North America. Muir made four visits to Glacier Bay, canoe trips in 1879 and 1880 and steamship journeys in 1890 and 1899, the last as a member of the Harriman Alaska Expedition, an ambitious scientific excursion funded by railroad magnate E. H. Harriman whose illustrious guest list included C. Hart Merriam, chief of the U.S. Biological Survey, *Forest and Stream* editor George Grinnell, naturalist John Burroughs, and photographer Edward S. Curtis, who would become famous for his portraits of Native North American peoples.

In the 1920s ecologist William S. Cooper found the retreating glaciers a prime environment to study plant succession. After delivering a paper on this topic to the Ecological Society of America in 1922, the idea of preserving Glacier Bay was born, and in 1925 Glacier Bay National Monument was established. It grew twice more, once in 1939 to protect brown bear habitat and again in 1980, when it became a national park and preserve. Today, Glacier Bay is one of the most visited places in Alaska. But we are early, and for a few more weeks it will be quiet.

APRIL 17

We carry two paddles each: wide blades for power, narrow blades for low resistance in headwinds. Our kayaks are nearly identical, skins of woven fiberglass and resin, painted a light gray, nearly white like the bellies of seabirds. A black stripe above the waterline cements the deck to the hull, dividing the craft like a horizon. The paddles, too, are these colors. The black graphite shaft, stiff and light, is as smooth as hand-polished wood. The backside of the blade is black graphite fabric, woven like burlap; its face, smooth and pearly, the latest in a long lineage.

Frosty and clear, then low clouds and rain. We snack at a cove of interglacial stumps that tumble from pyramids of glacial till. Freeze-dried and shorn, they are the relics of a forest that grew before the advancing Little Ice Age glaciers razed them some 3,500 years ago. Maren's hands are cracked at the fingertips from packing gear and the harshness of salt water on skin, and she has them taped like a boxer's, weeping blood. Mine are encrusted with salt and pruned from dampness. Across the inlet huge valleys open, and the shoreline becomes sheer, veined with dark basalt, waterfalls of snowmelt atomizing on rocks.

From atop White Thunder Ridge, a mountain goat surveys us, kicking cobbles loose that lob down into the water like mortars. It stares for a time, then disappears over a knob. Soon the water is somber in the deep inlet, the tiny particles of silt scattering the sunlight, turning the seawater turquoise. Small bergs float past. Stones continue to fall. The tide changes, turning to ebb, and we must paddle the eddy lines, pinched close to the crumbling rock. Instead of valley hollows, glaciers now appear—the McBride and, beyond it, the Riggs—where the inlet veers west and where we hope to find camp.

As we discuss crossing to the face of the Riggs, a crack rattles the fiord. A block of mountain, high above, free falls in an endless and noiseless instant. Then explodes into the water. Waves overtake us, and we paddle hard across the inlet, never looking back. When they have passed, a sound rises from the depths, a reverberation that is eerie and everywhere, like a cloud of descending locusts, as the avalanche tumbles into the depths some six hundred feet below. Safely across, Maren says she thought I was going to be pancaked.

We are lost in the scale of things and still face the ominous question of where to camp among the rockfalls. Below the moraine of the Riggs Glacier, we walk across the snow, every third step punching through to the thigh. Nothing. Rain again. Paddling around the pile of till, we land on the side facing the glacier. The tide leaks away, and we are stranded, cold and wet, and make camp on a patch of old snow in the hollow of the moraine. The place is disintegrating—creaks, moans, booms, and pops against the complacent calls of seabirds. As we erect the tent and cook shelter, a blue berg grounds on the tidal flats and settles to one side. Others drift out to sea. Finally, warm in the tent, I turn to Maren.

"Give me the ibuprofen," she says.

APRIL 18

The sun tinges the top of the tent; the nylon wall buffets as if breathing. Maren spreads the stove across a flat rock just outside the cook shelter and boils water for oatmeal. Last night we saw a starry sky, crisp and clear, the luminous ice beneath. But this morning I am nervous, and Maren says she can hardly look at the icy face. I have heard from the Tlingit that their teachings instruct them never to speak of or point at a glacier. What an invasion science must have been—the ropes, the crampons, the base camps, the sleds and scientists who not only talked of the ice but climbed it, wrote about it, dug into its core, picked among the crevasses, chipping away at this great wall. So for a moment I look away. Beyond the ice itself, this is a landscape *formed* by ice—smooth cobble, silt, gravel—and the occasional willow that somehow pries from beneath it all. The spring snow is patchy, broken by the heat of deep-black boulders. Some snow is corn snow—snow that successive meltings have turned into pellets of ice—a sign of spring in glacier country. At low tide the flats stretch nearly a quarter mile to a margin of green algae. At high tide our moraine is nearly an island.

During the last third of the flood tide, we paddle with unloaded kayaks, heading west into the deep fiord toward the

Muir Glacier. Snow packs the southern side, while the northern shore is melted bare and desertlike. The kayaks are agile, and we make good time. But I am anxious, waiting for the glacier to appear around the bend in the arm. It is the moment where we can go no farther, the northern ice. And then, as the granite walls roll away, it is there, almost smiling.

We nose up on the silt. The Muir is grounded and lies several hundred yards from the tidewater. Among the field of boulders, I take a pinch of silt and work it between my fingers. It is as fine as flour and hasn't seen daylight for thousands of years, the newest ground of the Inside Passage.

As I grind the silt, a memory visits. There was a rock in my uncle's backyard that we called "rock in the woods." It was at the bottom of a long, steep slope, and we would run into the forest, climbing over limbs and logs until we found it, sitting there like a shadow. It was huge and smooth and mossy and smelled like a cellar. There were no others like it. It sat alone among the trees. And every time we visited, I wondered where it came from.

My cousin said that it had rolled there. My parents said that it had been pushed by a mile-high wall of ice. This was fantastic news and I told my friends about this wall of ice but they didn't believe me.

Since that great spring of childhood, I learned that this rock in the woods is a glacial erratic, that I had lived along the terminal moraines of the late-Pleistocene ice sheet in Illinois river country and later, during high school, along the terminal moraines of the Wisconsinan Ice Sheet in Iowa. I had always known home precisely where the looming glacial faces once rose sheer to the sky. Maren, too, had spent a childhood among glacial scourings on the lakes and plains of Minnesota. And on the shores of Puget Sound, once again, we have made a home in the haunts of ice, where some 12,000 years before, the Puget lobe of the great Cordilleran Ice Sheet, the glacial mass that had spilled from the coastal mountains and shoveled out the fiords of the entire Inside Passage, had ground to a stop, paused, then retreated north.

APRIL 19

Since we arrived two days ago, the Riggs has calved hundreds of bergs, and the waters are clogged with ice. Not for more than a few moments has the rumbling ever ceased. Cliffs leak meltwater, and avalanche chutes stain the high walls. Drainage patterns form as the melt begins, and dirtied braids of alluvial trickles fan across the shores.

Across the inlet, White Thunder Ridge consumes the southwestern sky. Since the rockfall two days ago, several more immense blocks have peeled off and crashed into the inlet. White Thunder is more than a mile away, so by the time the sound arrives, we only glimpse a cloud of dust racing down the cliff into a froth of green splashes. Sometimes the falls begin as a lone rock tumbling down a thousand feet, dislodging others until the stones smack like thunderclaps. The avalanches build, triggering each other until the whole fiord seems to slide. The sound has no source; it simply shakes the air and nearly sends us to cover. Then, as always, as we feel the first pang of real fear, a distant trail of dust is seen, a stray splash, a dark rock skittering across the ice.

After Maren demonstrates our distress signal—a two-fingered SOS blast—I start across the outwash flat toward the face of the Riggs while she stays near camp to sketch and play her recorder. As I climb over the moraine, it is there, rumbling— the Riggs. The outwash is sorted: large boulders near the glacier gradually decreasing to cobbles, stones, gravel, and finally to silt in the outermost tidal flats, water carrying the lightest particles farthest. Every step falls on unstable ground. Pebbles and gravel give way in dish-shaped impressions. Silt and clay are slick and cover deeper and slicker round rocks. Cobbles upon cobbles shift and roll unpredictably, and when I lift my head, it seems as if I have barely moved. The outwash must be at least a half mile wide. At low tide the glacial stream divides into three shin-deep milky torrents so cold that it burns my exposed skin after the first step and numbs it after the second, so the third crossing is painless but rapid. In the

lee of a dirtied snout of the main ice, I lean against a small
berg that cools my kidneys, face to face with the glacier.

It gurgles and pops and shifts as if uncomfortable in a
chair. Low tide has stranded bergs, and I walk among them
as if walking among blue storms, their sharp angles softened
by yesterday's sun. The berg behind me is flattened like a
thunderhead. Its anvil top soaring out above a dark underside
drips water that was rain perhaps thousands of years ago. It
is honeycombed and bubbled and pitted on top, then slick
and solid and dense below. Small black stones near the surface
have bored tunnels as much as a foot deep as they have absorbed the sun's heat. At high tide, when this berg goes afloat,
only its flattened head will show.

The tide creeps across the rocky plain, advancing at least
fifty feet in the last half hour. Ice breaks and crumbles, constantly splashing into the mirrored meltwater pools at its base.
Gulls have colonized a rock at the glacial face, and their cries
sound like a schoolyard. Some bergs are afloat and drift
toward the ice wall. But I linger.

I am no more than twenty yards from the glacial wall. A
blue ring at its base marks the highest water, similar to lines
drawn to mark memorable floods. As I stare, the ice becomes
an infinite complex of fractures, layers, scales; the play of
light, a record of the snowy and rainy days for millennia.

A crack. A triangular blue block is in midair. Then a splash
so large that the water droplets seem to hang before coating
the rocks. Now a gaping hole, a window into a blue night.
Sitting here for an hour, I am anxious to see another huge
chunk break off, and I grow impatient with the glacier's pace.
On nature shows towering spires break loose on cue, and it
becomes clear that on television, nature is under pressure to
perform, a lifetime of miracles unfolding before the top of
the hour. If geologic time is perceptible to humans, it is seen
in the creep of glaciers.

My feet are warm but wet in the neoprene boots, calluses
building on what were hot layers of skin. Crossing from the
ice to camp takes at least twenty minutes on the open ground.
The tide has increased the stream level several feet, so I must

cross upstream through a shallow rapid. Maren is glad for my return. Over makeshift burritos and sharp cheddar, she tells me of her morning solace. Then she points to a swelling nimbus in the southwest, and we question the wisdom of taking a layover day this far north and stack extra rocks around the cook tarp and bury the tent stakes deeper into the snow.

As I brush my teeth, a splash erupts near shore, followed by a thrashing fin, a snort, and a plume of mist. Then the water glazes over. In moments, the water ruptures again, and an animal streaming with blood lunges in a spray of pink. I grab the binoculars. The huge back is red. Then it thrashes again, bloody and violent. Then it disappears. Sweeping the surface, I see nothing until the gulls circle. Where they touch the water in midchannel, I see a fin. Then a white belly. Soon the black hulk disappears, and the gulls disperse. Have killer whales maimed a sea lion? A young humpback?

The sun sets into a glacial valley, and the temperature drops fifteen degrees. We are anxious, unsure of our endurance. Tide recedes once again, bergs scatter across the bay, flecks of white on the stone-gray surface. Green tidal flats emerge. A day among glaciers. A wind pours from the ice. An insect buzzes my cap.

APRIL 20

Last night as rain beat against the tent, a deep boom reverberated through the mountains, thunderous and progressive. This morning the glacier face has opened, a gash of blue ice. Already the snow around camp has descended six inches from its level three days ago.

"There was a huge glass building with people in it, right here," Maren says, coming into wakefulness. "People watching the glacier and huge cranes and engineers with cables were holding back the rock and ice so it would stay this way forever."

Rocks are warm in the morning sun, and flies emerge and

congregate. As we wait for the tide to cover the flats, Maren wraps her hands. Again they have split open, and she is concerned that they are so bad after so few days. She is able to talk about other scars fondly and often, pointing to them and telling their stories, testaments to other journeys, of a youth spent abraded by wild country. Purpled sun blisters have swollen my knuckles from the hot paddle to the Muir so that my fingers are tight when I grab the paddle. Maren cuts the tape and wraps another finger, closing the cracked skin, praying for quiet water, for smooth and seamless fingers in the months ahead.

Slowly the tide floods the depression where we have placed our kayaks, and we watch the water curl about the pebbles, following the lowest contours, this miniature landscape sinking away as our loaded crafts are righted.

After a calm day's paddle, stopping for lunch along the low and gullied land near interglacial stumps, we camp on a cobbled alluvial fan. Here the land opens; it is green, thick with willows, and we ease, away from the tension of close peaks and rumbling ice. Tonight the land is flat and comfortable. To the west the summit pyramid of Mount Fairweather pierces a layer of high cloud as it once pierced the Pleistocene ice sheet, a nunatak—an island in the ice. Maren sings again, the first time in several days. The return of the crescent moon lessens the tides. Venus shines, a southerly wind sweeps the sky clean, and a deep night settles—a time of great thoughts. To the south, the snowfields of the bay are tinged with warm evening sun. If the weather holds, we will be there in a few days.

As we hold each other by the campfire, I gaze across the shore of light-brown grass, then slowly stand. "There they are," I say, too stunned to utter anything more.

Maren jumps up, "What? Oh, god!" Dark shadows tumble out of the willows, across the grass and onto the tidal flat. Fiercely silent, swift, as big as buffalo. There are five—and close. There is nothing we can do. "Hello bears," I sputter. One raises up high in the twilight, a bristled head against the alpenglow—brown bear.

"We are here, too," Maren says with a startling confidence. *Clap. Clap.* "Hey-ho. Hello. . . ." And we retreat
cautiously, sidestepping toward the tent, mumbling niceties.
Into the tent, into the darkness where there are no bears, two
membranes of nylon becoming walls of brick. We just breathe,
listening—the snuffles of a dark nose, a shudder on the rocks,
a weight in nearby grass—as the adaptive powers of fear and
denial and fatigue take hold and send us swiftly to sleep.

APRIL 21

Spooked by the sudden visitors last dusk, we eat no breakfast
and load the boats quickly. If I have a prevailing fear among
these lands, it is the notion that I, too, am prey.

Maren paddles ahead this morning, and after a squall ruf-
fles the inlet, the day clears with a brisk northwesterly. The
land is low and young. But beaches rise steeply so that when
paddling near shore, we cannot see the mountains above their
cobbled walls. Again, interglacial stumps fall from the eroding
piles of till. Sitka spruce infiltrates willow and alder. We are
coming out of the Ice Age and into the forest.

The tide floods against us, so we ride eddies near the rocks.
In a rustling willow, a marten nips spring buds. Then the *flip-
flip* of paddles—two kayakers approaching in a squat tandem.
We are eager to see people and talk as we float. "Usually we
are in the Arctic in April," one man says, resting his paddle
across the kayak. "This year, we just didn't go that far." They
carry skis and large duffels on deck and look dangerously top
heavy. Admiring our sleek boats, they say they have no kayaking experience and no plans; waving, they disappear behind
a point.

Adams Inlet is blustery, ripples building to dark waves.
Ahead is Muir Point, where John Muir erected a cabin during
his third visit to Glacier Bay in 1890. The point is low with
a small hill of spruce, thick with willow and alder just in from
shore. From here in 1890, Muir could see the expanse of the

glacier—named for him—a wall more than a mile across, so that his icy expeditions took place where now there is water. Suddenly a herd of perhaps thirty sea lions stirs from the shallows, surprised by our presence. They huff and rear up like periscopes as they swim, then plunge again for speed. Others are porpoising, propelling themselves completely free of the water as if fired from cannons.

Sea lions are like brown bears of the water, and the skulls of the two species are nearly identical, a sea lion's differing most visibly with rounded teeth. The herd continues to taunt us like a pack of thugs. We paddle hard. They are closing. Sea lions have been known to jump aboard fishing boats, seemingly unafraid of the human presence. We dig deep into the water. In the shallows, rocks race beneath my hull. We paddle for land. For all we know we are heading for their pupping ground. We bang ashore, pulling the kayaks from the water and running up the beach. But the sea lions are headed back into the channel. We pant and feel foolish, keeping a short vigil. Now they are fishing offshore, occasionally turning their thick necks and looking our way, snorting, threatening, then retreating.

Muir Point is evenly graded with small stones and two waist-high bands of blue mussel shells piled at high-tide line. They crackle and break as I climb over them, releasing a stench like carrion as my boots sink into their depths.

Though I am sure it is not here, I cannot help looking for Muir's cabin and tear through willows, past a bog of bear grass into alders and spruces. This time, for reasons I cannot fully explain, I sing Irving Berlin songs to alert the bears. "White Christmas" comes first. Then I stop, hearing a rustle in the bushes. Wind. Ellington comes next: "It Don't Mean a Thing If It Ain't Got that Swing." Deeper into the forest.

The willows cut the wind, and I scan the forest floor for fireplace stones and foundation logs. But there are none. With the postglacial uplift, if Muir's cabin still existed, it would lie much higher in the woods. Wary of surprising a bear, I make my way back to the open beach, waving to Maren, who has been guarding the boats, keeping them in the water as the tide drops. She is patient with my forays and knows that at times like this I am barely ten years old.

Snacking on dried fruit, we enjoy Muir's view. The afternoon is bright, and we can see the upper Riggs and Casement Glaciers and part of McBride Glacier. A few sea lions still eye us, but the herd has convened farther north. Finally, with the stink of mussels and the discovery of fresh bear tracks, we leave Muir Point and decide to cross the inlet to the beach near Caroline Point, where we had stopped briefly last week.

The afternoon wind is stiff, lifting the bright-green sea into splash and sparkle. Downwind we ride, fast with waves breaking over our sterns. Skimming at five knots, broaching, correcting. Adrenaline flows. "A ride for John!" I yell, and we laugh. At the point we slip among the offshore boulders that break the waves into foaming kettles, and the waves dissolve to ripples, then to glass, as we penetrate the bay. We pitch camp atop the second berm amid musket balls of elk scat, in view of the distant snows of Chichagof and the sheet of cloud that still cloaks the southern sky.

As we finish a chili-mac dinner, a lone brown bear appears on the beach. It sniffs and snorts, then looks back at us, pausing in midstride. It is a big bear but gaunt, famished from hibernation, its coat alternately matted and tufted. Then it ambles on, pawing aside boulders as if they were beach balls, hunting crabs. The encounter keeps us efficient, and we bed down early and distract ourselves by planning tomorrow's route. The indigo sky wedges between mountain and cloud. Tomorrow east, then south.

APRIL 22

Each day we get up, stare at the weather, stare at the water, debate, break camp, stare at the water, talk, eat, clean up, load the kayaks, stare at the water, and then after some debate and some more staring at the water, we paddle. Then we quit because of a change in the weather or to set up camp where we can find one or to eat and discuss the weather or debate paddling conditions. But no weather is the same, no tide, no campsite. The only constant is our spaghetti leather, which passes through time unphased. The old days of lake travel and hiking and bicycling seem simplistic. At night we light the candle lantern and relax for the two percent of our day not spent in sheer survival. The flame flutters, a constant chemical reaction, a stable form. Each moment it consumes new energy and completely remakes itself, a dynamic stability burning in the night.

A day of change. High cirrus press in all morning, and the water is restless with whitecaps. We realize that crossing the inlet yesterday was a mistake, and we abort an ill-conceived plan to paddle down the west side of Glacier Bay, cross Icy Strait, and head for the outer coast, opting instead to head down the eastern shore toward Bartlett Cove, a decision that will determine the weeks ahead.

Rising and falling in the green swells, the kayaks spin on each crest. Whitecaps suck from behind, and I watch over my shoulder, stabbing at them, placing the blade, as a brace into their rising faces. To kayak, you seek balance within a substance that is fluid, that has no inherent stability beyond the bonds of its molecules. Developing this poise is a lengthy process, for we do not merely float but must reach out at times for the water as one would reach for a handrail, to steady ourselves. We lean against the water with our paddles, pressing the blade into its surface and prying ourselves up again. The water is our element, and with a quiver of ready strokes, the paddle becomes our vocation, our velocity, our rescue, our stave upon the water.

Beneath the cliffs, the waves subside as we slip past snow gullies and avalanche chutes and head south to a protected cove. Again we fight flood currents and must hug the shore. Then more swells, part wind-wave, part tidal, rise steeply in the shallows. Needing fresh water, we turn into the cove and refill the water pillows from a small stream. As I pump the filter, Maren explores a bog and returns with a moose antler gnawed like a corn cob. A black bear paces the grassy berm across the slender bay, and another bear soon appears on the opposite shore.

The beach is shale, knives of gray rock, and walking to and from the water is like walking on the shingled slope of a roof. Storm waves heave shattered mounds of shells and seaweed higher on shore. A bear jawbone rolls in the waves. Its tooth sockets are smooth and fit my fingertips like thimbles.

Dark curtains of rain approach. The mountains have disappeared from view long ago. There is no horizon. We camp on a spit along the outer reach of the bay opposite the bears, stringing a tarp across the tent. It is forty-one degrees. My fingers fail to grasp, and I claw at zipper pulls, boot laces, and buckles with index finger and thumb. At high tide we are on an island, but now the tide is out. Rain drenches our tarp so that in five minutes we collect fifteen liters of water. Then it quiets. A complete calm.

APRIL 23

Dawn. A sheet of ice plates everything in crystal as we wait for the sun to rise above the high snows. No signs of bears. Thankfully the water is smooth, and we leave with the tide at 8:10 A.M. Clouds, curling and low, rise from the islands, tangled in the tall spruce that now cover the hillsides. My sun blisters have burst into sores that tear down my knuckles, and stinging saltwater slops over them with every wave.

Crossing Beartrack Cove, we aim between two flat islands. But as we near, a cul de sac of rubble reroutes us. We question ourselves, then head southeast into a cove that leads to another dead end of shoal and mud. Postglacial uplift, isostatic rebound. The Beardslee Islands are destined not to remain islands for long as they rebound from the weight of the Little Ice Age glaciers. Where my chart depicts a channel, now there are rocks or trees. The rebound here is the greatest in all of southeast Alaska, averaging about an inch and a half a year.

Scientists who have marked boulders in the tide line have returned a decade later to find them resting in a forest.

We retrace our paddle strokes, fighting a northwest wind. Around the outer shore of the Beardslees, swells rear up on the shallows and beat the shoreline. We are too close. In wave troughs I am less than a foot above the rocks. Then, pulling around a low point into calm water, I am amazed at how suddenly refuge is found or lost at sea. A single rock can often be the object of prayer and profound thanks.

Nosing through the flooding shoals, we encounter a floating carpet of fur. Sea otters. A curious few explore the hulls of our boats. We have heard that kayaks repel small sea mammals because our shape resembles that of an orca, with the paddler stretching skyward as the dorsal fin. But these otters seem to know otherwise, swimming closely, frolicking, rolling onto their backs, munching crab. Compared to sea lions, they are tame, even cuddly. Easy money for the Russians and Hudson's Bay Company, who nearly eradicated them in the 1700s and 1800s. There must be fifty of them here, together, like a log raft.

We secure camp on an unnamed island at the beachline, between the invading grasses and barnacled cobbles. Near the tent, a spruce seedling pokes through the grass. We guard this pioneer, walking around it, the first of a wave of spruce pushing into the grasses. Overhead, ravens croak at an eagle, wind swooshing over feather as they skirt the treetops.

Tent stakes drive through grass and moss, then grind to a stop. The soil and plant life is no more than a half stake deep, four inches. Maren cooks dinner in the intertidal zone as the wind and drizzle return. Although it is inconvenient to cook and eat and clean so far from camp, we are religious about this for the sake of bears. Bears are the same reason we have chosen not to fish. To do so would heighten the risk of a dangerous encounter, as wild bears recognize the scent of fresh fish much more readily than the aroma of lentil chili. With camp habits falling into place, we speak little when cleaning up or loading and unloading the kayaks. We are four days from the ice. Tomorrow, Bartlett Cove—and perhaps a hot shower.

APRIL 24

We cake on lotions and sunblock, smearing ourselves against exposure, preparing for the day. Wearing paddling jackets and wide-brimmed hats, with spray skirts curled taut over the cockpit, we armor ourselves, ready to receive the sea's falling blow.

We realize early that the tides will be off for crossing the narrow passage at the Bartlett River's mouth, which is only navigable at high tide. So we paddle slow, waiting for the sun and moon to bring us water. Navigating the forested islands, we follow an old boat that appears to know a way through. After a morning of showers, the water calms and the rain stops. Amid the polyphony of birdsong, our talk seems noisy and confused.

As we round a point, unsure of where best to paddle, we come upon the tuglike craft. Near it is the aluminum skiff we saw last evening, flying the red-and-white diving flag. We hover aimlessly around the hull of the boat until a man wearing toe rings and sandals leans over the railing and begins to chat. We stare up at his sandals, so misplaced in this environment. "Would you like something to eat?" he asks in a playful, parental tone. "How about peanut butter cookies?" He disappears into the galley and returns, tossing down half a package of Nutter Butters. Slipping away between the islands with no more than a foot of clearance beneath us, we find a steep beach that eclipses the ship and, respectfully out of sight, devour them.

Bartlett Cove is near, and we negotiate a narrowing channel of mud and seaweed. Countless gulls pick among the tidal flats. Then the dock appears. We beach within sight of Bartlett Cove and walk among the tide pools as the flooding tide spills across anemones, barnacles, and mussels, gradually broadening to a river. From a high rock, I hail NPS headquarters on the VHF. We are welcome. The sky darkens and a squall hits. Then a rainbow and warm sun.

Working against the shallow current, we scrape bottom every few strokes. But soon we are through and into deeper water, and Maren sings "Five Hundred Miles" as we enter the lagoon fronting park headquarters. As a terrific thunderstorm ruptures, she climbs ashore to seek Randy, the ranger who gave us the orientation. The barge from Seattle has just arrived, and Ben and Jerry's ice cream is melting. People trot through the downpour, arms stacked with boxes. I glimpse Randy running, then walking, then standing and talking to someone, slowly surrendering to the deluge. In a few minutes Maren returns, smiling. They can make space for us in transient quarters, a spartan room in the mail trailer. With hot showers and laundry, we are centuries ahead once more.

In Bartlett Cove and Gustavus

About two inches from my eyeball is some knotty-pine panel-
ing. From two inches it looks like a storm. From six inches it
is an eddy line. The whole strip, eyeing it upward from the
distance of a foot, mutates into currents swirling about islands.
We are warm and dry, sardined into a single bed. With the
luxury of a stove, Maren bakes scones and sets off the fire
alarm. As we fling open the door, a park employee shows up.
"Crisco in the oven?" she asks.

Even beyond a quick look, Bartlett Cove is little more than
an outpost of pallid trailers, well-kept ranger quarters, and
cords of spare plumbing pipes and auto parts, fronting a marvelous lagoon of green water. All morning, tall, lean, bearded
men with duffel bags come in to take showers—archetypal
biologists or geologists, arriving from various research projects.
Most are divers with NOAA studying Dungeness crabs, and
they talk of water clarity as they dry diving gear. "Good visibility before the algae bloom." "Lots of big Dungies in Dundas Bay." They dive at prescribed depths and count crabs,
trying to assess the population so that fishing regulations can
be established. "There's no baseline," says one diver, throwing

a heap of damp gear into the dryer. "That's what we're here to do, get a baseline before some disaster happens like the *Exxon Valdez*. It's always after the disaster that we count the dead, not the living."

Sitting amid crumbs left from hurried meals and piles of dishes, I go through the library, two shelves of tattered paperbacks beneath the mail boxes. James Michener's works are numerous—*The Novel, Alaska, Centennial*—a testament to dark, wet winters. A matrix of twenty-one mailboxes, each as big as a milk crate, occupies one wall. Most are unmarked and empty, a sign of various cutbacks and the absence of seasonal workers. But other boxes are jammed with packages. Mail is an all-or-nothing prospect here. Someone has said that a few years ago, weather kept the mail away for twenty days. "Some panicked. Others were blessed." By the door are ranks of knee-high rubber boots, X-Tra Tuf. When the tops crack and leak, the boots are cut down and conserved as clogs. Rows of boots stand by nearly every door in southeast Alaska, and life indoors is lived luxuriously in socks. We enjoy the time, chatting with personnel, recovering, reevaluating, making phone calls, generally drying and warming and desalinating.

Yesterday the food barge arrived, and today everyone is slow and satiated, speaking often of ice cream. When the barge comes, Bartlett Cove stops and unloads. Most of what is here has floated in. There are no roads among communities in southeast Alaska. Phone orders are placed and barges arrive. Barges of everything: food and clothing and dishes and washers and dryers and outboard motors and cement mixers . . . If it is urgent, it arrives at Gustavus airport some ten miles away.

Randy invites us for a lunch of caribou-lentil-cabbage soup. His home is walking distance from his office, and he enjoys the noontime solace. A trapeze hangs above the dining room table. "Winters get dark," he chuckles. "It's for the kids. They just go crazy on this thing." The home is compact, tight for a family of five. On the stewpot, Sally has left a note. She is in Gustavus for the afternoon with the children.

Randy is athletic and talks often of hunting, of working his way up the NPS ranks from a start in the parks of Montana, his Yellowstone days. As we eat caribou, he sees me looking around the room: a Dall sheep's head, a black bearskin. "These are not trophies," he says, "but reminders. . . . Sally shot the bear, her first. The Dall sheep is a reminder of that opportunity I had to hunt, of an interaction with an animal. I see hunting as a way of connecting ourselves to the world in which we live. It is something that has to be done with a lot of respect. It is part of our human history, and for us and for many people in the world it still is an important part of our life. We raise our children on some of what this area has to offer—salmon, halibut, and deer—and it is just a way of being part of the land and seascape. And, actually, our children are being built from these things, this area."

After one bowl, Randy rushes off. April is a busy time; summer staff will arrive within the week. "A season of many questions," he says, placing our dishes in the sink. "The number of permits for motorized vessels within the bay is limited from June through August, to protect park resources and the quality of visitor experiences. We have three Jet Skiers coming from Seattle. Should we give them a permit? It's a stunt."

Bartlett Cove is how I imagine a nineteenth-century frontier outpost was. Rather than horsemen departing to patrol the range, rangers now depart in speedboats. And like those early posts, Bartlett Cove is government funded. The difference seems mainly that of time. Yet, still there are questions about indigenous fishing and use rights, subsistence issues; still there are the travelers, like ourselves, who come through the country on their way to elsewhere, are shown hospitality and stop for a time. And the nearby town of Gustavus is a community founded by homesteaders. Perhaps in a genuine sense it is a frontier outpost. And where a few hours before all that had been wild in our world had seemingly vanished by warm bedding, it has again revealed itself in these questions about how we are to live on the land.

APRIL 26

A park employee lends us her four-wheel drive to go to Gustavus to resupply. That's what we tell her. All we want is chocolate. In the past ten days, we have devoured perhaps a pound a day. The drive is comforting and familiar, and John Denver sounds great. Roads around Bartlett Cove are all glacial till, as is the washboarded ten-mile stretch from Bartlett Cove to Gustavus. After only a week and a half on the water, I see the roads are built from the same rocks as the nearby shorelines.

For a small place, Gustavus is surprisingly spread out. It's not a walking town. There are some bicyclists, but mostly cars. Lots are generally large, and there is talk here and there about the white woodsmoke curling from a neighbor's nearby chimney.

On the exposed and windy dock that spans the flat Gustavus beach, a product of the old glacial outwash plain, a man dumps two halibut on the beach, white carcasses cartwheeling down, bouncing like rubber. Eagles hover in the stiff breeze, peel off and dive, flashing down, tearing loose strips of flesh in touch-and-go landings.

After returning the truck, we catch a ride back into Gustavus with a veteran national park service ranger, who delivers us to the home of Bonnie and Hayden Kaden. Bonnie founded Glacier Bay Sea Kayaks, and Hayden has been a lawyer and wilderness guide. The evening is delightful—lively conversations about adventures in Alaska, paddling and climbing glacial faces, questions and advice about our travels. At one point Bonnie tells of a flight tour she took with her parents.

"We ascended from Juneau," she says, her arms soaring like a plane, "up from the great tensions and political battles to the big green, then to the big white, the icefields. And, wow, Juneau was really invisible! And the stress down there, it all fell away. Then we floated back from the big white to the big green, circling, circling, until we found Juneau again and landed."

Maren and I sleep in a brass bed with silk sheets in the

top of their barn, a quarter moon dangling outside the window. Neap tides.

APRIL 27

This morning Hayden prepares enormous omelettes. "I used to do this on trips," he says. "That's what people want nowadays. Fresh food." We talk about our dried meals, the spaghetti leather, and he says the Mormons developed freeze-dried food for the coming of the Millennium. Then we hop in the pickup and head to the Mackovjak place.

We meet Jim as he works in a smoldering clear-cut in his backyard. He is clearing some of his seven acres for a new energy-efficient home. Within moments a drizzle sends us inside. The old home is cozy, and a woodstove cooks away in the center of the living space. Again the familiar trapeze hangs from the ceiling. After introductions, Maren and Jim's wife, Annie, retreat into the kitchen and quickly establish an intimate conversation. This is something Maren has an uncanny ability to do: sit down and talk from the heart. They drift into the shadows of the kitchen among the dried spices and canned goods while Jim and I visit in the living room. I tell him about our trip. He shows me a newspaper published by the Hoonah Indian Association with a clear-cut on it.

"Have you seen this?" he says, handing me the paper that protests the logging on the Native corporation and Forest Service land around Hoonah. "If there's one thing you should know about southeast Alaska, it is that whatever land you look at, somebody has a plan for it.

"Those logs are all exported in the round to the Orient. They have been logging for twenty-some years, and the Native corporations themselves never really wanted to do much but get quick dollars. So they will soon be done with the logging. But deer will be scarce, salmon streams damaged, the lack of tourism—the whole gamut there. They could have done things sustainably—I mean, there are plenty models to go by—and it's a tragedy."

He has run a fish processing plant for twelve years and says the fishing has been pretty stable, that the resources have pretty much been well-managed. "Some years this is good, some years that's bad. It kind of all averages out. You can't hang your hat on any one fishery to be certain.

"Resourcewise, southeast Alaska is probably one of the best-endowed places in the world. We have generally clean oceans, except for around a few facilities. The forests are losing fast, but at least twenty years ago our forests were in primo shape, at least around here. The streams were in good shape. There was a lot of game on the land. The climate is rough, but not that rough. A land of wealth."

When I ask what's happening in Gustavus, he is eager to talk.

"The big change around here has to do with two things. One is the growth of the tourism industry. We always had Glacier Bay Lodge, but that was kind of a sleepy affair. And what was going on in Gustavus was even sleepier. Now tourism in Gustavus is homegrown but pretty aggressive. It's not sleepy. This has coincided with an increase in logging on Native lands. They didn't start logging until about 1980 or so, and they have been going full bore ever since. And the Forest Service logging programs started in the late '70s, and they have been going full bore ever since. The two industries have collided because people who want not even a wilderness experience but just a nice experience are increasingly crowded in the few places that are left."

He pauses. "You'll see some incredibly beautiful places and some incredibly rough places. Were you to fly instead of kayak, I'm told that at five thousand feet you're never out of sight of clear-cuts; some are a pretty good size. I studied environmental biology and thought about working for the Forest Service. I'd love to be the manager of a well-managed forest. And managed is a funny word. I'm talking holistically managed. My guess is you just don't touch it too hard. Just admit you have to live in it and do what you can."

"Tell me about your backyard," I ask reluctantly, not wanting to offend his hospitality.

"I can rationalize my own cut," he says with bright eyes, as if he has been challenged with this before. "We had a real cold winter here, and our woodshed ended up empty, absolutely empty. So as we've been cutting down—and this is kind of scrubby stuff that I'm cutting—by the time we've cleared what we're clearing out, there will be about a hundred by a hundred feet that probably won't have any trees on it. And that won't even fill the woodshed. The woodshed holds about fifteen cords of wood. The new house that's going in there is being built with the wood that I got from Hoonah—all a blowdown sale from the Forest Service. A lot of the other stuff came off the beach. But the house will be really well insulated. Oriented toward the south, a large solar component. I figure our wood consumption will be reduced by two-thirds or more. In doing that, I think you save trees. And I am going to clear farther out toward the south. But then we'll replant that with trees that don't grow as high—crab apple or mountain ash. That's the rationalization, the compromise I made with my eyes open. You can rationalize about anything, but the whole idea is for the house to be more efficient to consume less over the long run. I just want to get it done before the birds nest in there."

Leaning back on the sofa, he talks of when he and Annie first came to Gustavus in the 1970s, how they pulled stumps out by hand. "I guess we have an intense history, not nearly as much as the homesteaders had. One of the differences in Gustavus is that when we were first here, you had to pretty much be able to do about everything by yourself. Halfway get a car running, halfway build something, halfway plant a garden, halfway repair something. . . . Now you could show up here with a pocket full of money and find somebody in Seattle to find you a car and the barge will deliver it here. There is a guy who is a decent mechanic. You could find somebody to build you a first-class house, everything to code and done well. Somebody to fix your computer.

"There's still a real identity to southeast Alaska, more so

than any place I've been. Especially if you live in the rural parts. You are so close to the water, so close to the mountains, the fish, so subject to the weather for everything.

"Annie and I traveled a lot and didn't settle down until we were thirty. As you get older, I think you get dimmer. But you do learn. You look at fish, you know the smells. When you look at a batch of crabs, there are different batches of color, and you know they came from this bay or that bay. They are subtle things that are enjoyable to know. It's like saying that this kind of flower should be blossoming over there pretty soon, and then when it happens . . . I think those are the pleasures in life, really."

In Bartlett Cove, we sit down to a dinner with the Kings. Over bowls of Ben and Jerry's, Sally likens the barge to the Wells Fargo wagon of the West one hundred hears ago. "You have this wish list going for quite a while," she says, laughing. "My whole perspective is pretty much with the children and the family lifestyle."

"This is the only place the kids know," Randy says. "Mackenzie was two years old when we moved here in 1990, and Dylan and Skylar have lived no place else."

"Their life here is almost a step back in time," Sally continues. "They are not exposed to a lot of the commercial things. Their idea of fun might be going down and exploring at low tide and throwing rocks. We have old-fashioned birthday parties. And they are out there with me harvesting, picking blueberries, trying pickled kelp. And when we travel, I don't think they feel like country bumpkins.

"But it's pretty overwhelming to go back," she says of visiting her family near Detroit. "I don't even want to drive the car for at least a week. It's just too aggressive."

Maren and I use the remaining daylight to walk the cove. A party of people spills onto the deck of Glacier Bay Lodge, the first tourist group of the year. Placid waters reflect the dock lamps, and as we pass the park-service homes, they seem carved into a slope. "It's really the only sledding hill around," Randy had said, the only small rise on the outwash plain of

Gustavus. And it strikes us that this plain may be the only basically level expanse in southeast Alaska.

As I repack drybags in the mail trailer, Maren prepares food for tomorrow: Gatorade, fig bars, oatmeal packets. Then on a desk: *Mac World*. "High-Speed Modems, Backup Strategy, Color Management, Fonts."

Bartlett Cove to Icy Strait

When we leave Bartlett Cove, the wind is already whipping from the northwest, gathering velocity in the western arm as the cold gusts drive down off the Fairweather Range and high mountains of the central divide. Sally and the kids see us off, Mackenzie, Dylan, and Skylar hopping out on rocks, waving. And marveling at our good fortune here, we paddle on, riding low in the water and confident. Beyond the tourist lodge and dock, the buildings slip behind a wall of trees, and the shoreline turns grassy, tan and bright as if ablaze.

The waves rise on a shallow shelf that extends offshore, the product of rebound. Again we are faced with the strange and challenging task of reading the waves, learning where and where not to paddle. It is as much a task of reading the sea as the sea floor. Shallows steepen waves, and when the water reaches a depth of a half-wave height, the waves topple and fall. Incoming waves build to steep breakers about two hundred yards offshore over a shoal, the depths determining the surface.

Our nautical charts are deceptive, for with the exception of occasional current and kelp markings, they map water mostly by mapping the land. Charts depict the shore: a gray area, shaded with dark blue, dots for mud flats and areas that dry or shoal at low tide. Plus signs and asterisks mark hidden offshore rocks that bare at low tide. Soundings—a galaxy of single, double, and triple digits spread across the waters— describe the bathymetry of the deep. But mostly the charted shoreline is a simple curving black line between blue water and brown land, a line we are only just learning to read.

We round Point Gustavus near slack flood and ease out of Glacier Bay, pleased to be making such geographic progress. We can nearly see the length of Icy Strait, and Point Gustavus continues as flat shoreline all the way to the exposed trestle of the Gustavus dock.

Waves slop against the kayak and pool on my spray deck. All afternoon we paddle in no more than four feet of water, no more than a quarter mile off shore, stopping occasionally to urinate in the shallows. The dock never nears. Against current and wind, it takes two hours. We debate about Hoonah, about how we should get back inside, about hazards of cross- ing various straits—Icy, Chatham, Stephens Passage. We are reluctant to cross any, but if we are to make this voyage, we must cross several.

At the Gustavus dock we arrive as strangers abob in the waves. A couple carrying their eight-month-old baby bends down to talk. "Hoonah?" he says. "Why? Do you want to see the clear-cuts? There's a bar here, a bar there," he ex- plains, weaving his hands. "Everyone walks crooked. Don't waste your time."

Next to them is a fishing boat, and we ask the same ques- tions. A woman wearing orange plastic pants cleans a halibut, rolls her eyes. "Gustaviors . . . Gustavus is not a typical Alaska town. It's too white. I almost didn't move here because of that. Why aren't Hoonah and Gustavus sister towns? They are only seventeen miles apart. Why don't we have Gustavus- Hoonah potlucks? There's some prejudice here. We keep our boat in Hoonah. Good harbormaster."

A Zodiac buzzes in. "The pressure's changing," says the man, gripping the throttle. "They say it'll blow southeast tomorrow at thirty, then southwest at forty later. A 'vigorous' weather system."

We depart immediately and have the luck to find a cabin. If the weather turns bad, we will be pinned here but perhaps dry. We need the time to decide whether to cross the four miles of Icy Strait and fight with the currents off Point Adolphus. Again people have warned us, and we hesitate at this major crossroad.

Thankfully, the unloading is easy. This is a good beach for us, steep and made of shiny pebbles. If a beach is too level, the tide leaks away, exposing a lengthy tidal flat—a great distance to carry gear. Many beaches are compromises, barnacled cobbles that descend to a low tide beach of sand. Others are shelved with boulders. With certainty we will see much worse, but tonight we have a smooth beginning to life on land.

After noodles and soy sauce, we listen to a radio, a small transistor with a wire coat hanger for an antenna. Through the crackle we hear "Take Five," and half waltzing, half two-stepping, we circle the iron stove in the candle glow, laughing. At the mouth of Glacier Bay, a Coast Guard cutter turns on its running lights, its white hull crossed with the familiar broad red stripe as if bandaged. As we contemplate Icy Strait, we are thankful, at least, for this floating civility.

APRIL 29

This morning I am on edge. There is no storm. Icy Strait is flat calm, and we are just sitting here. My tension irritates Maren. She wants to enjoy the day and relax. "Look at it. We could make it. Just two and a half hours," I say. We are in a silent scuffle. But we made a promise before we left: We would both feel comfortable with a situation before launching into it. How levelheaded we are! We will learn our lessons. Weather rules. "This may be the last calm day for a month," I say.

"The cabin is nice. I could stay," Maren counters.

We stay. We stay even though a front has stalled in a flat, gray day.

"If we are in a hurry," she says, "why are we traveling by kayak?"

After breakfast, I look to the far shore of Point Adolphus. It is nearly invisible. Fog. I sit down, relieved. Maren is relieved, too, accepts my apology, and we settle in for a day of weather.

The woodstove is rusted clear through in places and inefficient but homey. Rain pounds the roof. The weather collapses.

I read Darwin—a mistake. It turns my mind far too scientific. Seals eye us from the water, our constant companions, always staying about twenty feet from shore or our kayaks. But now primed, I marvel at their well-adapted hulks and go to watch them swim.

They are silky and agile in water but awkward on land. I am the opposite. Instead of biological change, I have summoned technology to exist and travel here. Binoculars are my eagle's eyes. For blubber, I wear neoprene. Again this pile of equipment, a mound that takes six trips to move. Explorers are notorious for lugging heaps of gear. Even John Muir, famous for hopping fences with nothing but hardtack and tea, relied on the cruise ships of his day, trunks of supplies, and a sled for his later rovings in Glacier Bay. Our equipment, shrunken to this bare minimum, measures my ineptitude here, my lacking in this environment, the distance between my physical self and survival. In most cases, it is a difference where the other, the adapted, have clear advantages and travel lightest.

After a third boat bake that is modestly more successful than those in Glacier Bay, Maren and I walk into the forest. A number of trees have bark missing on one side and have swollen and grown around the old wound. Maren bends down and sees ax marks. Tlingit used to plank wood from trees for boards, cutting notches at top and bottom at a desired length, then prying off sheets of split wood without killing the tree. The ax marks are from those notches.

"Culturally modified trees," Maren says, using the terminology of anthropologists. "CMTs."

Crossing Icy Strait

We are up before the wind. Last night, a southeasterly began to howl without warning, throwing waves against the rocks, and we slept easily, believing we would not have to paddle today. But this morning the water is placid. At last we decide to cross to Chichagof Island. We pack the drybags and scamper to and from the kayaks, needing the weather to hold for the next two and a half hours. We work silently, frequently peering across the water, reassessing conditions. By seven o'clock we are paddling, cocooned in drysuits, slipping farther from land, staring ahead at the dark-gray mass that is Point Adolphus.

Here, Icy Strait is four nautical miles wide, and we time the tides to hit slack halfway across, the ebb and flood canceling each other, minimizing drift. A nautical mile is slightly longer than a statute mile of 5,280 feet and is derived from the circumference of the earth. Of Earth's 360 degrees, each degree is divided into sixty minutes, and a nautical mile is equal to one minute, 1/21,600th of Earth's circumference, just more than 6,000 feet. Nautical miles are a direct measure of the planet, so as we paddle from shore, the great expanse ahead carries the emphasis that we are traversing a portion of the globe.

We have been warned about this crossing by several people, who say "just pick your weather." The weather is dark but calm. We scan for boat traffic. A tug works east with the flood, distant and not a hazard. We paddle together as always, within twenty yards, speaking encouragements. I take a range, aligning the dark hulk of Lemesurier Island and the Inian Islands farther west. After most of an hour, Lemesurier has slipped slowly backward, and all shores look distant.

Our kayaks are narrow by most standards, crafted for swiftness, efficiency, and agility on the open sea. But paddling quickly goes beyond equipment. We study the water's topography, the troughs and crests, the escarpments of waves, the peaks crumbling to whitecaps, laid out before us and read like elements of a fluid geology. The job is never passive. You can never lose the feel for the water, can never fail to follow an incoming wave. If even for a moment concentration drifts too far, you could be swimming. And in the wrong place at the wrong time this could prove disastrous. In this way the sea is unforgiving and selfish. At the end of a day, you are both sharpened and dulled by the whole business of paddling, like reading an entire book in a single sitting.

Off Point Adolphus, tidal swells—strange waves that roll from several directions—steepen considerably. We are not drifting, though, and the waves are not breaking. But it is unsettling, and, ready to burst with urine, I power ahead. This is stupid because Maren is keeping a steady pace, and she is now out of shouting range. I keep glancing back, waiting, but too anxious, I keep paddling. It becomes obvious that we are far east of Point Adolphus, drifting with the flood. Ahead the smear of Chichagof Island has materialized as a ruddy stone fractured like paving bricks. I can see branches on trees. But it still takes a half hour, the longest half hour. Then one hundred yards, fifty yards, stroking . . . looking for the best place to land among the cobbles . . . twenty yards, ten . . . "Oh, jeez, at last!" I say aloud, and I bounce ashore, crawl out of the kayak, tears pouring from my eyes.

As Maren approaches, I see the distance and scale. She is frighteningly small, a fleck of white and green among the waves. She approaches endlessly as if on a treadmill. Then comes her song, "Shenandoah." She hollers, and when she scrapes ashore, she kneels and kisses the rocks. We strip down to long underwear, casting drysuits onto the rocks where they land like deflated corpses, and eat: dried apricots, Hershey bars, gorp. Drinking. We are elated and relieved and swelling with a newfound confidence, looking back at the far shore.

"We need to stay together next time," she says, peeling Band Aids off her hands. "I'm glad we made it across, but just wait for me."

Paddling east, along the coast of Chichagof toward Port Frederick and Hoonah, the afternoon squalls bring four rainbows, beams of sun, terrific headwinds, and dead calm. Two humpback whales rise and sink near land. Three brown bears emerge from the forest to rummage among the tidal flats. A startled seal splashes my kayak. High ribbons of geese fly above. The flashing backs of harbor porpoises gleam ahead. It is all grand, and I feel that we have shed something in Icy Strait, the sense of lacking and ineptitude that such a gargantuan landscape evokes.

We are paddling strong when we confront a clear-cut, a cone of red dirt that marks the beginning of Native corporation land. It is the same clear-cut I saw in the paper at Jim Mackovjak's place. CMTs. A thin wall of guard trees is all that remains of the forest here. And suddenly the solitude and pristine qualities of Glacier Bay seem contrived. It is a park, after all, a land managed for specific reasons. Crossing Icy Strait, we have crossed into another management scheme. As Jim had said, there are always plans for the land.

Soon the hills drop away, and Port Frederick opens into the heart of Chichagof. On the chart it is a gash that cuts southeast, nearly cleaving Chichagof in half. Slowly, the water fills with wood debris: branches, splinters, and needles that gather in the eddy lines. An axiom: When the land changes, the sea changes. There are many clear-cuts now. We make camp on a small island in position for tomorrow's paddle into town. Twenty-five miles today, twelve hours. Our longest.

A southerly wind stirs at dusk. Camp is dirty, full of trash. As the moon fills the hollow of shadowy peaks, Hoonah's dock lights snap on, twinkling.

In Hoonah

MAY 1

We awake to chain saws. Trees split like popping bone, then
fall in a crash. But we are blinded, fogged in a world of audio,
and can see no farther than nearby spruce boughs. Our island
has large trees, and I walk into the spongy woods and stop.
At my foot, a deer leg, severed from the knee down: dark
blood, fur intact, glossy black hooves. Overhead, the *kruuuck,
ah-ho, ah-ho* of ravens.

As the fog rises, we load and make our way to Hoonah.
It is strange going in and out of civilization, like a sewing
needle punching through the fabric of wild. Leaving the island, the hillside is uncloaked, red earth dripping with trees.
Once across the inlet the day burns bright, and Hoonah unfurls, stretching across the water on pilings, the fuel dock,
store, dozens of fishing boats, and homes stacking up the hillside. A paintless wooden speedboat rots in the tide, its ribcage
sinking into the sand, still tethered to the dock as if it might
suddenly resurrect and flee.

People are out enjoying the midday warmth, and the entire
town greets us, waving from docks and boats, as if we were
proceeding down a parade route. We take a shag-carpeted

room at the Snug Harbor Lodge, lug the kayaks to safe ground, shower, and walk. It feels good to use the legs.

Days are longer now, and twilight lingers past ten o'clock. Kids race down the main street, two on bikes, one riding in a plastic car, and several on Big Wheels, skidding their sneakers along the asphalt, squealing with joy. By the time we pass over the hill, they have sailed down three times.

Unlike Gustavus, Hoonah has a definite center, and we follow this bright street along the water and through the heart of town. It is three weeks until summer break. A girl dances on the oxidized hood of a blue Camaro while a friend stands by and giggles. At the wheel, a teenager blares "Beat It," increasing the volume as we walk by. He stares at the legs pounding on the hood. A fat, grubby dog barks at the exhausts of 4x4 trucks. "She's been run over twice," says the girl dancing on the Camaro. A man sees us watching this pitiful creature and says, "Hoonah is a town of nine hundred . . . two thousand if you count the dogs."

The clerk closes the grocery store after we purchase some cheese. He knows we are new in town and welcomes us, and he replies to our travels by saying he is a high-school senior training for a trip to Glacier Bay with his classmates and a teacher who likes kayaking. He is full of questions and enthusiasm, following us out to chain the parking lot, then returning to help a final customer.

Hoonah is predominantly a Tlingit town, and traditional form-line paintings adorn occasional sheds and window shades. We follow roads that turn to gravel as they branch into the residential streets of modest homes. In 1946 a fire destroyed most of Hoonah, sparing only the perimeter of town. Before the fire, the town was built on pilings that curved in a crescent along the beach. Elders say the fire started beneath the old shoreline homes. In those days not everyone had their own smokehouse, so some people smoked fish under their houses. One day a wind blew up, and one of these fires ignited fishing nets that were stored nearby. The wooden houses were so close that the fire spread quickly beyond control. When the smoke cleared, the devastation was so great that the United States government redirected prefab buildings being sent to the Philippines up to Hoonah. These homes lacked insulation, however, and that first winter was terribly cold.

The town backs against a high hill, and looking across Port Frederick, almost every slope is cut into brown rectangles. Whitestone logging camp, to the south of town, bustles with loggers from Washington and Oregon who came north with the prospect of work. We are reluctant to ask about the logging, however. It is an explosive issue, and we are vulnerable, so small in the water and traveling so slowly.

Most notably, Hoonah lives off the sea. The Tlingit have a saying that "when the tide is out, the table is set." And during these sunny days, yards fill with broad tables of drying seaweed that was gathered at the zero tide level from traditional sites in the area. People smile and tempt us to try some. We eat it like popcorn.

As the moon rises, we meet more children on the sidewalk. "Are you new?" they ask, jumping rope. "Glacier Bay is where we're from."

They hopscotch among chalk drawings, and Maren says that spring is here for sure. When the town is quiet, a cat darts across the road. Then out of the stillness, a generator fires to life.

MAY 2

This morning we meet a big man with a broad smile who is full of stories. "Did you see the whales bubble feeding yesterday?" he asks, resting his shovel. "They were here, but Nacho wasn't here. Nacho is a humpback we all know. He's got a notch in his dorsal fin from a boat accident, or maybe he was born that way. So his name is Nacho. Once when I was in Hawaii I saw him. He traveled all the way down there. But we haven't seen Nacho for several years."

Then he tells of a raven he trained. It would tap on his

windows when it wanted food. It would land on his shoulders. "I helped save it when it was caught in some string. Then it wouldn't leave me alone," he says. "One day it just didn't come back. Time for raven to move on. It, too, went away."

A tree by the cemetery in front of town blossoms with eagles. I stop counting at thirty.

MAY 3

After flapjacks, we meet Kenny Grant, president of the Hoonah Indian Association, over a cup of coffee. He has a thin, peppered beard and wears a ubiquitous Ray Troll T-shirt—DON'T WORRY, BE HUMPY—which seems as popular as salmon along the entire coast. We tell him about our travels.

"Sounds like a great journey. I used to live in Seattle," he says, sipping from his mug. "For most of us in Hoonah, Seattle is the wilderness. And for Seattle, this is the wilderness. So you see, it's reversed."

He is soft-spoken and articulate, cupping his mug with both hands as he talks. "Glacier Bay is imbedded in our history. It's inescapable. All of our stories, our songs, our personal names, our regalia, everything has its origins in Glacier Bay National Park, not just the Bay proper. The outer coast. So you know it is hard to separate the homeland part of it from our people here in Hoonah.

"The creation of Glacier Bay National Park definitely affected the Huna people. No one knew what was going to be the outcome when it first started as a national monument. No one knew what a monument meant. I asked the elders what they thought. Of course, a lot of our people didn't understand the English language then. No one knew the ramifications of the word 'monument' or the word 'preserve.' Elders said that it was explained to them that they would be allowed to use it in a traditional fashion—'You can come and go'—and if the elders that were up there needed any assistance or help of any kind, they could call the rangers. The preserve gradually grew down to the entrance to what we know as Glacier Bay. And just a few years ago, in 1980, it became a national park. And it was slow moving like a glacier. Gradually moved our people out. And that's the metaphor I use, too. Ice Age. Second Ice Age. Cold federal policy."

"What kind of access for traditional use do the Huna people have now?" Maren asks.

"As we know it, it has been a very undefined line as to what we could and what we couldn't do over there. We signed a memorandum of understanding with the park, and we're working on the Huna presence in the park. None of it has been clearly spelled out yet, but based on the document, we agreed to meet and resolve the issues," he says.

I shift in my chair. "You must be in the middle of those questions as president of the Hoonah Indian Association," I say, concerned that I am pressing things.

"I think whoever holds the position and sets the goals we have, it will be the same. I think it's not unique to Hoonah. I think anyone who steps out of the realm of the norm becomes a target immediately—a little more so when you are in a little village around people that you know and love and communicate with. It's a little harder. You feel the pain a little more than in a large city.

"I must be pushing the bounds, but I thought it was necessary. The squeaky joint gets the oil, you know. We had to raise our voices. We had to do something. The Glacier Bay place naming was a good thing to do because the realization that our culture is . . . the sun is setting as we know it. It will go on, but it won't be the same. The traditional Tlingit place naming was done just at the last moment when it was most effective, I think. If we would have waited a few years . . . a lot of the elders have passed on now. They were buried with the names, you know, but we were able to gather a good portion of it. It's like Linnaeus said, 'If you do not know the names, your knowledge of things perish.' Brilliant words.

"Our names are not like the English, the Euro method of naming. There are certain places where things happened, and the place is named after it. It's not superficial; it's deeply rooted in the culture. It's not just a person's name.''

He takes another sip of coffee.

''If you study the Tlingit place names, the name itself speaks of a consciousness. 'Sit' Eeti Gei' is the name of Glacier Bay. It was translated by a few people to mean 'the place where the glacier used to be.' But in my upbringing, in my knowledge of the Tlingit language, I take it one step further. That 'i' at the end shows possession. If I were to say, 'This is mine,' I would say, 'ux aadi.' Add that 'i.' If the house was mine, I would say, 'ux hiti,' the house that *belongs* to me. Because Sit' Eeti Gei has that possession on the end, I would say it translates to 'the place that *belongs* to where the glacier used to be.' This gives the bay a consciousness. It's not just a place where the glacier used to be. It is a place that *belongs* to where the glacier used to be. We give it the credit, a consciousness, that glacier has a right of possession. It owns that place. People call it a spirit, but it's not a kind of pantheism. I call it a consciousness. The ice has a consciousness. That's why we treat it with reverence. We have so much respect for Mount Fairweather, for the glacier, that we don't point at them.''

We tell him of our camp at the face of the Riggs Glacier, of our time with ice, of inadvertently following John Muir's travels.

He smiles as I say this name. ''John Muir occupies both ends of the spectrum from my perspective. I think he was remiss to not give the Natives credit for having used and occupied Glacier Bay, and to claim credit for discovering it. He may have discovered it for the naturalist community. But I give him a lot of credit. He saw something that should be protected. And knowing today's society, the development mentality of our market forces, you know . . . Today after seeing what's going on, I say, 'Thank God! Thank God!' that he was able to enshrine the naturalness of that country, probably forever. I would hope forever. So that's the other end of the spectrum.''

''Good perspective,'' I say, pleased to learn that we

share a similar take on Muir. Soon the talk drifts to his travels in Icy Strait and southeast Alaska and to places we have each known well. We remark how rapid change is, how so many people see familiar landscapes altered, even obliterated, in a lifetime. "It was a shock to encounter the logging in Port Frederick," I say, before I can think to stay clear of the issue. "People in town seem upset." Kenny recradles his mug.

"I think I wrote in my declaration of harm to the Forest Service that the bottom line to me is the damage that it does to our psyche, if I could put it in that term. There is a futility factor that nobody talks about. For myself and for others in the community that are concerned, it is an awesome task to even suggest to preserve the trees. There are so many people accustomed to the paychecks and the benefits of what the income can do. It alters our level of thinking. Is our culture worth it? Maybe not. Look what's happening: We claim that our culture is woven into our environment, the trees around us, the deer, bear, everything, you know. And yet it's being cut. Nobody has addressed this. So maybe we aren't worthwhile. Maybe we aren't worth it. I think it's an unspoken level of mentality that's happening, that weakens our culture. And to me that's the biggest harm. We try to strengthen our culture, but we are not really connected to the land anymore."

As I grub for a response, Maren asks if the Native corporations and the Alaska Native Claims Settlement Act caused this situation.

"Well, it's all part of the big picture. An elder gave a metaphor of the waves that hit our shorelines. And I see the land claims as one of the waves that erodes our shorelines. I think it was meant for assimilation. And it was pretty effective. Money is a very powerful drug. It splits families. It splits cultures. And it is doing it. I think separating or giving property to a corporation was the biggest mistake that was ever made. The land should have gone to the tribes and been held in tribal trust.

"There are many waves that erode our shorelines. The first

was Columbus. Then the diseases came and wiped out many of our people. The preserve, the park was another wave. It was very silent. Then statehood. Then land claims. Of course, we never like to talk against the churches because they are very much a part of our community. The churches, of course, advocated making young English gentlemen and ladies out of us." He laughs.

Kenny's smile gives me the confidence to ask about the controversial legacy of the residential schools.

"A lot of fond memories from people who have been there," he says. "I went to Sheldon Jackson. I think getting a bunch of young people together and growing up in a location like Sitka . . . I know I have very fond memories of going to high school and boarding school, rubbing elbows with Eskimos, we called them, and the Aleuts and Athabaskans, Haidas and Tsimshians, and non-Natives, too. All put into this melting pot. It was crazy. It was a lot of fun. I think there was a common ground we all shared. It was one of the unspoken things: We were Alaska Natives."

"Where did you learn to speak Tlingit?" I ask.

"We grew up with our grandparents, and we spoke it. My grandmother, when my younger brother and I would come home from school and be speaking English, she'd swat us on the rear and tell us in Tlingit to speak Tlingit. We were so little that by the time our feet touched the floor and running, we would be speaking Tlingit. We didn't even think about it, just switched gears."

He peers outside into the clear day. "In the great chess game of life, Hoonah is in the middle game, in the state of flux, not knowing what our end result will be. At least we're surviving."

"And now it is spring," I say.

"Yeah. Upbeat. Like a bear coming out of a den and shaking his hide. Stretching."

And we shake hands and are off into the sun.

I meet him later in a café, where he is finishing a burger. He is a fisherman and owns a fine vessel, studied business at the University of Washington, designs his Tlingit artwork on the computer. Penning his E-mail address on a card from the Hoonah Indian Association, he says, "Everybody has a homeland, a home. The land they grew up in. A landscape of home. But today . . . hmm. Landscape is becoming Netscape."

Hoonah to Tenakee Springs

MAY 4

Sometimes on a journey you have an encounter that changes the whole course of events. It comes when you have thought things through, planned sufficiently, yet still hang precariously undecided. Then a person steps from the crowd. And you listen. And you go as they have directed.

After a morning of indecision and debate and staring at charts, wondering if we should return to the familiarity of Juneau and paddle down Stephens Passage, we have resolved to cross the portage to Tenakee Inlet, praying that the postal service is able to forward our next month of food from Juneau to Tenakee Springs in a timely fashion. Many have told us that the portage can be a long trudge through the mud if the tide is too low, that there can be brown bear problems. Others have simply said that it is a powerful place to be. Tomorrow, when we arrive at the portage, we will arrive at the highest daytime tide of the month. It is a decision, however, that places before us several long and exposed crossings: Chatham Strait and Frederick Sound.

The decision came at noon with the tide in, the kayaks loaded and floating. I ran to the lodge to make one more phone call. And there he stood—a man we had met two days ago, covered with fish pins—impeccably dressed. He had been at the head of a table in the café, dignified, in quiet command. We had noticed his presence from several tables away. As his table departed, he had come to us.

"So you are the kayakers," he said, having seen us paddle into town.

We nodded.

"Are they ocean-going kayaks?"

"Yes, quite."

"Good," he said. "I'm Byron."

"So am I."

"Ah," said Byron, beating lightly on his chest. "Breathe deep, Lord Byron." And then he left, smiling.

Now here he was again, wearing his fish pins. "You're leaving?" he said.

"Yes."

"Where are you headed?"

"Juneau."

"No," he said shaking his head. He spoke of an old familiar route. "Take the portage to Tenakee—you'll be protected inside Chichagof. Then cross Chatham when it's quiet, and say hello to Angoon. Admiralty will shelter you when the southeasterly blows up. When it's quiet, cross Frederick Sound. Then to Kake. Through Rocky Pass and down to Ketchikan."

Then he took our picture and drove away. We were dazed. There was no questioning this advice. In fact, it wasn't advice but command. I fumbled through the charts. By piecing together a small-scale chart of Chatham Strait and a Forest Service topographic map of Rocky Pass, we could chance it.

As we leave Hoonah, a freighter floats in Port Frederick, heavy with logs, the bow nearly rising from the water. Stevedores tow log rafts alongside and load the hillsides into this iron hull bound for Japan. Then, beyond a point of land, the scene disappears, and slopes—still shaggy with forest—wedge the sky, the water quieting to the still of a lake as we paddle into the heart of Chichagof. In Salt Lake Bay a humpback huffs, leaving a silvery plume against spruce. For an instant the droplets are suspended in the great breath before vanishing.

We camp in a Forest Service cabin, a rude structure wallpapered with centerfolds and littered with unopened cigars, bottles of maple syrup, and shotgun shells. The beach fountains with clams. Interior Chichagof is a land of smooth hills, high rock, and fantastic pebble beaches, the familiar sculpting grounds of glaciers.

Spending the evening planning for high tide tomorrow, we pray that the weather holds, that there will be no bears. The moon rises over the hollow, full and bright, pulling at the water. Slowly, rocks submerge, the beach disappears, and a repose that has been absent for three days returns.

MAY 5

Gorgeous day with a brisk northwesterly blowing twenty knots, and we see the wisdom of this sheltered route. Timing is crucial, and we must arrive at the portage at high tide. Once across, we will ride the ebb as it empties from Tenakee Inlet. In this way our days defy the notion of carefree timelessness that so many people must imagine them to be. Each morning we wake to our alarm.

Following the path of a long-vanished tongue of ice, we leave for the portage, fighting the westerly component of the northwest wind until the inlet bends to the south and finally closes off the wind altogether. The land rolls into low knobs, a tumbling forest, remote and mostly roadless. With every turn, the land falls away.

As we near the portage, the inlet becomes narrow and riverlike, the water once vast enough to float trans-Pacific cargo vessels reduced to an ankle-deep stream bubbling over rocks. The tide is still rising, and we must line the kayaks through the shallows, walking beside them on the grassy shoreline knolls and towing them like pets on leashes. In a few hundred yards the water diminishes to a snaking channel, just wider than a kayak. Maren sings to the bears. Within a quarter mile of the portage, we can see the water's end.

At a shallow lake we again take to the paddles. The water is stagnant—too high to be flushed by the tides—and we pass over sunken limbs festooned with algae. At the lake's finish, we nose ashore on a patch of spring snow and drag the kayaks across a short stretch of mud and grass to a small rise. We are here. Log steps ascend the rise, placed here by hand trollers of the 1920s and 1930s who slid their boats over these wooden rails. The mud is black and ripe with decay. Over the arc of land, no more than fifty yards away, shines the brilliant blue water of Tenakee Inlet.

It is a powerful place, a meeting of waters. Like most paths in the wild, it was gleaned first from animals. In some translations, *Tenakee* is Tlingit for "killer whale crossing place," and their history tells that their ancestors discovered this passage when they observed killer whales carving a channel through the isthmus, a time when the land was lower. Isostatic rebound and the earthquake of July 10, 1958, have raised some areas in this region as much as ten feet, draining the tidewaters. Plant succession is clear, too. Grasses invade the brackish lake, and the forest closes with small seedlings among the grasses.

The trail notches the small hill. The Tlingit frequently used this neck of land as a portage for canoe travel, and John Muir passed through here in 1880 following his second visit to "Sit-a-da-kay, or Ice Bay," as he recorded the name of Glacier Bay from the Tlingit. We heave the kayaks onto the logs and slide them over and into the sparkling inlet. The maneuver is remarkably easy. We had prepared for unloading at this point and packing everything through muck. But in twenty minutes we are over. From the Tenakee side, the portage is deceptive, a side stop on the long Tenakee Inlet noted only by a dip in the land.

The inlet is treed to the water with high, snowy mountains above its southern side. And all afternoon we ride a tailwind, slipping beneath avalanche chutes of willow and rock. The shores here are suddenly rockier than Port Frederick, and beaches have become cobblestone. As we pause to consider camping on a particularly nice beach with a grassy rise, a brown bear strolls across the glade.

Finally, we pitch camp in near dark at the top of a steep, sharp beach, tramping around with bear repellent in hand, clapping and singing. Admiralty, Baranof, and Chichagof Islands, collectively known as the ABCs, have one of the highest concentrations of brown bears in the world.

A seal splashes offshore into the night, and Maren reads the poetry of song lyrics out loud. High tide comes with Venus and the moon rising over snowy caps. Calm and clear. Quiet and cold. Now no sounds.

MAY 6

Last night the tide crept to within two feet of the tent and food cache but no closer. This morning it is out again, lying low like a mischievous boy who has done wrong but admits to nothing.

Our morning is still. While the south-shore beaches are warm and yellow, the sun has only gradually begun to fire this beach, advancing from stone to stone as if the curve of the beach were the curve of Earth itself. We must move on at some point this morning but have no marathon ambitions. Our food will not arrive in Tenakee Springs for two days. Also, our schedule has changed with the change in tide. While yesterday we traveled with the morning flood, today we must wait for the afternoon ebb to help propel us out of Tenakee Inlet. In this way, crossing the portage has reversed our days.

More than anywhere else so far, Maren enjoys this inlet. It is more predictable and intimate than Icy Strait, more accommodating than the stark upper reaches of the Muir Inlet. Also, her fingers have begun to heal. So today she is elated as we breakfast, knowing she will have a leisurely morning to sketch and sun on beach logs.

After an easy paddling day, sailing beneath the high mountains and drooping cornices, I break branches and clear driftwood embedded in soil to make room for the tent. The impact on the land seems great for a single night's stay, but there is no other place. We have likely fallen into a routine that will last the rest of the journey: While I beaver away at pitching the tent and unpacking camp gear, Maren cooks. We eat. Then I clean dishes in the tidewater while she readies the next day's breakfast and lunch. In the morning, I roll sleeping bags and collapse the tent while she prepares breakfast and makes tea for the Thermos. She thinks it is funny that we have found such traditional roles for ourselves. She has also become utterly consumed by timing the tides and must know by memory the exact moment of slack for the next day. She eases at slack and is agreeable to paddling most anywhere if the wind is not up. Falling asleep, I hear her penciling a schedule for tomorrow's ebb ride into Tenakee Springs.

In Tenakee Springs

MAY 7

We come to Tenakee Springs on a clear, breathless day, and town unravels as we round a subtle point of land. It looks strangely abandoned and scrappy, as if we are seeing it from an alley, a town with its back to the sea. We grab the seaplane dock as the mail arrives on a Beaver and are told where to get a cabin and unload.

Inside, the town is alive with the first bright days of spring, and the people have come onto the pathway among the daffodils and dandelions. We settle into a cabin, and a woman from Snyder Mercantile lights the oil stove. We are checked in. On the wall is a sign:

Welcome to Tenakee Springs
Heating is by oil heater . . .
Cooking is electric . . .
In winter, tap water will probably freeze. Water may
    then be obtained by bucket at Schoolhouse Creek.
Turn left from cabin to the creek bridge.
Toilet facilities are "out back" on the beach side.
HAVE A PLEASANT STAY

"Out back" means that over the intertidal zone, and behind several dwellings gangplanks lead high above the beach to an outhouse, and we realize that we unloaded our kayaks in the town sewer. But the town is small, less than a hundred residents, and the tidal exchange so great in the thirty-five deep miles of Tenakee Inlet that every high tide gives the town a complete flush. It is little different than our practice during days in camp when we squat behind intertidal boulders, emptying bowels onto the beach cobbles. When we ask about hygiene, we are told that no coliform has shown up in any water tests. On my first visit over the tides, I find an old magazine with my name in it, a short piece I wrote about a tent maker named Byron. Through the toilet seat, I see beach rocks far below and feel that the whole town is watching. Near the bakery is an outhouse known as "the long drop."

A single trail runs level among the colorful buildings, a gravel path for pedestrians, dogs, single-gear bicycles with baskets, and a few golf carts driven by longtime residents who are no longer ambulatory. When we mistakenly call this trail a street, we are informed that it is very much not a street or road. That it is not made for cars. And several proud residents joke that the only car in town is "maintained in an unusable condition." When we go to the post office, a man rises from the bench out front. "You must be Maren and Byron. Your package is here."

When I buy Kit Kats at Snyder Mercantile, the clerk steps to the old cash register and turns the crank. "Made in 1917," she says.

Most homes are built on pilings, a practiced style in much of southeast Alaska, where all materials must be shipped in and building a foundation can cost more than the house itself. Antlers and nets, net floats, and aging tools cling to the exteriors of older homes. Some are log cabins, originals, built when Tenakee Springs was established as a cannery town near the turn of the century. The town is almost mystical, and the friendly people and old cabins seem to evoke the ideals of a different era.

Tenakee Springs is often called a retirement community,

but many people have simply lived here for a long time and are merely old. There is some new blood, however, some recent retirees from Juneau, some seeking odd jobs, some having second homes here, summer folk, who, depending on the year, arrive sometime after the first of June. We meet the "year-rounders," residents who are coming off an Alaska winter into the first few bright days of spring.

The town exists because of the springs, a natural hot bath that bubbles and burps sulfurous smells from the bare rocks inside an austere concrete bathhouse. It was closed for three days for painting and reopened just the day before. Everybody in town seems to be going to or from the bath. There are strictly defined women's hours and men's hours. Although we are eventually told that it can be co-ed between midnight and 4 A.M.

We parboil our bodies in the spring at every chance, soaking up benefits from the Tenakee fault system that cuts through Chichagof Island. We are always thinking ahead. The next food shipment will arrive in Wrangell. I'm anxious about moving on, making time, but that will surely come. From Tenakee we are on our own for several weeks. But with a Chatham Strait crossing just ahead, it is an easy decision to stay in this town where nobody needs to go beyond first names.

In the afternoon I am naked in the tub of rock, talking easily among strangers. Shoulder to shoulder, I can see that I am turning fit, deltoids now shadowing the biceps. Before entering the spring, we dip rinse water from a decapitated Clorox bleach jug. A man slips into the tub, introducing himself as Pete. He is into our trip. Into living in Tenakee. "It's like you're in outer space sometimes; the stars are right there."

He is engaging, friendly, and sharp and talks of friends building human-powered craft, a catamaran that can be made into a treehouse, Native sweat lodges and painting and drawing, which he does all winter. I ask about the fishing.

"It's stone-ax simple. Small operations can't compete with things getting larger. Another local fisherman here called it quits last week. No computers. Regulation fees. They can't afford them like big corporations.

"People get caught up in their machines. But it's all done by humans. People show me their new computers. I say, 'Make something. Show me your creations. Build a trail. Shovel snow.' "

Another man slips into the bath. He introduces himself as Roger and is excited about black walnuts. "I read a story in *Mother Earth News*, a great take on economics and investment. A father planted a black walnut tree every year for forty years, then gave them to his son, saying that he had to do the same. The kid harvested one tree every year for forty thousand dollars, and planted another one. Talk about sustainability!"

He has been renovating a building in town to make a bike repair shop, and he and his wife, Elizabeth, have bicycled across the United States several times. He tells me that logging roads almost connect Hoonah and Tenakee. Some want to have them joined. Others say that will change the character of town if you could drive here from somewhere. Tenakee is adamant about keeping the roads separated. "People can portage by bicycle," he says, sinking up to his neck in the tub.

"Tenakee is a liberating place if you have a notion toward sustainability because you have a chance to practice it. You can go human powered all the way here. You don't realize what it is not to have cars around until they aren't around, how much they stink. Keeping this place without cars becomes a mission sometimes. It's difficult to ever make a reversal. Once you're in a place that has cars, you don't get rid of cars. A whole industry gets built up around the cars and a whole way of living. The very few places left in the country that are carless and roadless become jewels, really to be thought of as something getting more and more special because it's getting more and more rare as roads are punched through everywhere. The water is our highway, and boats have taken the place of cars. And the boats are very utilitarian, not pleasure craft, and people use them to participate in the subsistence harvest, which is a very big deal here."

When I return from the bath, Maren has spread our food

shipment across the floor and is packing Ziplocs of macaroni and spaghetti leather into the bear canisters. Hungry for calories, we have already gorged on candy bars and must purchase even more at Snyder's. Then she heads for the springs.

MAY 8

A bear was shot in town a few weeks ago. It had been drawn to a cabin where the occupant had been careless about storing food and garbage, and the bear began breaking in for food. Someone was joking that they should have given it a brick of cheese to constipate it so it wouldn't come around anymore. But eventually, as happens with so many "garbage" bears, it was shot as a danger to the community. It limped down to the water, where nearly the whole town saw it collapse into the tides to soothe its wounds, and there it died. A massage therapist in town says she has worked with several bear skeletons to see how ligaments and tendons and bones move together. She wants to improve her technique, rotating limbs, flexing digits. She says words that I remember—marrow, palsied, sinew, manipulate—as she describes her art of healing the inner by working the outer.

People in Alaska are always eager to tell of disasters, and we hear of three. A few years ago the Tenakee fire, started by an electrical short, burned the inn and old tavern in seven hours. It had been dry and windy, and loggers arrived with the National Guard and Forest Service. Without them, it would have consumed the whole town. On Thanksgiving Day some years back, the town had a flood, a spring tide combined with high onshore winds. Waves invaded the back doors. And in somber tones we are told that the Forest Service has plans to log more of Tenakee Inlet, around the portage, which many people cherish as an historic, even a sacred, area.

Hail and showers fall all afternoon, and we are glad to be soaking again in the warm spring. The town enjoys a panorama of snowy slopes and smooth valleys. A towering three-pronged peak at the mouth of the inlet is said to be a place where the Tlingit escaped the great flood. And clouds around this peak have been used for ages to gauge winds on Chatham Strait.

In the bath, I hear of an elderly Native man who died of a heart attack at the Fireman's Ball. His father was one of the last Tlingit owners of the Tenakee area. The town was spooked. There were reports of eagles sitting on poles where they were never seen before. Whales surfaced in the harbor in great numbers. This man had known every cove and sandbar of the inlet, and all the young pilots had learned from him. They put his body on the ferry to Hoonah. One day, a month and a half later, dozens of people spontaneously showed up at a potluck. The Tlingit mark the end of mourning with a party forty days after a death. The potluck had been going for some time before someone announced in astonishment that the Fireman's Ball had been exactly forty days before.

Tonight Pete stops by the cabin, and we talk about books into the twilight. Then he reads one of his poems. "Sudden hummingbirds . . ." he speaks into the cooling air, "materialize as messengers from a better place. . . ."

The tide floods at night, now. A solitary light flashes on Tenakee Reef, and mine remains the only light burning in town.

MAY 9

I hold a final boat bake today, bracing the kayak's hull with boards and carrying the craft into the cabin, holding it over the oil stove, turning it slowly on a rotisserie of arms. When the braces are removed, the hull at last retains its shallow arch.

In the evening we visit a family who lives on a home-built barge. "If the world goes, we're on the jumping-off point,"

Kerry says in the comfortable and compact kitchen. "There are a lot of little hidey holes up here."

We talk for a while. He is peaceful and kind. His wife, Eileen, sits behind us, watching TV with an ankle wrapped in bandages. Earlier today, home medicine dictated that a cyst had to be crushed with a dictionary, and she is recovering. Kerry spits out a tide table for May on his computer. "We've got a microwave, too," he says. "A home of the '90s."

They have embraced the challenge of subsistence living and stock a large freezer with the meats of deer and fish. We talk about paddling routes and plans. Where to camp on Chichagof? How to cross expansive Frederick Sound? His finger traces the chart, down the rugged coast, pausing at possible campsites along Baranof, good landing beaches on Admiralty. Then he taps on Frederick Sound. "When you get here, watch out," he says without smiling. "Kayaks are just speed bumps to fishermen." Then he retrieves a block of halibut from the freezer and slides it across the table. "Here," he says. "This should help."

Crossing Chatham Strait

MAY 10

As we load the kayaks, a man burns a terrific pile of trash on the beach, flames licking up into the blue. The friendliness we have found here tempts us to linger, but it is a banner-blue morning, and we have just begun to travel the great distance south. The villages, still set along the shores a few paddling days apart, have become small refuges for us as they have been for paddlers for centuries. In Tlingit country, we paddle among the traditional territories of the various "kwáans," or tribes, who owned and controlled their respective regions from a permanent winter village in the area. In Hoonah, we were at the center of the Xunaa Kwáan. From Tenakee, we are no more than a three-day paddle from Angoon, the waters of the Xutsnoowú Kwáan. As we leave Tenakee Inlet, a woman waves from a far shore. This pleases us greatly and leaves the lasting impression of the place.

After such seclusion and quiet waters, Chatham Strait feels exposed. The sky is open again, and we can see north to Point Couverden, where Icy Strait meets Chatham, and in the hazy east, the sloping shores of Admiralty Island. Among southeast Alaska's Alexander Archipelago, the major straits are wide with little protection, and we must stick to coves and crannies and assorted offshore rocks as much as possible. Here in Chatham, however, the shoreline sweeps from beach to rounded points that do little to block the following waves. As we enter Chatham, a floatplane flies low overhead. "I wonder if the planes ever see us?" Maren asks.

"They are probably looking for us," I quip. But she does not find comfort in my sarcasm.

The waves build in Chatham Strait, following seas that twist the kayaks, and we must rudder with the paddle every third stroke. The bows rise and fall, sinking into the back of the next rolling wave. We are limber and less rigid in the water than when we first encountered such seas in Glacier Bay. But after riding the waves for a few miles this windy afternoon, we are eager to find camp, and we pull to a pebble beach at the foot of an old spruce forest. Beds of moss drape like tablecloths over the shoreline. It is a good, sheltered camp, one where we can stay for several days if the weather sours while waiting to cross Chatham. From shore we can see south to the open Pacific.

At dusk, a great white cruise ship plies south along Chatham Strait. Immense and surreal against the distant shore, it glides, nearly flying, seemingly unmoved by the waves and water. In twenty minutes it has traversed our field of view and leaves only a trailing wisp of blue smoke, an apparition.

MAY 11

We awake at 4:30 to a great indigo. Last night my snoring and the deep breaths of a humpback just offshore kept Maren awake, and she teases me through breakfast with snorting sounds between bites of granola. I heard the whale's huffing all night, too. Despite the lost sleep, we are full of energy, and Maren is eager to paddle. Again it is a crossing day, and we must break camp quickly.

When we pull from shore, Admiralty Island is still in the

shadows, a dusky-gray form some six miles ahead. Beneath, Chatham Strait deepens abruptly, plunging some 1,800 feet in its center. And so departing Chichagof, we sense the first frightful weightlessness of flying.

The Chatham Strait fault is one of the largest in southeast Alaska, straight and deep, extending through the Chilkat River valley near Haines to the Pacific in the south. Land on the west side of the fault is slipping north. In geologic time, Chichagof and Admiralty Islands are pedestrians strolling past. Rocks found on the western edge of the fault often match those on the eastern side that are nearly one hundred miles farther south. In this way, perhaps the beautiful beaches we have found on Chichagof are previews to what we may encounter across the fault and farther down. It is always good to know which way the land is moving.

Again, we have heard the horror stories. Chatham Strait is known to roar. During high pressures, the winds funnel down from Skagway and the interior, blowing unobstructed to the open Pacific. Storm winds bellow in from the ocean. Of all the straits in southeast Alaska, Chatham is the longest, straightest, and often most tumultuous. But this morning we are lucky. Chatham is glass, as flat as a millpond.

As I pull ahead, two whirlpools stir to life. One spins clockwise about the blade, the other counterclockwise, like the great high- and low-pressure centers that govern the seasons. As I glide ahead, slipping farther from shore, the small twisters soon spin themselves out, dying somewhere behind my kayak in the friction of salt water. In their wake I mark a distance, rather like noting a stride, a forward movement, incremental and repetitive—a cadence. It is nothing I ever measure by science but rather something that is settled into unthinkingly, like walking. An endless procession of reaching out and cupping the water.

I have my eyes on a peak and guide the nose of my kayak toward its dark horn. After most of an hour, Admiralty's shoreline is still cloaked in shadows. Glistening backs appear. Porpoises! With puffing breaths, they change course as they near our kayaks. Ahead, they are mere flashes of light.

Without the occasional flotsam slipping past, there is no immediate way to determine speed or distance or if we are moving at all. The water is mesmerizing. All I have to go by is Maren's kayak and the steady wake streaming past my hull. The morning sun burns just off my bow, a fire in the water. My knuckles are purpled and hot again, now scarred from the blisters of Glacier Bay. My face is reddening, and I am dripping sweat inside this plastic drysuit. At times, it is as if we are paddling into oblivion.

Near midchannel we pause, surrounded by distant land. It has been more than an hour's paddle to this point, and we rest between tides, in the center of a complete calm. Rafting together, we stretch and eat dried apricots and gaze north to Skagway and Haines, where an arm of the Inside Passage reaches for the interior. Then we look south, along the high snows of Chichagof and Baranof on the west, along the lesser and drier slopes of Admiralty to the east, to the far Pacific. For some time we float at this quiet center until the first stirrings of the ebb begin. And then we move on, the lower forested hills of Admiralty seeming to rise, eclipsing the higher peaks. Only one other small vessel, a fishing boat, putters along the Admiralty shore. Far behind, the Alaska State Ferry has steered into Tenakee.

Slowly land focuses. At last the sun breaks over the peaks and illuminates a point of land directly on our course. The point is white in the sun, and for a remarkable hour as we near the island, the sunlight remains focused only on this single bright shore. Maren begins to sing: "My Bonnie Lies Over the Ocean," "I Dig Rock 'n' Roll Music," "Java Jive"— whatever falls into mind. And when she sings, I know we will make it.

Admiralty's shores are bold white outcroppings and beaches of smooth egglike stones. About twenty yards from shore we fly over an immense kelp forest, brilliant green ribbons streaming in the wind of tide. We follow their arching stems down through the turquoise to the depths where they are rooted, anchored on stones the size of grapefruit. Then we nose ashore.

Still the entire strait is tranquil, the haze of early morning burning away. More than ever we believe that we can do this, that the water ahead can be paddled, that days like this do exist, and we collapse, drying on the beach, enjoying a solace together. For nearly an hour we marvel at how we have powered ourselves across something so wide and have landed on the luxurious shores of marble.

After lunching, a loud snap in the forest sends us scurrying for the kayaks, and we continue south, the shore protruding far into the water in aprons of rock. On a headland near a nice beach are three crosses, most likely fishermen who have lost their lives. Despite the amenities of the cove, we should not camp here, and as happens every day in late afternoon, we must decide where to camp. It is difficult, for all of the momentum that it took to move camp and paddle must be channeled into setting it up again: What took so long to set in motion must now be ceased. To camp too near Angoon could mean bear problems, especially on Admiralty, which has an average of about one brown bear per square mile. Admiralty Island was named in 1794 by Vancouver, but the Tlingit knew it as Kootznoowoo, "fortress of the bears." Near towns we run the risk of running into a garbage bear, one that has learned the equation: People equals food. Bears elsewhere, while posing a very real danger, usually do not wish to be around us. After some discussion and the lack of a good beach, we paddled into town.

All afternoon Angoon is visible, boxy homes stacked like milk cartons on the hillside. It lies on the mouth of Kootznahoo Inlet, a maze of tidal streams that fill and empty the vast waters of Mitchell Bay through a narrow channel. By the time we reach Angoon, the flood has begun. A fisherman in a small skiff says we should go through before the current gets any worse. "You've got eighteen minutes and more guts than I do paddling that thing," he says.

We enter the outer rapids, and clearly the rush has increased to a steady roar. We pull near shore and ask another fisherman about the current. He has only enough time to point before leaping toward his engine, firing it just in time to keep off the rocks. We are drifting, too, much faster than we can paddle against. And so we are going through the narrows.

Water wraps around a reef, then flows over a ledge like a river into the bay. My speed relative to the water is unchanged. Leaves float past at normal velocity. But shoreline rocks are a blur, and ahead the water actually spills downhill. The current grabs the kayaks and slings us forward, spitting us into a powerful eddy, which gives way to more current that propels us to a dock. We float a bit dazed, knowing that we cannot leave until tomorrow at slack tide. A man steps from his home and examines us through binoculars. "Welcome to Angoon," he says, waving. "Saw you from our floatplane yesterday, coming out of Tenakee Inlet."

"Where do we go?" I ask.

"Here. Right here."

We unload the kayaks, tie them to a dock, and sit down with Gil and his wife, Gail, to a tray of two dozen drumsticks, homemade bread, and heaps of chocolate cake. "Ha! Isn't that something?" Gil says wiping his mouth. "We saw you yesterday, and now you're here. I guess it was meant to be."

"The tide brought us," says Maren.

"That's how Angoon gets visitors. Eat! Eat! You must be starved."

In Angoon

MAY 12

"You travel at a pace that is challenging the new world," Gil says over breakfast.

And I feel its tug. Even in these smaller towns, what we are doing seems foreign, although just a hundred years ago many people who lived in these villages canoed these waters, perhaps paddled the entire coast. Now that time seems distant, separate, and we are greeted as adventurers, as risk takers, as interesting but novel people—a notion we have begun to like.

Gil is from Salinas, California, an ex-Hollywood stuntman who began his career busting broncs with Slim Pickins and has been in films such as *East of Eden* and *Winterhawk*, television shows such as *Baretta*. He loves to talk on a cordless phone and strolls around the house in lively conversation whenever it rings. Gail has been a television and radio reporter in Juneau and Unalaska. She, like Gil, was "adopted" by Tlingit families in Angoon and from them says she has learned reverence and respect. She is keen and honest and works long hours for the emergency clinic in town.

With them, we attend the Presbyterian church. We are

introduced as visitors along with a tug captain who has not been in the church for forty years, and the pastor carries the image in his prayer, saying, "Help us all, Lord, for we are all people of the boat." The sermon is fiery and articulate, built from the passage about putting on the armor of God in Paul's letter to the Ephesians. At the end of the service, we receive red long-stem roses, which we carry about town. It is Mother's Day, and it seems appropriate to be in an old Tlingit town, among people who have for so long lived within a matrilineal society.

Angoon is the only Tlingit village left on this island where once there were many. It stands on an isthmus, the old clan houses of weathered clapboard facing the beach on Chatham Strait. Killer Whale House was built in the late 1800s, and its whitewashed and formline killer whales have been repainted many times by the descendents of that family. The traditional chief's title is Guctahín and relates the swift, billowing water around a killer whale's dorsal fin.

All afternoon Chatham remains flat, and skiffs are out fishing for kings. But they probably will catch Dolly Varden, someone says at the dock, which they will give to the dogs.

We climb to the base of the highest point in Angoon, the antenna (marked on our nautical chart as Angoon's conspicuous landmark), its receivers and transmitters covered taut like Tlingit drums and painted with formline figures. Angoon has been jolted from an almost entirely subsistence community to one connected with distant places only in the last thirty years by three big catalysts: telephone, television, and the ferry service. "Now everyone goes to Juneau shopping," says a man working in his yard. "Those who remain subsistent fishers compete with the new predators of sport and commercial fishing." He adds, "We have six miles of road and about seven hundred people here, and new cars are everywhere, maybe seven hundred of them. There are seven hundred at the dump, too."

Although a number of people in town can speak Tlingit, children may only learn to count in Tlingit. Few elders are living. A student here has created a computer program where you can enter a Tlingit family name, and it will output the clan lineage.

Hearing that there was a bear in town earlier, we keep to the open streets. Near the radio tower, some boys spill out from a driveway with a litter of soft kittens, which Maren lets crawl on her shoulders. When an animal peeps from beneath her hair, it sends the boys cackling. This small creature somehow eases her from the thoughts of paddling Chatham tomorrow, and for several minutes she holds the kitten close before we continue.

We attend the last moments of the Angoon Baccalaureate at the Assembly of God church, with its thin, unornamented spire. The crowd is mostly relatives, and there are four of the seven or so graduates in attendance. Afterward, the sun is setting across Chatham Strait, and we are worried about the walk back to Gil and Gail's in near dark. We are not used to the threat of bears in town. But in Angoon the distinction between wild and settled is obscured. Earlier, when we passed by the dump, a brown bear was wrestling with a Buick.

Angoon to Tyee

MAY 13

At 7:15 A.M. we tune to the VHF weather channel and get no reception. There is also no need. Calm and sun prevail. A deHavilland Beaver, the single-prop workhorse of the coast, glides in over Kootznahoo Inlet, teetering its wings, adjusting, then skimming across the glaze into Mitchell Bay. It is a perfect morning to paddle, but when in Angoon, we must wait for the tide. So, while Maren catnaps, I amble across the rocks to study the torrent. The tide floods, and shoals boil to a foam. A white-water river has a brighter timbre and is somehow less substantial, even dainty in comparison. A tidal rapid is massive and powerful, with deeper tones in its fury. It thunders. And its surge varies, making it unwieldy and less knowable, a current powered by the gravity of another world.

Gil says there is a trench in the middle of the rapids, and a utility pipe used to run along the bottom. When repairs were needed, when it would be torn apart by the stresses of the tide, divers would have to fix it, able to work for only fifteen minutes at a time during slack water. Today our fifteen minutes would begin just past noon.

The shore is gouged by current. Inland, the intricacies of

Kootznahoo Inlet are low and grassy, with tidal marshes and flats of spruce forest. Among its upper reaches along salmon streams are numerous fishing grounds and summer fishing camps. The tidal rapids guard these places, as they have long done when salmon and herring would simply come to the people—as did we—with the tide. Seaweeds, mussels, and clams were gathered along the intertidal zones, and women and children picked salmonberries, huckleberries, and blueberries by the basketful, dug roots, and scraped the edible cambium and inner bark of Sitka spruce and hemlock, while men hunted bear, beaver, and deer. They often dried food, berry pastes, and fish, to preserve for leaner times. Plants gave them medicines and building materials. It was all part of an annual cycle of life, where people lived in permanent winter villages and made seasonal rounds, gathering what they would need throughout the year. Like few other such complex cultures in the world, the Tlingit required little developed agriculture to sustain them. They lived in a luxury of abundance known to few of the more nomadic inland peoples. And until this century, the Tlingit and other Native peoples of the northwest coast largely relied, with the exception of small gardens, on what they had learned to gather from the shore and sea.

As we leave Angoon, we paddle past the front of town and drift. From somewhere near this spot on October 22, 1882, the U.S. revenue steamer *Corwin* and the *Favorite*, most likely the same ship that Beardslee had piloted into Glacier Bay in 1880, leveled their guns, then opened fire. It was neither the beginning nor the end of violence, merely an explosive middle that had erupted earlier with similar incidents in Kake and Wrangell. Although many versions of the story are heard, all distill to a misunderstanding among cultures at a time when the American presence in Alaska was young and the territory largely ungoverned.

A general rendition of the story goes like this: A harpoon gun aboard a Northwest Trading Company whale boat accidentally exploded, killing a Tlingit shaman. When the company refused the customary Tlingit compensation of two hundred blankets for the death, the Tlingit seized a company boat, nets, and two crewmen. Still payment was refused. Armed vessels from Sitka arrived, and the people of Angoon were told to pay twice as many blankets themselves for seizing prisoners or the village would be destroyed. The next day it was. We are caught in the gravity of the scene—the small village, rickety from the water, as if still propping itself since that day. Starvation followed in that winter of 1882. In 1973, the United States government paid the people of Angoon $90,000 in reparations.

After fighting a terrific headwind, we camp in a cove that holds a deer spine, bear paw prints, and old spruces that were chopped long ago for planks. George Vancouver's crew landed at this same cove for breakfast one July morning in 1794 and met Tlingit looking to barter furs for guns and clothing. Earlier today we passed Killisnoo Island, once a refugee camp for Aleut families displaced during World War II when the Japanese invaded and occupied the Aleutian Islands. Nearly every bay or island or point of land in this often-advertised pristine Alaska wilderness holds a human history, a legacy of many cultures, and their relationships and interactions and traditions are as complex as an ancient rain forest, as the network of inlets, coves, fiords, reaches, and straits of the Inside Passage itself.

MAY 15

The morning is breezy, and we stay in a channel between rocks and a mattress of kelp. It is our narrow paddleway, the kelp softening the waves into a billowing sheen. Kelp leaves stream like ribbons with the current, and they become our windsocks of the sea.

For two days Admiralty Island's shore rises in forested knobs and drops into blue bays shored by moons of white pebbles. We stop often and luxuriate in the midday warmth. It is drier here. Admiralty is in the rain shadow of Baranof Island and receives some three feet less precipitation per year than the sopping outer shores. The idea of a rain shadow is powerful—even one island can alter weather.

We are beginning to read the shoreline well, by chart and by sight, more easily locating landing sites, places that must surely have been visited often in the old days. The canoeing Tlingit valued what we do: steep, protected beaches. Slowly we begin to learn where paddlers have lived and landed before us.

Villages have been abandoned all along this shore, and like many place names on our charts, they carry the parenthetical ABAND. It is a testament to the uprooting that has happened in the last two centuries—Native villages decimated by disease, reduced in size then consolidated, then the countless canneries and whaling stations, mining operations, logging camps, various boom-and-bust enterprises. Even today, more people come to travel along this coast than to live.

While expecting to see many brown bears along Kootznoo-woo, we have seen only one—a haggard mass—pawing through the tidal boulders last evening. By the time we near Point Gardner, we are thankful to have had quiet nights.

This southern reach of Chatham Strait rolls with silver swells, just perceptible as they lift the kayaks. Exposure grows as we confront the Pacific, its power seeping in between islands. Shores are rugged rock, chewed basalts, with no place to land. Another crossing, our largest, looms ahead—the twelve miles of Frederick Sound.

For several hours, Point Gardner, the toe of Admiralty Island, stretches out before us, lumpy and low, a dragon's snout drowned in the waves. It is a smooth and familiar form. But the great ice has only given a unified look to these otherwise disparate lands that form the Alexander Archipelago and the rest of the Inside Passage. Despite all their seeming permanence, these terranes have drifted north for some 200 million years, gliding with the Pacific plate as if on a conveyor, gradually colliding and melding with the westwardly advancing plate of North America. They have traveled a great distance, some from as far as the Galapagos, and nearly every island is a jumble of geology—limestones shouldering basalts, young rock fronting old—a mosaic at its heart.

As the plates collided, the Coast Mountains rose, scraping moisture from the winds blowing in from the Pacific. Rain and snow fell against the mountain wall, the highland snows accumulating and compacting over seasons into glacial ice that has periodically descended to overrun the lowlands, then retreat. As the Wisconsinan glacial stage of the Pleistocene reached its maximum between twenty thousand and fourteen thousand years ago, sea levels reached a nadir, their water sealed in the vast ice sheets, and the continental margin lay bare. As the ice melted, it unveiled a landscape of rounded hills and smooth valleys that we have been passing for a month now. Sea levels rose and flooded the troughs quarried by glaciers. More slowly, as in Glacier Bay, the land rebounded from the great weight of ice. Eventually salmon populated the rivers, and the beginnings of a temperate rain forest cloaked the land. And somewhere near this time, people appeared.

Debates rage about how they might have first gotten here. The idea that Ice-Age hunters moved across the once-exposed plain of the Bering Land Bridge and came to the coast from the interior has long been a dominant theory. But in the past twenty years, some have argued that a coastal route could have been possible when the sea levels were low, that marine hunter-fisher-gatherers could have traveled from Asia into North America along the exposed shorelines.

Although this idea is gaining a following, many coastal Native peoples have oral histories that tell of coming from the interior, of riding the great Taku, Stikine, Skeena, and Nass Rivers through caverns of blue ice to the sea. Rising sea levels and the thick rain forest have all but erased traces of early coastal human dwellings. If evidence is still to be found, perhaps it lies atop the highest peaks and occasional headlands that were once ice-free refugia. And there, some finds are turning up. Native traditions do tell of a great flood, of living atop mountains throughout the region when the waters rose. But some elders have said that this was in a time before this latest rise in sea levels, a time, perhaps, before time.

As in many inquiries, oral traditions and science do not always converge. They are separate entities, hold distinct values. In a region with such complex bedrock, it is unsurprising that people here speak of many stories, many origins.

The ocean swells have intensified. Small, disfigured trees line the shore, and swells belt the rocks. They lift and carry us dangerously toward shore, so we must paddle another two kayak lengths from land. As we round Point Gardner, we are nervous and vulnerable. The water churns, and swells disassemble into high breaking chop. There is no place to hide. A time to get to know yourself. Squalls, dark lines, race across silver water. A southeast wind howls in our face. We can do nothing but drop our heads and paddle.

We haven't spoken much all day, focusing on this, the day's major event. At the point we are at a definite place on the map, where the end of Admiralty falls to the sea. The area is gnawed by storms, broken into three fingers of rock and two bays. The first bay, Surprise Harbor, is deep with a flat shore of spruce. The second, where we will stay, is Murder Cove, smaller and more protected, where a Kake Tlingit avenged his brother's death by killing two settlers, an incident that led to the shelling of Kake. Although slack flood on Frederick Sound was less than an hour ago, the ebb is well underway, and we can barely fight the swift river that the sea has become.

Drift logs, fleshy and limbless, are jammed into cuts on the west side of Murder Cove. The chart says TYEE (ABAND.). We pass the caved-in buildings of Tyee cannery. Yet in the distance a building is under construction, and we paddle up to its level beach.

While I sit in the kayak, Maren searches for some time before finding the caretaker, who lets us sleep in a rustic loft above the toolshed. He has spent the winter alone, and we are the first people he has seen this spring. "Soon this will be a guest lodge, for people to take it easy out here," he says, surveying the weather-wrapped buildings he has helped construct. "But there is no taking it easy out here."

He is generous but seems nervous by our presence, unaccustomed to living with another's routine. His hair that was once feathered has grown long, retaining only a vestige of its former style. "I'm headed back in two or three weeks," he says. "Then a buddy of mine will come up here."

He opens his kitchen to us, and after we watch *Naked Gun 33⅓*, he breaks brown raw hamburger into chunks and sends them sizzling across a skillet.

MAY 16

Weather day.

Dark storms toss Frederick Sound with whitecaps, and all day, rains hammer the metal roof just overhead. Downpours begin and end within thirty seconds, and in the quiet following the rain, the cistern—Tyee's water supply—burbles with fresh rainwater, a coolness that only moments ago was five hundred feet above.

Maren and I walk to the old cannery and whaling station, a tumble of weathered clapboard and rusting pistons. Broken bottles of heavy clear glass are embossed IMITATION FRUIT ACID. I put my head into a piston chamber, long ceased with rust and salt. On shore I find a softball-sized float: I AM HERE X. SEND HELP. THIS IS THE ONLY THING KEEPING ME ALIVE.

Back in the caretaker's cabin we find magazines, several months old, stacked near the kitchen table. Three rifles and a new spotting scope rest against a sill. On the wall is an old cannery sign with the image of a mermaid. He found half of it last summer on the rocks and the other half this winter, blown ashore by a cold southeasterly. When I ask about the long winter, he cracks a smile.

"I'm content," he says.

While we have good radio reception, able to hail the marine operator on Baranof Island, we call family on the VHF. It is a quick and startlingly clear call, and I can't help but marvel at this small black box and the invisible circuitry of talk. As we disconnect, I turn to thoughts of tomorrow's crossing, and the outside world again seems distant, nonessential. But in this handheld device lies the infrastructure for our modern world—the filled wetlands, the cut forests, mined hills, smogged skies. It is all here in my palm and undeniable.

The evening is still. Without the customary wind, a shower washes the forest. Clouds on the horizon mushroom with great winds aloft, sprays of thunderhead atop blue cells of power. Conditions must stabilize if we are to cross. I lie awake for hours listening to the cistern trickle full, then overflow.

Crossing Frederick Sound

You can paddle with agility, skill, and endurance along a shoreline, but that is entirely different from letting go of that shore. On a crossing you confront that which lies beyond, a vague and distant land, exposure, changes in wind and tides, and after a point, no returning, no chance to abort. When you have crossed open water, no matter how calm or tempestuous or how often, you have crossed something in yourself, confronted and conquered and transcended a fear, a doubt, and passed into the gracious shores of new land and known water.

We are awake at 4 A.M. Clouds skim across Frederick Sound, but overhead it is clear. Maren and I walk to the cannery to survey the water. This morning it has flattened, and as the tide nears slack, a calm settles beneath the portal of blue. Today we will cross.

Between this southern tip of Admiralty and Kuiu Island, Frederick Sound is nearly twelve miles wide, at least four hours of exposed paddling. It will be the longest crossing of our entire journey, and it is the one crossing that John Muir's

Tlingit guides feared most when they canoed from Wrangell to Glacier Bay in 1879. "They spoke of it repeatedly," wrote Muir, "as the one great danger of our voyage."

We, too, have feared its expanse. In a deeper sense, crossing Frederick Sound will somehow mark a transition, for it has long been a division in the lives of many who have lived here. Its vastness divides northern and southern Tlingit dialects. North of Frederick Sound the Tlingit are split into two moieties, Eagle and Raven, while to the south are Wolf and Raven. Red cedar, used to make the great dugout canoes, is abundant to the south of Frederick Sound, but suddenly scarce to the north. And Frederick Sound is also where salmon migratory patterns diverge. As we load the kayaks, we cannot help but read a significance into this body of water, into this placid morning, as if by day's end we, too, will be changed.

We begin late, just after slack ebb, but as the tide begins to churn, welling up from six hundred feet to race over shallows of less than seventy-five feet, slipping from Admiralty is somehow smooth and fast. I fix ranges on the open Pacific, Yasha Island, and Turnabout Island to the east. For nearly three hours we will use these imaginary lines of sight to help us gauge progress and drift. I make a third range that touches Cape Omaney on Baranof Island, Kingsmill Point on Kuiu, and bisects our course. When the Pacific disappears, we will be halfway across.

From Admiralty, we cannot distinguish our destination on Kuiu. I have marked a compass course of ninety-five degrees, but it simply points toward a shadowy mass. Between the south of Baranof and Kuiu's outer coast lies the open Pacific, a haunting void. As we cross, it will pour into Frederick Sound.

A pair of loons follow us a mile or so from shore, diving and yodeling, then suddenly turn back, having reached the edge of their world. Sometime in the next hour, a northeasterly rises to near ten knots against the flood current, stacking the waves into whitecaps. We are about four miles off Admiralty, some eight miles from Kuiu, and break the steady cadence of paddle strokes to make a decision. The wind holds steady. Our momentum high.

Soon all shores are shadows, and every third or fourth wave curls over, smacking the side of the kayak, pelting me with icy droplets. As I look into the wind, the waves are foreboding, breaking faces and shadowy troughs, advancing in dark ranks. But downwind the sea is silvery, deceptively calm, the shiny crests traveling away toward sea. Stains appear across the water, rafts of rockweed, undulating green mattresses swarming with flies. They reek of decay, having been torn from their intertidal footings and cast adrift. For some time these rancid pads become the only measure that we are moving at all.

Almost imperceptibly the open Pacific closes behind Kuiu, and we stop, floating in the center of this seamless blue. It is time for a bathroom break. We struggle with the drysuits, unzipping them and sticking an empty drinking bottle between our legs. For Maren this is the only choice, and I stabilize her kayak for this awkward maneuver. After seeing her struggle, I choose to rare up and fountain overboard. Relieved, we munch on gorp and king-sized Snickers.

As we near Kuiu, as the dusky shores become forests and the forests at last become trees, a particularly tall tree I had been using to reference drift has disappeared behind a hill. We are moving eastward with the flood and must ferry slightly westward to compensate. But other trees vanish, and we are soon drifting so fast that the hills themselves seem to move, the nearest slope occluding the ridge behind.

Something is very wrong. The water roars like a wind tunnel, and within moments waves that were manageable are unruly, steep, and irregular, some towering nearly eight feet, toppling haystacks of freezing sea. They are so steep that rather than floating over them, my kayak sinks into them, and I am inundated as a wave passes through me, my kayak entirely submerged. I wobble, slapping at the water for stability. I look for Maren. She is gone.

"Maren!" She appears briefly on a high crest paddling rapidly, then drops from sight, bobbing up again, yelling.

Less than a mile from Kuiu we are in a tide rip, fighting a whorl of white water. Waves twist and heave the kayak, then sling it sideways into the next foaming crest. The VHF radio is strapped to my life vest, but I cannot take a hand from the paddle to reach for it. I rehearse the Mayday call; our location: drifting east, fast.

From the crests of waves, Maren and I shout to each other:

"Are you OK?"

"Keep paddling!"

In an astonishing feat of clear thinking, we stop ferrying completely and head straight for shore, perpendicular to the current, toward a silvery strip of calm. But another wave sucks through my kayak, and I tip way over. Shaky, pressing into the wave, pressing hard, I am running out of paddle stroke. The kayak rolls, and I tuck my head, braced for the numbing sea. Somehow it stalls. A wave drops, another lifts, and I am righted, still scooping, still yelling. And then as quickly as this came on, the waves subside, and we have made it across.

In the thin eddy, we are visibly shaken, crying. Not more than ten feet away, the flood tide rushes past. We pause momentarily but paddle on, perhaps foolishly, bypassing a small beach, paddling toward a sheltered bay, away from the rip.

For most of an hour, exhausted, we negotiate strange and shifting currents, spooling streams among rocks. The land is mysterious, sculpted and dank. Tides and waves have undercut the soft-gray cliffs into smooth hollows and deep vaults like a rot corroding the gums. When the water at last quiets, we glide across a deep-green pool bathed in mossy light. A frayed rope dangles from a tree. And high on the rock, a pictograph, an ochre sun, drips with lichen. We have crossed to another island, another world, one of limestone.

The bay is ovoid, its outer reaches wrapping around the inner waters like a crab's pincers. Beneath white and weathered bluffs, we collapse on warm slabs that have tumbled from above, gulping at the water bottles, saying little. We came too close. In the occupied idleness, I finger a beach rock. It is chalky and ribbed. Lifting it to my face, I see it is a fossilized shell, a brachiopod. I sit up and lift another. It, too, contains a fossil. Another seems to be made entirely of silicified shells. And as we probe among the stones it becomes apparent that every rock holds a flake of extinguished sea life, that we have landed in a kind of Permian cemetery. It is stunning, yet unsettling. But we can go no farther. Then, staking the tent behind a berm, I clear a plate of earth. The soil is ruddy and brittle. Siltstone. And removing a rock to level our bed, I raise a relic that nearly crumbles beneath its own weight, the gossamer imprint of fan coral.

The evening is full of light, and when the routine of making camp is thankfully complete, we walk the beach, passing among the fallen blocks of ancient seafloor. It is warm and windless. The bay and Frederick Sound are glazed in twilight. The dropping tidewater has pooled in cavities in the slabs, stranding predator and prey in small fossilized bowls. As we peer into a pool no bigger than the cup of our hands, a sculpin settles beside an anemone. The fish is soon propped on its pectoral fins, gills fanning in measured breaths. And for a rare moment, we seem to hold its gaze, inexorably bound to its ephemeral world between the tides, to all those living among the dead.

Kuiu Island to Kake

MAY 18

A clear, frosty morning. To round the treacherous point at slack tide, we must hurry. And though we pack and nearly finish loading the kayaks, we cannot face it again so soon, and we collapse together on the white rocks in silent agreement.

As we sit, an open skiff speeds our way, nudging ashore at our feet. "You seen a barbecue grill up here?" shouts a middle-aged man hopping over the bow.

I point to the left of our tent.

As he climbs the beach, the other man in the boat introduces himself as Glenn Wilson, new pastor at Kake Presbyterian, and he invites us to stay there if we visit Kake. When the first man returns with his grill, he grips our hands. "Rick Mills," he says. They have been gathering seaweed on the west coast of Kuiu and discovered a beached humpback. "Beached whales are rare," Rick says. "People remember their occurrence with the strange affection of a tremendous windstorm."

We tell them about Frederick Sound.

Rick nods. "That probably gives you an indication of the life of the people in the old days," he says, stepping over the gunnel. "It doesn't matter how close you are to land; if you are not there, you are not safe. And that was life."

Then they depart.

"I guess tomorrow we go to Kake," Maren says.

We spend the hot day reading and writing and sleeping. Mosquitoes are out, and voles probe the shadows of a great beach log. By midmorning it is nearly eighty degrees, and for the first time this season I go shirtless. Along the beach, parallel stripes mark high-tide lines. Last night's line is crisp and brown, an assortment of ribbon kelp, rockweed, and bleached twigs that pop and crunch underfoot. The daytime high line is six inches lower and is a lesser collection of the same elements, still green and damp.

Maren suns with a cup of tea, writing, looking out to the arms of the bay, then back into her notebook, enviably relaxed so soon after yesterday's terror. The tea is chai and echinacea, her own loose-leaf blend. When I call it high-tide tea, she delivers a wide, teasing smile, her lips flecked with tea leaves.

In the west glare the Baranof snows, icy hard with successive spring melts and freezes, high snows of a mountain range that surfaces farther south as the Queen Charlotte Islands and then as Vancouver Island. We will see this wall again. In front of camp is the immense graying log, half sunken into the berm, sawed square at one end, broken and ragged at the other, an iron bolt driven far into its heartwood. The log must be six feet in diameter and some twenty feet long, an old spruce cut from one of the islands, used as part of a fish trap. When traps were outlawed because they were so efficient at exterminating the salmon runs, no doubt it was cut loose to drift in the tides until it washed ashore. Behind us, the acreage is a recovering forest of alder and Sitka spruce, clear-cut some fifteen years ago.

The giant log serves as an eating perch for river otter and mink, and bits of shell and small bones are strewn about its length. For us, too, it has become a lunch counter, and later, a drawing table. I make rubbings of fossils into my notebook, the ribs of the shells darkening against a cloud of scrawl.

MAY 19

The VHF radio crackles to life: *This is national safe boating week. The U.S. Coast Guard Auxiliary and the National Weather Service are reminding boaters to think safety on the water all year long. Check the weather before leaving shore. Listen to the National Weather Service weather radio for the latest forecast twenty-four hours a day. And remember: Personal flotation devices and survival suits are the most important safety equipment. They can save your life only if you use them.*

Willow pollen powders the tent, the yellow dust scattering as I slip out the poles. Leaving shore, I peer into a school of transparent jellyfish. There are perhaps a hundred the size of half dollars swimming a foot beneath the surface. The tide is very low, and the littoral zone descends into the water in a spectrum of gray, green, and ochre tones. The lowest strata are red with coralline algae, giving the shoreline a raw appearance. The plants and animals in this lowest intertidal level—the kelp and eelgrass, limpets, snails, chitons, bivalves, spoon worms, and sea stars—endure threat from terrestrial predators only four or five days a month.

The point is quiet, and we round it uneventfully, slipping into Keku Strait. For a break we stop at a steep, rounded midden beach rimmed with grass and sprouting new fingers of devil's club. It is a place where people have lived before. No matter what the weather, every old settlement site has held calm water. In those days a superior canoe-landing beach was most highly prized. Today, as some villages have grown into cities, we have run out of these ideal places and instead try to remake them. Shorelines are filled so that flat land is available at the water's edge, and imposing breakwaters calm the inner waters where once tree-tufted islands did the job. Yet still there are these unfrequented pockets, known most often to those with paddles.

After spending an hour here, watching rain showers drag north along Rocky Pass, we cross to Kake in big drops that fall without wind. For more than an hour the town is there before us, a collection of buildings spread along the strip of flat shoreline at the base of a hill, a plat that typifies so many southeast Alaska towns. We speak again of Byron in Hoonah, Kerry in Tenakee. We have followed their guidance all this way. The influence of a wise voice can never be underestimated. We do not battle conditions but live within them, acknowledge them, nod to them. And with this, I have noticed an opening, a willingness to believe that if we continue in this way, we will pass safely from island to island and down the passage. The coast is somehow connected, and we are just beginning to see how.

The Presbyterian church fronts a beach of black cinders, and Glenn helps us unload and stow gear in the fellowship hall. Tonight the Kake High School Baccalaureate will be held here, and Glenn is folding the fitted sheets of drying seaweed that he and Rick gathered yesterday.

After showers, we ride with Glenn to the grocery store and purchase the following:

4 Dove dark-chocolate bars
3 large Hershey bars with almonds
6 king-sized Snickers
1 one pounder of M&Ms
5 assorted cheeses
2 bags of egg scroodles
1 bag of macaroni
6 Pop Tarts
Total = $78

We burn somewhere near five thousand calories a day now and luxuriate in dipping chocolate into peanut butter before bed.

During the baccalaureate, Glenn joins the other pastors of the churches in town in delivering variations on a common message: Don't let people tell you no. You can do anything. Don't ever give up. Simple, steadfast advice. At the reception, I meet a cheerful graduate who is heading to Anchorage to start his career in the army. "Artillery," he says. "More promotions from that line than any other." Eventually he will head for Hawaii, which he says is another reason for the artillery decision. I do not ask him about the shelling of Kake, and after grabbing a cookie, he drifts into the arms of his father.

Among the finger foods we find Rick, who is eager to talk. He spoke to the graduates about faith and teaches high school math and courses in Alaska history and Tlingit studies. It is good to see him, and sharing the chance meeting on Kuiu Island, we get along with him easily, as if we have known him for a long time.

"Traditionally, in the Tlingit ways it would not be me talking to you," he says, illustrating a point he often makes in class. "It would be my clan speaking to all of your clan. So when we spoke, we would make every effort not to insult one another because that starts wars. If we abuse things around us, it comes back on us manyfold."

"Is that sense fairly alive today?" Maren asks.

"No, it isn't," he says, biting into an oatmeal cookie. "I'm trying to get people to realize that.

"There were two types of European people who came to Kake: people who had financial interests in mind and people who had church interests in mind. The people with financial interests were bootlegging, basically. It is interesting, the dynamics here. You have one group coming in and corrupting the people and one group trying to save their souls.

"The people who came to save the soul taught respect and honor of God. And so there was respect and honor taught whether you were a diehard traditionalist or if you went the new way with the church. And that was in place even when I was a young man. But we have a whole generation of young people who are not getting the respect and honor taught to them. And so kids come to me as a freshman in high school. . . . Well, it's a little late. Choices have already been made."

Then he brightens as if in a sun break. "We do have a culture camp that is fairly well attended. Kids talk about that throughout the year. And when you ask the youth how you prepare a seal, they could describe it for you. It is a wonderful opportunity for the kids to learn from the elders."

But when we ask further about education, the brightness dims. "One of the ways I learned how to be a parent to teenagers is by being a teenage child with my parents. And many of the people that went to boarding schools never learned that. The other downside is that kids go outside the culture for school. In my case, I went to Pacific University down in Oregon. I was encouraged the whole time to go to school, to get an education, but when I came back, I was an alien. I didn't fit. And that still happens.

"So change goes on. . . . The elders who made those first decisions to change from traditional ways went in with both eyes wide open. They knew that it was change or die. They took it upon themselves to make the call."

He quiets before talking again.

"I am only speaking of my understanding of these situations. I say these things with much awe and reverence of the people that have struggled to bring me to where I am and the people to where they are."

MAY 20

We breakfast with Glenn and his wife, Diane, enjoying conversation over hearty portions of eggs, bacon, and toast. They have recently moved to Kake from Florida, where Diane was a lawyer and Glenn a lay pastor. They speak of adjusting to Alaska life, learning to harvest and eat seaweed. The rain. Glenn says that the Presbyterian church here is still funded as a mission, which surprises me, having thought that the era of missions and missionaries passed a century ago. "But this status may not be for much longer," he says.

Glenn has a robust voice and discusses issues of his ministry with care and compassion. As he laments the many suicides in Kake, he searches for answers. Unlike many pastors in town, Glenn works to integrate Native culture into the church, believing Christianity is an enhancement of the Tlingit religion. Sensing a tension among churches, I ask about the cohesiveness of the religious community. "Essentially the Tlingit people here in town are one big family—and were for centuries—and they had one religion," he says. "And then Christianity came. But there was a splintering eventually because there became two churches here, the Salvation Army and the Presbyterian, so the families divided between them. And now there are six churches, so there has been more splintering. The churches don't really speak with one voice, and that makes the spiritual voice in the community weaker than it once was. I think it was much stronger before contact. It was stronger fifty years ago. And it seems that this splintering has dissolved some of the family relationships."

At noontime Maren and I walk around town, along the wet gravel roads meandering through the rows of clapboard homes that front the shore. A truck honks, and Rick stops us in an intersection and leans from his pickup. There is no traffic, and he shuts off the engine and begins a story.

"We were down working on my uncle Albert's boat, painting, getting it ready for another fishing season, and no matter how hard we tried, we couldn't work through coffee time because old Morris would show up. Well, things led to things, and you get a couple of the old boys together and they start telling stories. . . .

"I can understand enough Tlingit that I could follow things. Albert was telling about a fishing trip, and as he was going through the story, he was pointing to a certain place on his hand. I think everybody who was in tune with the story knew what he was pointing at, what he was talking about. But Albert stopped. And he got embarrassed. Morris said in English, 'Go ahead, I know what you're saying, I know.' And Albert said in English, 'I forgot the word.' And Morris said, 'So do I.' Here were two of our elders, and they could not come up with that word."

For Rick the loss seems as if a rock had tumbled from the cliff into the sea, the old culture eroding word by word. He says that words come and go from a language, that any revival of the Tlingit language as it was once known, the nuances, will be all but impossible. "The Tlingit have many words for types of water, as the Yupik have many words for types of snow," he says. And as he continues, I envision the scene again, the pointing, the vacant stares, and the embarrassed eyes that marked the passing of the Tlingit word for that small cove.

Then a car honks, and Rick turns the ignition, jolts the truck into gear, waves, and heads toward home. It is the last we see of him.

Kake to Wrangell

In the fellowship hall, Glenn has left us two Ziplocs of dried seaweed. Beneath a bag of smoked fish we find a handwritten note: "May this dried halibut give you plenty of strength. —R. Mills."

On the water again, and it feels good to pull at the paddles. As faces and encounters play through memory, Kake falls slowly behind. The land closes as Keku Strait funnels into Rocky Pass, the narrows that separate Kuiu and Kupreanof Islands. For two days we will be protected again, and it is a relief to obsess less about the weather. Maren is thrilled, too, though she remains guarded about currents, maintaining a keen reconnaissance for deviant puckers in the water. Huge tables of rock sail beneath our kayaks. Once my boat scrapes, punching the hull upward as I pass over it undamaged. On shore a mortally wounded pleasure craft, the *Shane Boy*, has been caved in to the pilothouse.

The *Coast Pilot* advises "Local Knowledge" for navigating the waters of Rocky Pass. It is a phrase that appears frequently in discussions of sea navigation, but rarely on land with as much authority, except in guides to remote mountains or canyons. And it pleases me to see it here— emphasized in bold type—the relationship between people and place recommended.

We make camp on an isthmus that floods at the highest tides. Two animal trails divide our camp, the only passage to and from the peninsula. Calculating tomorrow's tides through Rocky Pass, we must time it exactly: flood in, ebb out.

MAY 22

This morning air and water are one. Eagles dive into the sea, fish leap skyward shaking off sea lice, and the atmosphere becomes an impenetrable swirl of morning fog. Occasionally, a skiff buzzes out of the cloud, its pilot standing behind the windshield, riding high like a horseman, bucking across the waves. The skiff stops at floats in each bay, and the solitary captain bends across the water, pulling in crab pots. Wearing large gloves, he picks out the snapping crabs, replaces the bait, and heaves the pot overboard. Then he motors away to tend another.

Today, like the Tenakee Portage, tides rule the agenda. They meet at a summit, the highest point of the channel's basin, so we plan to ride the flood in, hit the summit at slack, and ride the ebb out into southern Keku Strait.

Into the mouth of Rocky Pass the land closes and flattens, and the current increases until it is like paddling down a river. Gradually the fog thins, revealing a succession of distant points. Overhead, a dome of perfect blue opens, and there is fog everywhere except above us. The water shimmers in the new sun. We are moving fast, twice our normal speed, and it is difficult to tell where the channel leads. I pull over to Maren. "My chart shows that we should stay to the left."

"No," she says, pointing at the islands. "We are here and have to go there."

The water is less than a half mile wide and narrowing. Landmarks are indefinite, and I feel the pang of being lost. Islands fade behind points, and points slip behind islands. Where there should be water there is land. Shoals rise three feet above the surface, fences we cannot peer over. I must read the map and project myself flying above, like the Landsat satellite, to find the way. We are drifting fast, so my perception of how far we have traveled is skewed. We raft together again.

"I think we're at this island. Or is it this one?" Maren says.

"That one. Unless . . . Essentially, we just stay to the right and follow the shore."

It sounds like slapstick, nonsense conversation. Shouting above the noises of water and wind from kayak to kayak, Maren will say, "Look at that."

"What?"

"That."

"Oh, *that*. I saw *that*."

Now it is just a conversation about confusion.

"The current takes you, doesn't it?" Maren says eventually. "We should follow the current." This is the answer, and she is elated. She treats the current like river paddling, the islets comparing to rocks in a stream with eddies looping behind.

At the summit the water is quiet. We have timed it superbly. And in moments the ebb takes hold, dragging us at six knots. "Hey, this is fun!" Maren shouts. "We're flying!" All around, the water is swift and sudsy. Devil's Elbow, a hideous S curve with rapid currents, has been a worry all day, but it is smooth. At the bottom of Rocky Pass, as it widens and empties into southern Keku Strait, we sail over shoals in inches of water. We have made it. Ahead, Eldorado Peak rises from Prince of Wales Island. A true summit.

Crossing to the shores of Kupreanof, we find camp in soft hemlock needles twenty-six miles from where we began the day. Minks scamper to the water as I clean the dishes. A colony of acorn barnacles fans for food until the tide sinks away, when they seal their conical shells. There are no boats across Keku Strait tonight. No one. As I fade to sleep, Maren reads lyrics to "Morning Morgantown."

MAY 23

Points and capes are almost never quiet, never calm. They are, in the deepest sense, turning points, and rounding them or crossing the straits are the most significant events of our days. We time them meticulously, rounding or crossing at slack, watching the weather far too long, and burning a thousand calories on nervousness and speculation, always looking for a promising beach, a sheltered cove.

This morning we awake to eagles chirping and flying through the forest, and every few minutes we hear the rush of feathers. As I load the kayak, an eagle lands no more than twenty feet above, so close that I hear its talons grasping the branch. Its chest feathers flutter in the tiniest breeze. I see the pupil of its eye, the sharp hook of its beak. Then it takes a deep breath, one that I hear, and leaps into the sky.

When we depart a southerly breeze gusts, and already the familiar haze of a frontal system has swept away a third of the sky. South along Sumner Strait and the Pacific, surly clouds build against the islands. As we near the exposure of Point Barrie, the headwind increases. We almost abort, stopping among the steep aprons of stone to talk strategy. On some days wind and waves make me nervous, make me question this whole endeavor. On these days, of which today is one, every ripple in the water nourishes a question, a doubt, a reason to leave the brine and head into town. But just yesterday this was all bliss. We continue, although Maren leans toward staying back. I want to push ahead, to get past the point before the real storm hits. My assessment of most conditions: "It's not that bad."

At Point Barrie we bend eastward into Sumner Strait and weave between shoal, islet, and kelp, following quiet water. In places paddling through the kelp is like poling across a bowl of spinach. Then we float over the green ribbons as if flying through clouds. Suddenly the kelp opens and reveals a school of herring, perhaps fifty silver fish swimming in formation as if aligned in a magnetic field. Then the kelp closes, reopening in a few strokes to disclose a rock purple with sea stars.

Outside our quiet channels of kelp, the sea is raging, and the first waves swell at our quarter sterns, lifting the kayaks as someone might lift you by your belt loops. Shoals line Kupreanof from Point Barrie east for several miles. On the chart the continuous billowing symbol for a shoal takes the appearance of a roll cloud. For a time this shallow shelf dampens the waves of midchannel, but as the tide rises, the waves carry farther and farther inland, and soon we must race from rock to rock, across steep and breaking seas, for safety. But as more waves infiltrate our slender paddleway, this hopscotching among rocks and foam is more risk than protection. For more than an hour we paddle in these fast sprints until at last they run out. Over our right shoulders the white-caps crest in the shallows, curling.

My mood rises and falls with the waves. I am anxious and uneasy, believing I can handle this, but wondering how soon it will be until I cannot, when finally I am turned and rolled with a crest of sea. Maren is holding steady, paddling twenty yards ahead, but I know this wears on her. We are both dreaming of sunny days in a grassy yard, living life at dandelion level on our stomachs, reading simple books, playing softball. . . .

We are skidding, almost surfing. An island blocks enough of the seas so that we can land and rest on a pebble beach. We hope to camp, but the beach is ruined with the wreckage of a log raft sunken in a tea-brown mire. No birds are out, no eagles. They know best. Onward. The waves are rough, and the shores are battered organ pipes of columnar basalt. Then a magnificent sweeping beach unfurls, a steep, even slope of fist-sized agates. Off the point the water roars with foam. We gulp water from our bottles. Loons yodel, and an otter's tail flaps. A safe place. Then over the forest, out of nowhere, thumps a Coast Guard helicopter. It hovers, a person in a white helmet peering from the side window. Circling. Then it is gone.

"They come once we are safe," Maren says.

The beach is walled with drift logs, and we make camp on a high grassy berm at the edge of the hemlock forest. Unloading the kayaks, we must carry our gear over the stacks of bone bleached wood, old 2 x 4, 4 x 4, 4 x 6, and 6 x 6 lumber, long, limbless trunks as straight as telephone poles, yellow cedar that glows as if sunlit. They are fleshy and barkless, heavy, slick, and full of water with ends ground to splintery nubs. The whole pile is at an uneasy equilibrium, and stepping across the jumble varies in degrees of stability and safety.

Where there are drift logs, there is logging nearby. Although drift logs have long existed—most often produced when blowdowns toss live trees into the sea—this volume was unknown until recent times. Behind the old-growth hemlock here is a clear-cut, and at the head of the bay the south side of Kupreanof Island has been cut to about eight hundred feet and is now filling in with the lighter green of alder. Across the strait, Prince of Wales Island appears shaven in places, patchy, like a distant leper. Some peninsulas have no trees and other areas are simply swaths of earth with a zagging road. Most of the logs here have probably strayed from those operations, from broken Davis rafts, blown here by storm winds, brought in with the tide.

All evening clouds scrape north in furrows. Low on drinking water, we spread a tarp across the drift logs to catch rain. But no rain comes, and we must cook with a quarter seawater. Around eight o'clock, a cruise ship, white with a red-winged stack, pushes through waves, water ruffling around the bow, lights blazing. The wind shifts. To the east the last sun tints the high peaks of the mainland in a dirty light, mountains we have seen before from the ferry.

MAY 24

Radio: *The synopsis: A weather front offshore of southeast Alaska will move through the panhandle Friday night. . . . Area 1A, inside waters . . . Sumner Strait and Clarence Strait: small craft advisory. Southeast winds to twenty-five knots diminishing to south fifteen knots Saturday. Seas five feet, subsiding to three feet Saturday. Showers. Outlook: northwest winds fifteen knots, seas three feet.*

Wind glances the water and shudders our tent, tossing limbs and bending grasses, whose frantic shadows mime across the nylon walls. The day off brings comfort after yesterday's rough waters, and we relax, warm and humid inside the sleeping bags, unfolding charts and cracking books we have not read for days. With a transistor, we take turns listening to the one radio station we can get. After *Car Talk*, comes a crooning Nat King Cole. Then Pearl Jam.

Maren and I remain in good company, even in the small confines. Chores are efficient. Such obvious weather days are easy because there is no decision about whether or where to paddle. But yesterday . . . For that I have apologized. Maren drives sense into me, breaks my driven self. And I perhaps push her ahead when she would rather not go. So together we press ahead both cautiously and daring. It is a fine balance to maintain without coming to fisticuffs, and when the waves build or the sea calms, we side with our tendency and orbit each other like pugilists until a decision arrives. And then slowly we ease, seeing that we have made it at least this far together.

MAY 25

A blustery day of sun and squalls. With a system blowing out, we stay and dig among the agates. They are almost translucent. Their swirls of color seem caught in unfinished motion, a handful of the great gas giants—Jupiter, Saturn, Uranus, and

Neptune. Looking close at the red and creamy bands, I peer into the Jovian cloud.

MAY 26

Today is Maren's thirtieth birthday, and I would like it to go well. But it does not. By the time we reach a deep, ragged bay, the wind is up again and on the next point she is bawling and yelling and soon ashore on her back in tears. We are at a breaking point. "Why are we doing this?!" she cries, curled into a ball, rocking herself. "It's my fucking thirtieth birthday. Why must we be so bold?"

I open my mouth but have no answers. I do not feel very bold. I kneel and stroke her hair, thick waves of amber. For three days we have gone virtually nowhere. Now it is not even noon, and we must soon quit and unload and make camp. Perhaps it is time to throw it in. Abandon ship. It is one thing to sit around on beaches for days on end and marvel at the rocks and quite another to maintain an inertia. Even Ketchikan seems distant, probably three weeks away. And that's not even the end of Alaska!

Eventually Maren agrees to continue. For now, we will aim for the Stikine delta, then Wrangell. I am awkward in these moments, knowing that she just needs to let it out and be comforted, but I feel that the curiosity that propels this wild scheme has finally sprained us. This is my father's birthday, too, his sixtieth, and I ache with a homesickness that I have not felt since scout camp.

With the kayaks bouncing on the rocks, we reboard and look for camp. In Douglas Bay we stop at an island for lunch. Among the black rocks, it is calm and hot and our moods improve. But there is nowhere to unload. So we slip across the turbulence toward a not-too-distant point, perhaps a mile away.

A skiff that has been speeding around the bay intercepts us. "What are you doing out here?" shouts the man in a flannel shirt and suspenders. "Mitchell Point can get pretty snotty, I wouldn't go around on a day like this. Maybe not any day in one of those." He and his partner are salvaging beach logs for a local mill, and we can hear the revving chain saw on the gusts of wind. Then he speeds off, his Bayliner having slipped anchor. We paddle two bays farther and pull ashore, just out of the wind.

At the head of our notched cove is a glade and a river delta that turns the water blood red. At first I believe it is red tide, but there is no stench. In the center of the bay stands a treed pillar of basalt, shingles of red rock. Streamers of kelp and seaweed flicker from the branches of a fallen spruce. We cook on this downed tree, setting the stove and pots among the branches that arc skyward like mammoth tusks.

The sunset is saturated with rain and orange light. Kupreanof Island's southern shore is shallow, a light blue on the chart, less than ten fathoms deep. If the wind blows on shore to any measurable degree, rounding Mitchell Point will be a replay of Point Barrie. In mid-Sumner Strait is a reef called "The Eye Opener," and I imagine the surprised captain who discovered it. It is one of the best-named reefs in Alaska.

Camp is a challenge course. Our tent is pitched in a tiny clearing among the devil's club, beneath a fallen hemlock that bridges the understory. Exiting the tent, we each smash our heads against its gummy underside and extract particles of fungi, moss, and spongy wood from our hair all evening. And the only way to shore is by stepping down the steep roots of a willow.

Before sleeping, Maren climbs onto the kitchen log and tries the marine operator. They cannot pick up our signal. "Try twenty-four," I say. Nothing.

She climbs out farther, clutching one of the branches, and flips through the likely operator channels again. Success. And after a string of beeps and payment confirmations, her face brightens. "Happy Birthday, partner!" she says. And out of the hiss there comes a clear and reassuring voice, "Happy Birthday to you!"

MAY 27

Maren has nicknamed the bear canisters. The heaviest is "choc/cheese/brd" (chocolate, cheese, and bread), and I carry it in the stern of my kayak where it is cool, often saying, "choc cheese brd, choc cheese brd," just for the pleasure of sounding it. Maren's favorite is the canister that contains the spaghetti, aka "the spag."

Finally we have a calm morning and round Mitchell Point with ease, paddling in no more than two feet of water. The shoals extend several hundred yards off shore, spilling half-submerged boulders before us like marbles. As we stand in ankle-deep water swallowing a Snickers each, a tremendous flock of surf scoters alights from the water, grouping as a squadron, circling toward the sun. Ahead lies the hilly gate of Wrangell Narrows, a place we remember from the ferry. Something known and therefore of comfort.

At Kah Sheets Bay the shoaling subsides. It is slack tide. The water has changed from brown to green. Logs bear blatant cut marks with squared ends or are stumps sawed shoulder-high above the roots. I look up Kah Sheets Bay to the familiar smoothed knobs of land. Their recurrence marks a unity to our days.

Every fifteen minutes we are washed by squalls, periodic cleansings like the showers of town. It is Memorial Day. And in the blue breaks between clouds, I remember grandparents, all that I have come to cherish about our daily world because of them. After lunch on a pocket beach, we paddle east all afternoon, crossing the Wrangell Narrows, a freeway of boat traffic. Several fishing boats and a cruise ship enter as we arrive. By stopping at a stream to get water, we miss a clear crossing time and must wait another twenty minutes. Sport-fishing boats line the opposite shore, kids pressed against the windows, entranced as we paddle by. In a morning we have gone from the solitary to the trafficked. We are on the outskirts of town, our largest yet.

The wind picks up at three o'clock, steep waves from the south. For two days the weather has forecasted a northwest wind, which would be ideal now, sheltered to the north by Mitkof Island. But it has not come. After a time, we learn the errors of weather forecasters, and they quickly fall from omnipotence. Besides, if a front approaches, we know it. We are on the water. We are learning the ways of weather. Forecasters are never quite right, anyway, and of course can never tell us what to expect in a kayak.

We find camp on an outcrop of smooth volcanic rocks and hoist our kayaks onto two immense drift logs. And walking along these beached logs, a smell we had noticed since we arrived turns putrid, the stench of carrion. My first thoughts race to bears. Have they made a kill? Was a deer wounded and came to our shore to die? As the smell gets stronger, I look down. On the depths of the beach is a dead eagle, a collapsed tangle of black and white feathers, a mustard-colored talon clutching the air. It is damp and dirty, disgraced by the tide. Could it have drowned in the waves while fishing? Shot, as so many are?

A first gibbous moon shines tonight, drawing the tide higher. With binoculars, I scan the outlines of craters and dished shadows. A cloud fired with evening sun passes before it, dimming the moon and tinting it the color of ripe peaches. I see spherical qualities, the dark side is visible with my naked eye, and, most fantastically, the tops of crater rims are illuminated at the line of light and darkness, like the tops of peaks in alpenglow.

Clear-cuts are all around, moonlit bands on mountains, squares, a patchwork. To the east lie the snowy mountains of the mainland. We are out of the exposed, out of wind, away from shoals. At last we are back inside.

MAY 28

A warm, sunny morning beneath spruce trees. I cook Maren a belated birthday breakfast: rainbow oats (Maren's mix of oatmeal with powdered fruit and soy milk), granola, raisins, and green tea. We each take second helpings, enjoying the moments of dryness and sunbeams, reclining on the black rocks still cool with night. For once, we have an excess of food, and the bounty is splendid. We will pick up a food shipment in Wrangell in a few days, and we still have another one and a half bear canisters, roughly a little more than a week's supply, to eat through. So we set a relaxing pace for the morning and are underway when the tide rises to camp. At 9:30 we have almost an hour of the flood to ride eastward toward the Stikine River delta, a migratory stop, a meeting of the inner and outer waters.

Occasionally, solitary drift logs, unusually large, rest alone on a rock, sprouting saplings. Sometimes this is a headless stump, with roots reaching like stricken tentacles, or a downed and knotted spruce, its torqued grain once a strength in winds now cracking open like worn pavement. The bashing of wood against rock is especially marked on these hulks. They are marred along their length and soft with splinters, bruised like dropped produce.

Past a slough, a stream spills across a delta of moss and sparkling schists, and we fill both water bags—twenty liters of fresh water. When we reboard, an orange construction truck clamors toward us. The noise is strange and unexpected, and we stare at it as if we have never seen one. Then a road, the No. 7 from Petersburg, swoops out of the forest and along shore. Here we see our first sedan since Juneau, an American-made coupe. It stops in the road, the driver probably staring at us, thinking we are either whales or nuts. Beyond a wayside, an olive-green outhouse, and a boat ramp, we feel the first nudges of Stikine current.

In a half mile, sediments flushed from the high mountains and glaciers of the Stikine ice field turn the water brown and silty. We work the eddies marked by lines of turbulent bubble and drifting debris—unanchored kelp and rockweed torn loose by the powerful flow. Hiding behind a point or a boulder, I trail Maren, who launches out against the full brunt of current.

Soon the water is shallow, tan like a desert. The tide is

falling, and sandbars emerge as sweeps of shadow. Following a kayaker we saw at lunch, we linger near shore. Where the bar seems to touch land, we just clear between the riprap road bank and sand. Now, perhaps, we are trapped. The bar has diverted most of the main current far to the south, but a weak current indicates that there must still be water ahead. Our charts are filled with shaded channels and vagary. We do not have the proper scale for this navigation. Few exist. When George Vancouver sailed through here in 1793 on his carto-graphic journey, he made no map or mention of the Stikine. He was after a Northwest Passage for trade, and such a shal-low river mouth must have afforded little promise of com-merce with the Atlantic and Europe. His error was one of perspective, for the Stikine Tlingit—the Shtax'héen K̲wáan—have long prized the Stikine as a trading corridor with the Tahltan of the interior. Vancouver just missed the market-place.

We are in a maze. Rounding the Blaquiere Point beacon, the compass spins northeast. And finally the northern winds arrive. Against both wind and current, our speed is cut by two-thirds. Sand walls rise all around now, and we edge the shore. The Stikine delta opens, a broad basin circled with snows aloft.

Slowly, channels reveal themselves among sandbars, and like salmon we track the current. Even knowledgeable locals must relearn the river delta every spring, as winter floods shift the shallow channels. Near the dune that is Dry Strait we meet Mark, the other kayaker, and stick together. He has a slightly better chart for this purpose—actually, a topographic map—and together we seek the northern arm of the river through the winding delta's sand and mud.

The silty banks are baffling, abruptly curving to dead ends, or if they appear to lead somewhere, we suddenly nudge against the bottom and must get out and line the kayaks, dragging them across the shallows. With most of the heavy camping gear, my kayak grounds often, and I lag behind. Fi-nally the sand parts to the east, and we find a tendril of the

Stikine, King Slough. We are no more than a quarter mile
from the Forest Service cabin circled on Mark's map.

The current is fast, flowing at two and a half knots against
us, and we power along the tall banks of caked mud, Maren
leading the way with Mark, who has just embarked on his
journey from Wrangell to Glacier Bay. For several hours we
paddle and pull kayaks through the muck and river. The mud
is grainless and slick and nearly sucks our boots off with each
step, leaving clouds of silt swirling behind like nebulae.

After an hour and a half, we reach the island, but no cabin
exists where one is marked. The island rises from the flat
plains abruptly, and stepping from the marshland onto the
rocky slope is like going ashore for a second time. There is
no camping. Every flat spot near the island is soggy and mired.
Mark continues upriver and disappears around a bend. Eventually we paddle on, too. The delta is flatter than the Gustavus plain and strewn with whole trees ripped loose during the
spring floods, carried downriver and stranded. They are surreal
in this otherwise treeless basin, lying toppled in the grass,
the gray of tombstones, the dead of the interior delivered to
the sea.

Around a turn we spy the dome of Mark's tent. He is
warm and eating. "Come on up," he calls, waving us in, and
we make camp on the flats near the river. Tonight will be
comfortable, a level bed upon flattened grass and cracked
mud.

As tide fills the slough, the current slows, then reverses
and drowns the bars and mudflats in a sudsy flow, inching up
the bank. With binoculars I scan the savannahlike expanse,
expecting to see a moose or a lone bear. Instead, clouds of
insects, mosquitos and flies pepper the glowing sky. Birdsongs
waft across the plain—hooting grouse, cooing ducks bedding
down for a clear, cold night. In the distance a beacon flashes
at the Wrangell airport; behind it, the town, a soundless twinkling amber.

MAY 29

Clear, hot day. We enjoy the complacency that comes with this great openness. Drying gear is scattered all over as if camp exploded. Yesterday no mosquitoes were biting; today, one.

Near high water, Mark and I set off upstream, leaving Maren to write beneath the shelter of our blue-and-white cook tent. Remains of old skiffs, red and white and wooden, litter the shore. Moose prints and mud. A grove of cottonwoods slowly sinks into the river. Mark says he takes a journey like this every two or three years just to get away. I do not ask from what. This is no place for shop talk. Over the bank plunges a black bear, and it begins to swim across, but seeing us it turns and bounds away, a thundercloud racing through yellow grass.

At the confluence of King Slough and the Stikine's north arm, we stop for a snack on a trail of fresh bear tracks still trickling with sand. The north arm tumbles in a shallow of white water from the interior of spiked peaks whose trees reach no farther than three thousand feet up the slopes, well below the gorges still caught with snow. The tidal influence here has only softened the muddy prints of earlier bears. Not far upstream, the north arm joins the main Stikine, the artery to the interior. The Tlingit know the Stikine as "the great river," and it is one of the mightiest on the coast.

From its source, the Stikine flows nearly four hundred miles, descending from the arid interior of British Columbia among pinnacles, glaciers, an unnavigable canyon, and alpine valleys before fanning to its delta. Human history entwines this river. Ancestral Tlingit stories tell of riding the Stikine from the interior, at times through caverns of glacial ice, and the legacy of trade between the interior Tahltan people and the coastal Tlingit was well established for millennia. In more recent times, the Hudson's Bay Company competed with the Russian-American Company for fur-trapping grounds here, and the procession of explorers, missionaries, Klondike and Cassiar gold seekers, and tourists have descended upon the enduring Tlingit backdrop. Mark and I linger for a time, peering inland, our boots sucking across the river bottoms, before we scrape away the ooze and peel into the slough's brewing current.

Paddling downstream is unbelievably fast, slipping around the outer curves of swift water as if banking turns in a velodrome. As we round a bend, a moose, a tall and lanky cow, clomps toward us in midriver. We hesitate and fumble, drifting sideways in the current. I have always thought moose a comical name—MOOSE—and I wonder what a herbivore could possibly want with me. But we are close, fifty yards, nearing that interspecies zone of defense, and perhaps she has a calf to defend. Mark describes a video of a moose stomping that killed a man, and I thank him for sharing and drum the deck. The cow is tall, ribby, stilted on her long stomping legs. I paddle to the shore opposite the moose and catch the fastest current. She looms—ten feet of hoof and hide—swooping her head toward me. I can do nothing in the crucial moment but drift. Then she breaks into a canter, up and over the bank, alone.

Sighting the bear and moose have made me nervous for Maren, but when we arrive back at camp, she is writing. "I've had a wonderful day," she says, finishing a letter to friends. "Now, who's making dinner?"

The moon rises big, a day brighter on its left, and the tide initiates its upward creep. Water churns with silt and sediment, too murky to drink or filter, and I go to the banks to watch it boil. Clumps of grass collapse to the mud like dough. Our beach is scuffed with deep footprints, which have softened as if melted in chocolate when the tide recedes, a record of the day's joy and errands.

We share time with Mark over dinner. Then while I clean up, a powerful thing happens. As Mark tells us a story of how he once howled and drew a wolf from the woods, he howls again. And at that moment, not more than a hundred yards from us, a wolf—big and black and gray—saunters toward the riverside, sits, and turns toward us. In an unbroken stare, it shows us a courage that is stunning to witness in the wild. Its confidence undermines our own so that even as we are turned

to wonder, we are turned to doubt. We do not go for the
camera. We do not talk. We simply meet its gaze. Then,
having graced us with a dignity, it returns to the forest.

The water is high now, 11:30, and the moon has just
swept past the meridian, casting a dusky sheen across the
delta. Its wavering reflection shines across the river, an invisible pull that we can describe but not yet explain. Through
cold, dew-drenched blades, I walk to the bank. The river is
less than a foot below.

MAY 30

In the hot morning sun we leave with the rising tide and say
good-bye to Mark, who will paddle upstream for a few days.
As we retrace our route, it barely resembles our journey in.
The tide is high, and the sandbars we trudged along two days
ago are now covered by a broad river. The mud banks that
towered above us are filled to their grassy rims, and all the
way to Wrangell we paddle in no more than a few feet of
water, edging these strange mirages of salt-marsh delta that
are flooded like rice paddies.

In two days this place has gripped me, the open ground
that is all but absent along this coast. The Stikine is a confluence. Beyond the faint green of Sergief Island, the ragged
peaks of the interior Coast Range come into view, the main
channel of the Stikine, a glimpse into the Pleistocene. Our
drift increases in the main current, and we ferry slightly to
adjust. Above Wrangell it is pleasing to see the mackerel sky.
For once we will be in town during bad weather.

The shores of Wrangell are black schist. The homes are
older, many with aluminum roofs. On an outcrop kids fire
slingshots into the water. Gradually the town forms, a new
and unfamiliar place until we get to the ferry dock. "We
walked over this!" Maren says.

Teens in skiffs speed dangerously close, and as we track
beneath a second wharf, they follow our route, weaving

around the pilings like slalom gates. Having enough of this, we stop at the foot of the public dock. Scrambling up the steep bank of riprap, I am suddenly in downtown Wrangell. From Gil and Gail in Angoon, we have a name: McCandless. A woman in a pickup truck knows the name and points to Eagle's Wings art gallery. "They know the McCandless family." A few moments later, something picks at the back of my life jacket. I turn, facing a man more than six feet tall.

"I had to sew these pouches on my life jacket when I canoed from Wrangell to Seattle in 1975," he says.

We have a new friend. He is excited about our trip, and as Maren joins us, he says we might be interested in what is in a nearby shed. As he cracks open the door, the sweetness of cedar escapes, and in two strides we are deep in cedar chips, studying a canoe being carved by the Wrangell Canoe Project. The craft is still months from steaming, but it has been hewn to a definite form—the high-reaching bow and stern, the rounded hollow.

"Traditionally, a clan would own it, so carvings would show the clan ownership. But that would divide the community. We'll probably paint it black or a smiley face on one side and a frown on the other," he chuckles. "Tlingit are always yin and yang. Raven and Eagle. Happy and sad. No, mad. Happy and mad."

His name is John, and he drives us to his home for a shower. He is a quarter Tlingit and a fourth-grade teacher. He has an aura of genuine friendliness, a compassion and certainty characteristic of the most highly respected men. He is on the board of the hospital, and Dave McCandless is a doctor.

Once we are clean, we walk the gravel roads of town in the warm and light evening. As we ascend the hill behind John's house, he tells of his mother, who had eleven children. "She knew when it was time to deliver one," he says. "She'd take a nice hot bath and get all cleaned up; then she'd start walking the block up the hill here. They'd look out the hospital window and see my mother coming and say, 'All right, get ready. . . .' And she'd come in and deliver the child."

Then his voice steadies. During his mother's second pregnancy, the doctor said the baby was positioned wrong, and she wouldn't be able to deliver. If the baby did not make the necessary adjustments overnight, they would have to operate. "That was 1940," John says, "and surgery was a risky prospect, especially in small-town Alaska. So she came back down to the house, and told my Tlingit grandmother what was going on. And Grandma left and got a Tlingit woman who was the local midwife. So this woman came in and started massaging my mother's stomach and singing to her very softly in Tlingit, just kind of a cooing sound. And my mother fell asleep. When she awoke, my grandmother said that everything was going to be all right, that she would deliver tomorrow.

"The next day, the doctor was amazed at the changes that had taken place. The midwife had repositioned the baby with this light massage technique. 'If she could read and write,' the doctor said, 'she would make a wonderful physician.' "

Soon we arrive at the McCandlesses' place. "Sure, you can stay," says Valery. "Dinner is almost ready. John, you come back for ice cream."

In Wrangell

MAY 31

Dead clear and difficult not to paddle.

Ben McCandless is making biscuits, a secret variation of a Betty Crocker standard. He is worried that the supplies for his baidarka will not arrive in time to complete the project this summer, and in the garage, below his parent's foldable kayak, he shows me the jig he will use to bend the aluminum framing for the skin-covered craft. Ben, a young teenager, is fascinated with our kayaks, and we lean over the porch railing, talking design. "The Aleut boats were flexible at the joints, able to bend easily over the waves," he says. "Yours are fiberglass."

"Yes," I say, looking at our two kayaks in the front yard. "But the stiffness keeps them efficient when loaded heavily for the long haul."

"Hmm. I don't know," he says. "The Aleuts were onto something, I think."

Dave left a geology career to attend the University of Oklahoma medical school, and after his residency in Pennsylvania, the family decided to move to Wrangell. "You make choices today that will affect your future," Valery says, painting toilet-paper-roll binoculars for the vacation Bible school's "African Safari." That is how *our* journey goes: Each crossing leads to new land.

We see no television in the home, and every night the McCandless family reads together, children gathered around parents on a couch. And soon Maren and I are inducted into the readers' circle. The kids are bright and communicative and seem engaged and endlessly fascinated. They manufacture toys—swords and shields from wood scraps—and stage clashless fights among the foundation of their new backyard ship, a replica of the fabled *Dawn Treader* from C. S. Lewis's *The Chronicles of Narnia*. When complete, the ship will be fully rigged and include a galley for picnicking, a hold for bedding down, and a lookout for waterfront surveillance.

There is a great reciprocity here that Maren and I rarely find in a family, the ability of parents and children to listen, learn, and play together. There are the usual tussles among the children—Ben, the oldest, Trina, the youngest, and bright-eyed Will in the middle—but most notably, Dave and Valery seem open to all that their children are teaching them. And so home life is electric and slothless. The home itself is elegant yet basic. The dining table is a picnic table under wraps and gives each meal a festive spontaneity, like eating out-of-doors.

On Ben's recommendation, Maren and I climb to the top of Mount Dewey, a small forested knob behind town overlooking the small bustling waterfront. This is the mountain where John Muir built a fire in 1879 so that he could better see the sway of trees in the midst of a storm. Like him, we were drawn north to see the ice, and here we will finish trailing his Wrangell-to-Glacier Bay canoe route. It is a path that we had not expected to follow, for we are not on the heels of Mr. Muir but, rather, directed our travels on knowledge of the old canoe route that came from Hoonah. Knowing that the general way is still the recommended passage is meaningful, however, and the connection to the Tlingit paddling days seems strong. From Wrangell, Muir boarded a southbound steamer in 1879. We will continue to paddle, and from this gentle summit we look out across town and the narrowing of Zimovia Strait that we will travel in a few days.

The descent is soft, padded with spruce cones, and we walk around town. Blossoms and buttercupped yards line Wrangell's streets, and we pause at the corner of Church and Grief. The whole town seems to be on summer recess, and around the rollicking kids I feel young again, reflecting often on school days and dodged chores. It is this youthful sense of possibility that Wrangell itself seems to recall at this turning point. With the mill closed and fishing uncertain, the town seems eager to free itself from these old economies, to stretch in new directions.

John's wife, Cindy, an artist who owns Eagle's Wings gallery, says this is a time for ideas. "People are starting things. A post-office clerk just began a desktop publishing business. There is good energy here." We have heard, however, that if the large cruise lines come in, they will demand a share of profits from the businesses. And if Wrangell refuses, the big ships and big bucks may not come. "You'll notice that as you head south, the towns get more and more like Seattle," she says.

On the bridge crossing to a replica of Chief Shakes' Tlingit plank house, a woman wearing a silky sweatsuit stops us. "Has someone told you that there is an eagle in that tree?" She points with a hand strapped to a video camera. And there it is, perched among the highest branches, farthest from the dozens of name-tagged people who are also pointing upward, scoping it through viewfinders, zooming in and zooming out, talking to themselves, narrating the experience. Her question reveals the great distance between these people and this environment. While the presence of an eagle is no small occurrence, we have seen so many that we seem to live among them, not apart from them.

At Chief Shakes house we pay our fee and duck into the dim room, joining a talk already in progress. " 'Shakes' is a title taken by successive chiefs," the guide says, "a title that was won in a war with the Tsimshian. The name Shakes has been passed down for generations. . . ." The talk is informed but expedient, and its conclusion flushes the tourists back into the daylight.

"I'm proud of this house," the guide says as I step down the cedar benches toward the fire ring. "This is living history. But so much of the history has been lost over time, you know. I guess that's true of everybody's background, no matter what nationality they are. We're too mobile. We don't pay attention to any of our customs—oh, except on certain days. It's true of everybody. We never seem to appreciate who we are."

JUNE 2

In the evening Valery drives us south of town to the crumbling Wrangell Institute. It stands to the west of the road, striking in its solitude and vacancy, a building like few others in Alaska in its large architecture, as though Mr. Jefferson had drawn the plans. For decades this was the elementary boarding school for Native children brought here from all over Alaska. Behind the chain-link fence are broken windowpanes. Someone has stolen the weather vane. The front walkway is mossy and extends across a lonely yard of dandelions.

Emptied and weathered, an expanse of dreams both resented and beloved. Like its sibling, the Sheldon Jackson School in Sitka, the Wrangell Institute changed the Native communities more than can be quantified, and the building unearths all the questions of how one culture understands and treats another. There is both laughter and sorrow in its halls, triumphs and failures in its administration. The town is unsure of what to do with this magnificent but decaying building. Some want it destroyed to abolish bad memories, the loss it brought to the Native cultures. Others want to renovate it, convert it into a community hall.

Near the institute a lone dog trots down the roadway, as if traveling across country.

Wrangell to Meyers Chuck

JUNE 4

As we leave Wrangell, the rains commence. John loads every-thing into his Trooper and drives us to the floatplane dock in downtown, the same dock where he left on his canoe trip twenty-one years before. "Guard your momentum," he says, then disappears to make some cabin arrangements to "help ease us back into the pace" while we pack our gear. Ketchikan is some ten days away, and again I am concerned about progress.

The dock is wet and oily, and we nose the kayaks over the wooden edge and into the water, the bow submerging to the front hatch. John returns to say good-bye. "There aren't many times in your life when you can do this," he says. He lingers around the kayaks, rain spotting his jacket, an old flower dangling from the pocket. As we dig our first strokes, he turns and ascends the plank.

A southwest wind builds, blowing hard through Chichagof Pass as we near the Wrangell Institute. Sheltered in a park, we eat a lunch of cheese. The traveling dog is here again, flinching when we step toward him. Nosing the air, he snarls and circles. He sniffs the ground, zagging among garbage cans, gnawing on a melon rind he finds beneath another picnic table. The institute is exposed, rain pouring into its windows.

At the Wrangell mill, black barges create a confusion of reflection waves, and I yell, "Keep paddling," but want to quit myself. Within an hour of leaving the town, we are drenched with sweat and seawater. Beyond the pass the wind waves persist, but within a mile even these subside, Zimovia Strait slickening with current, and soon I can see the reflection of the sky in the water.

For nearly fifteen miles we parallel the road south of Wrangell. Homes extend as far as the road, and beyond this, cabins, where we will sleep tonight. Not long after Chichagof Pass, an old flat-bottomed Stikine riverboat is stranded on shore, sturdied by piles, its red-and-black hull peeling apart at the seams. In the pilothouse a man tends plants, and seeing us, leaves from view. All day a feeling has persisted: Wrangell has many decisions ahead.

JUNE 5

As is typical when we stay in cabins or in town, we get up late with no chance to beat the wind.

The tide ebbs all morning, a -2.8, exposing the limp eel grass. For the first time the shore ascends in nothing but steep rock from the stain of intertidal life to forest, thick with spruce, hemlock, and cedar. There are few places to land. Instead of sand and shallows, river deltas are mounts of cobblestones braided with silver water where the flow has broken the shoreline rock. Where a tea-colored stream gushes over the granite, I climb on boulders above the barnacles and moon snails to the high-tide line and dip the water bags into the flow.

On a nearby island we have heard that an old dugout canoe lies in partial completion. The Forest Service cannot helicopter it out because it will disintegrate, so they have left it, one of the relics, over there somewhere, melting into the forest floor.

The southeast wind bellows again, and we are stopped by a speedboater. He says he is going to Thoms Place to smoke dope at a buddy's house. "I used to be a kayaker," he says. "But I got a job."

"And a motor," I say. He dislikes this response and jabbers about nothing I can remember, keeping me tight against the rocks. Then he guns the two hundred-horse Mercury, bouncing us in the wake. The encounter erases any fantasy I had about all people living in harmony with this beautiful area. His small aluminum speed rod roostertails ahead, a waterborne muscle car. A hot-rodder. A motorhead. Dull and wasteful. We must go by Thoms Place, a bay farther south, and hope we do not encounter him again.

Much of the forest has been cut to the tree line, and brown grass and shrubs climb to near three thousand feet. Remaining trees warp with headwinds, and we work along the rocks, no more than a paddle-length from shore.

As we approach a solitary home, a man rows from shore to get clearance for his motor. "Where you headed?" he asks.

"Seattle."

"Ah, I see." And he rows on.

A woman waves us in from the yard. "You need to see this," she says, and she guides us through the tall grass to a slanted tree. I can hardly pick anything out, but then it becomes strikingly clear: a totem pole split by a living Sitka spruce.

"You can't tell that it's a bear on top now," she says. "But forty years ago you could sure tell. There were no trees growing on the site then." She says it is the oldest standing totem pole in southeast Alaska, in its original place since around 1820. A mortuary pole. It is called "Bear up a tree," and as she shows us in a book, it is the same pole John Muir sketched in 1879. "People say that someone should fix it up, but these were made to fall down. Old giving way to the new." She gives us smoked king salmon in a mason jar. "Smoked with apple wood," she says.

And soon we are paddling again.

Outside our night's cabin I split firewood, the straight grain of yellow cedar, aromatic and spicy, and recall the yellow cedar of agate beach. This journey is gaining a cumulative effect, a summation, experience enriched by all that has preceded it. The days are crammed with details, things that I would have not imagined in any way important before paddling this far: the ruffle of an eagle's feathers, the fanning of kelp beneath the surface, the particular folding of waves, an approaching spray of cloud, the broken or unbroken shoreline where a stream empties, where we can gather water.

Beneath the bed I find scores of musty 1950s and 1960s *Life* magazines and discover an article, "How to Write a Postcard." After a lengthy introduction that asserts "one of the most important skills in this busy world is to keep people informed," I discover the next page has been ripped out.

The cabin is constructed with vertical logs and a shake roof. Fifteen pairs of deer antlers provide prongs for drying clothes, and we have used them all. In the kindling box is gift wrapping left over from Christmas day. I find written on a name tag SONDRA, my mother's name, and place the tag on the counter, selecting another piece to throw into the fire.

Flipping through the cabin log book, we notice an icon, a perfectly drawn "Opus" from *Outland*. Indeed, Berke Breathed stayed here one night, racing up from Seattle on a powerful speedboat in just eight days.

The cabin has perfect shelter for a stormy night, nestled among three islands, a God's Pocket. Few cabins are locked, an Alaska tradition.

JUNE 8

After crossing a blustery Earnest Sound, we skirt the steep rocks and beaches of the Cleveland Peninsula for two days in the lee of a strong southern wind. Great blue herons—long, slender birds—lunge into the air, flapping forward, then landing again until we violate their distance of alarm, when they once more leap and fly.

These are days of looking after points, distant points, and staring at the low, flat land of Lemesurier Peninsula. The nearest point is always seen in color; the next one, a charcoal smudge; and the farthest, a light wash of rain. Amid one of the squalls the sun appears, and with it, a low rainbow, its bright arch just above the waves, so beautiful that we must stop paddling and stare.

At high tides we are raised to the lower branches of cedar, and we glide beneath the belly of the land, into pockets of sweetness, the smell of green. As we paddle on these long days, the mind is swept into its own currents. It responds to the tug of memory, of experience, of those who have helped shape our journey and our lives. I find myself remembering the old people I knew when I was young, grandparents. Of large hands leading my small hands across dark soil. Of days when I walked among the plants, looking up through the veiny leaves at the sun. Then the vision ebbs and another floods, a memory of a fish caught or of stargazing. Maren's melodies dance to me in the wind. Thoughts spin off in mid-channel, then quiet behind a boulder.

This morning another system pushes through, clouds bringing drops that plunk down through the old cedar, and Maren says she has had another dream about high tides sweeping our camp away.

All day we paddle toward Lemesurier Point in the shifty winds, toward the hamlet of Meyers Chuck. Murelets bob and dive, and Maren insists that the sea stars clinging to the undersides of rocks are practicing yoga. Clouds swirl from the hills. Eagles that hover against the wind visit fish as sudden shadows.

At Lemesurier Point bull kelp signals exposed waters, the first kelp we have seen since Point Barrie. Coves on the point are slots with beaches pushed to their heads. On the tip of Lemesurier, a generator hammers from a small home among the stunted trees. A tarp forms a crude boathouse. It seems the residents have little but rock and prayers.

"Here's our wind!" Maren shouts as we circle the last rock, and we buck the froth once more. As we near the village and the chuck's narrow opening, a distant whine manifests as three Jet Skiers. They whiz past. Jet Skiers? Is this the party headed for Glacier Bay? They are motionless on their craft, freezing in bulky survival suits. One looks windburned, his face nearly peeled away.

Once in town, Maren convinces the owners of the Meyers Chuck Lodge to open for the evening, and we are warm for the first time in days.

The most striking feature of Meyers Chuck is the complete absence of a main road. The only way around town is by a footpath that snakes by the general store—closed for several years now—a generator that spews diesel, a post office, homes, and out to the shores of Clarence Strait. On the post-office door is a poster declaring EXPECT A MIRACLE along with MAIL PICKUP IS APPROXIMATELY ONE HOUR AFTER PLANE. GARAGE SALE RON'S DECK JUNE 22. TUESDAY POST OFFICE 11 A.M.–2 P.M. We laugh at the miracle of mail delivery in this remote area but sober up when we later learn the miracle is meant for the schoolteacher who may die of a brain tumor. The school will soon close in Meyers Chuck, enrolling only six students last year. Just twenty-five people live in town year-round now.

Linda, who has stepped from her house to welcome us to town, soon leads us to a cedar cabin that has been converted to an art gallery and sits in a chair, an instant proprietor. "It's not a good day," she says as we survey the wooden bowls and greeting cards. Today her husband has left for the outer coast of Baranof Island to fish for the summer, and the seas are rough. She says that fishing "out front" is no longer very good, and people must move north or to Ketchikan or be absent all year. Signs around town read: RESOURCE DEPENDENT COMMUNITY: LOGGING, MINING, FISHING, RECREATION. When in talking of our previous paddling days we mention the Cleveland Peninsula, she bristles and says that nearby areas may be logged soon.

Waves pound the rocks with white surf while the chuck remains a complete calm. "It's screaming out there," says Joyce, who runs the lodge with her husband, Cliff. She has made a hearty meal, which we share from the lazy Susan. We discuss their charter business, how sport fishing brings in more money than the declining commercial fishing. "In history, consumers went from canned fish to frozen, and now they are going to fresh," Joyce says as the Parmesan cheese spins her direction. "The demand for fresh fish favors the farm fish. Farms have a steady supply, where commercial fishing doesn't—and can't."

Cliff enjoys the hummingbirds that mob the feeders, and he watches them intently, pointing out species he knows, mostly rufous, marveling at their iridescence. "They really swarm at dusk," he chuckles. "Getting tanked up for the night, I guess." There must be fifty or more whirring about, dipping into the feeders, then rushing on. Outside, they dive at our bright-red paddling clothes, mistaking them for flowers. Joyce prepares sugar water for them every day, and each day the birds drain the feeders. With such a high metabolic rate, hummingbirds must feed almost unceasingly during the day to stay alive. And at night, they reduce their metabolic rate to survive the cold and long duration between feedings. Tonight, I clean three plates of spaghetti.

In Meyers Chuck

JUNE 9

"This thing doubles as a squirt-gun base," Ryan says as we climb the makeshift ladder to the tree house. On the tiny porch, semiautomatic squirt guns are strewn about on beanbag chairs patched with duct tape. The tree house, known as The Spruce Needle, is made of found wood, half painted, unused hinges clinging to boards, a louvered door.

As we are shown to our window-side card table—indeed, the only table—Ryan explains, "The Spruce Needle is a spoof on Seattle's Space Needle. Our motto: No attitude. Better food." Ryan, with his friends, Noah and Sam, assembled the tree house, and now assemble a breakfast burrito with eggs and hot pepper sauce. Today the cord from the propane stove is missing, however, so they must cook below in their home rather than tableside. We are their first guests of the year, a time to break them in.

There is an entrepreneurial air about this young trio. "I realized in Juneau it wouldn't work," Ryan says. "Insurance, property, a big kitchen. Two hundred and fifty thousand dollars just to have a restaurant in a tree house." He is frighteningly businesslike for someone who has not reached adolescence. He operates on a natural cunning. Although Ryan is the spokesman, somehow all three manage to work together, and have for several years. Before The Spruce Needle, they ran Joe's Dreamland Diner, which served muffins and coffee at 3 A.M. for the fishermen leaving early. Nowadays they produce perch prints, catching small perch in the chuck, then coloring them with paint and pressing them on cardstock paper. It is a Japanese art and leaves impressions much like fossils. Today they must make 210 perch prints for an order in Juneau. Seeking shelter in the chuck, tourists simply return to them like the salmon.

We add our names to one of the three signature boards above the table. The guest book. Scanning down the list we stop at a curious entry: the Galloping Gourmet himself, Graham Kerr.

In early afternoon Maren and I follow Ryan, Noah, and Sam to their clubhouse, the Drift Inn. They want to fix hot chocolate for us. As they start a smoldering fire with candles, Buddy, a stout compassionate dog, slouches against Maren, and she must hold it up at times with both arms.

"It's kind of fun that there's only one path around town," I say.

"Yeah. No cars," Ryan says. "What's going to happen? You get hit by a dog? There was a bear that got into some food here, and they shot it with a thirty-thirty up the rear. Then all of us had to go over there and watch someone skin a bear. Quite a nature study, watching someone skin a bear.

"I like it here because you can get away from most of the things that you really have to worry about, like how people view you or anything. You just kinda are able to get back together with yourself. Not as much problems to think about here. I got great friends here. I came out here from Juneau when I was two years old, Noah was three. Probably the biggest reason I'm here is to give Noah somebody else to be with. Watch TV, play games like Star Wars, games that we invent. You pick a character and you roll for how smart he is."

Sam speaks softly and laments that he hasn't sold many perch prints yet this year. "But I make necklaces, too," he says. "And earrings and candleholders from purpleheart and bird's-eye maple."

We turn to Noah. He is less flamboyant than Ryan but enjoys the spotlight nonetheless. "I've been here a long time," he says. "It's not the city, which I really like. You know everybody."

"What do you like to do here?" Maren asks.

"Build forts. Get GI Joes and play guns. We hardly ever meet kids from boats. They are old people. We're the only people, just about, who are not summer people. There are about four other families who are not summer people. Now we are going to be summer people. The school only went to the twelfth grade, but because there are so few students, they are going to close it, so we might go to the high school in Sitka. We thought we were going to go to a place with more kids, but there's only six kids in the same grade there. Forty kids total. Now forty-two. They probably have to order two extra chairs. I'll probably get sick. In second grade I caught everything. Living out here, there isn't much that can get to you, until somebody comes that has a cold. I remember a friend of my mom's that came out here and got the entire chuck sick."

Clarence Strait is whitecapped all day. At night the weather radio tells the tale: *Looking at the evening weather map, the parade of storms continues to march across the Gulf of Alaska. Looks like another storm will approach and move through southern southeast Alaska tonight. We've had measurable precipitation every day so far this month of June, and it looks as though that could continue not only through the early portions of the week but possibly through the entire upcoming week. There's a big trough of low pressure situated in the upper atmosphere, and there is no indication of that weather pattern breaking. So here's the forecast for tonight: Windy with rain.*

Southeast winds fifteen to twenty-five miles per hour. Lows in the upper forties. The chance of rain one hundred percent. For Monday, windy with rain. Winds fifteen to twenty-five miles per hour. Highs in the mid fifties. Chance of rain, one hundred percent. For Monday night: Cloudy with showers. Lows in the upper forties. Chance of a shower, ninety percent. Tuesday: Cloudy with showers. Highs in the upper fifties. Chance of showers, eighty percent. . . .

JUNE 10

The southeast wind blows dark across Clarence Strait at 4:30 A.M., but we pack anyway, and by the time we are ready, the wind has fallen. Skeptical, we walk the path around the village to the outer beach. It is quiet. Brightness glows in the south. We stare and exchange pragmatic comments about tides and loading time.

"I bet we could make it to Ship Island if we started now," I say.

Maren shrugs. "I just want to stay and write postcards."

Still undecided, we tramp back, and Joyce has a fried potato and gravy breakfast whirling on the lazy Susan.

"How can we leave this?" Maren says.

Cliff studies the strait through binoculars and says the weather will do what it is going to do when the tide changes. Within fifteen minutes of slack water, the shoreline foams with chop.

Then over their VHF: *Break. This is United States Coast Guard Juneau Alaska Communications Center. This is bulletin number one from the Alaska Tsunami Warning Center. A major earthquake of magnitude seven decimal two has occurred in position five one decimal five north, one seven seven decimal zero west. Three zero miles southwest of Adak. A tsunami warning is in effect. . . . A tsunami may have been generated, and intensity cannot be predicted; however, this wave could cause great damage to the Alaska area. The danger may last for several hours. Esti-*

mated local times are as follows. . . . This is United States Coast Guard Communications Center in Juneau Alaska. Out.

This is something we have not considered. We stay, and everyone bustles about their daily work while we wait for the huge wave to rise in the west. Finally at noon someone says, "The warning? It was cancelled hours ago." We nap in the afternoon, and when I awake, cruise ships, oblivious to the waves, are slipping past in the strait, great hulks of steel as white as toothy smiles.

At dusk Joyce turns on the generator, aka the "gen," that will power the lodge until about ten o'clock. The solace of night, which one expects in such a place, is obliterated by the generators. Where even voices can carry for a great distance over the water, their hammering sounds like factories.

Looking for something besides navigational books to read, I find H. G. Wells's *The Time Machine* among the paperbacks and read in bed. "I saw the moon spinning swiftly through her quarters from new to full, and had a faint glimpse of the circling stars. . . ." says the Time Traveler.

Our time, too, is spinning and seamless. In these javelin craft, our days are cycles, the moon orbiting Earth, tugging at the tides, Earth revolving, sweeping day into night, high tide and low. The tides advance about fifty minutes each day, pacing with the moon's twenty-eight-day revolution around Earth. So we depend on the tide books less and less. The tidal cycle has become intuitive, internal, as if the nearly two-thirds of us that is water also bears a tide. Every few days, when the tide is low in the morning and evening, beach carries are longer, heaving more work on us. Then for several days as we leave and arrive near high tide, carrying gear up the beach eases, and life is luxury. As we head to Ketchikan, the tide will be ebbing in the afternoons. A week of longer carries. More than anything, tides fix our days, sway our moods, set our clocks as they rise and cover beaches like shadows.

Meyers Chuck to Behm Canal

JUNE 13

With a whistle call to charge ahead, we left Meyers Chuck two days ago. But the weather has been difficult. Ocean swells racing from the mouth of Clarence Strait and the Pacific beat the Cleveland Peninsula, rousing the waters off steep headlands into chop and confusion. When squalls hit, we head for beaches and gripe, crouching on logs, shivering, nibbling at smoked cheddar. Then we somehow grind on, only to make camp and go to sleep early and wet, hands and feet like prunes, nearly bloodless and white. Miraculously, the books and charts are bone dry, double bagged and kept in the hull. We dry by our own heat at night, but we can savor it only long enough in the morning to confirm the tides. Then it is into the sopping neoprene and clammy Goretex for another run with the sea. We have been out for two months now, and though the calendar has advanced twice, the weather seems to reside permanently in April.

Today we are awake at 4:30 and paddling by 7:00. It is clear, but as we reach Caamano Point, another front has assembled in the south, and the forecast has increased its wind prediction to twenty-five knots. While it is relatively calm, we round the exposure of Caamano Point. But slowly the winds build, and I carelessly let two large crests carry me near the rocks. When a third wave drops, my kayak crunches. I scream and try to pry away. Scream and pry again as new waves pin me against the stone. Again I shriek and stroke, finally freeing myself as a larger wave belts the shore. I have had enough, and past Bond Bay we are literally blown into a cove, surfing the five-foot breakers into a slot of rock no more than four feet wide. And my kayak has an added gash to its underside. Though it does not leak, the gelcoat has been scraped clean away, and through it I see daylight. It is not speed that will wreck you in a kayak but ego and neglect.

Today we watch our destination from afar and pitch the tent in the lee of an elderly spruce. An assembly of white buildings and fragile lights in Behm Canal is a submarine test station, and the chart marks a restricted area that intersects our camp. They require a zone of silence for their secret work, but I do not see how this tossing water could allow them much quiet. By the time we get to Ketchikan, it will surely be clear and calm.

JUNE 14

Weather day.

A dull, half-lit morning with furious winds and pounding surf. The forecasters report thirty-knot winds, but the gusts seem greater, hissing through the trees. The voices of the forecasters are scientific. They sound cloistered and over-worked, spent by the odd hours, numbing statistics, and end-less routine of weather itself. Only when the white noise of spray mingles with the scratch of frequencies does it seem that they are sitting by the same plangent sea. Their transmis-sions reduce the great cyclonic storms, exploding surf, and relief of calm rain into wind-wave and swell height, decimals and digits.

But that is their job. Ultimately, we regard these voices

that travel to us across the surf and unnamed bays with the same affection given to hometown baseball announcers, and we are disappointed when a companion crackles and fades out of range. Their transmissions—taped loops of weather information recorded one over another—often slip in moments of yesterday's broken sun and cloud with today's howling front, and we laugh and remember the sun. I am sure they wonder, as anyone does who talks into a microphone, if anyone is listening. On these days of storm, they broadcast from the same center of loneliness as a fog horn.

The FM radio brings "My Sharona," then women's folk music, and then a discussion in which someone says tourism brings $1.7 billion to the state of Alaska each year. No cruise-ship sightings yet today, although they will come, ghosts across the water. Ketchikan is one of the busiest tourist hubs in southeast Alaska.

When the rain eases, I leave the tent and am astonished to see two orcas just off our point. One surfaces and blows as the other leaps into the air, exposing its entire camouflage of sun and shade. They work the line of foam where the currents mix about fifty yards off shore, passing three times, before knifing away. *Guctahin*.

Fog descends all afternoon, and Revillagigedo Island soon vanishes. The middle hours of these weather days have become a time of silent preparation for what may come to be. Cooking chores are done. There is no camp to be made or broken. Maren likes to read, sketch, and write. I, too, turn inward and tread the shore, breathing the ocean air, knowing the days will warm, the sea will flatten, as this system presses on. So often I speculate on tomorrows, trimming the limitless day ahead to fit a theory, an expectation. And this is when my life deadens. Yet on this beach I am most alive. Perhaps with these great crossings, the sheer leaving of land, I have shed something. So slowly I see that this journey is not a quest but an opening, a trust, an awareness.

Evening is dark and rainy. But near sunset a solitary bird whistles a beautiful and complex song, one we have not heard before. A call, it seems, of fair weather.

In Ketchikan

JUNE 15

A cell of storms mushrooms over Prince of Wales Island, far to the west. To the east, the plume of a whale.

When we arrived at this beach two days ago, we floated onto the rocks. Now the tide is out, and we must lower the kayaks down the daunting ledges of seaweed to the water. Stepping flat-footed and carrying a kayak, I slip and sit hard on a rock, bruising my tailbone. For a moment my breath is gone. Seconds later, Maren falls, too, and is surprised that her elbow has not shattered.

After days of high waves, the water is flat again, and we cross Behm Canal as if crossing a mirror. On the far shore, we must weave among a fleet of salmon trollers and tourists and ask permission to use a beach to change and snack. The fishermen stare.

Arriving in Ketchikan, we are dwarfed and uneasy—the pilings, the iron hulls, the breakwaters, the weight, the impact. I wince as a jet thunders overhead. We work our way down Tongass Narrows, past elaborate homes of glass and steel of the latest vacation architecture. We are overwhelmed by scale even after two months, even in Ketchikan.

At Totem Bight, we pause for a snack on the park's inviting beach. Then paddling around front, the scene takes on all its irony: clear-cut, forest, totems.

A tremendous horn blasts, and from around the point emerges the bow of a cruise ship. It is frightening at this short distance, knowing that the propeller blades exceed my height, that they are thrashing somewhere beneath. We prepare for the wake. The ship glides by, eclipsing the western sky, people standing on the high deck, the glint of camcorders just visible. Water folds around the bow, then seems to suck beneath the hull. Behind, a boiling slipstream. Then plies the *Columbia*, the ferry, our ship. A hum in the water is all we hear.

Outside Thomas Basin, I ease toward a docked Princess liner and reach for the white wall of steel. Sighting down the hull, I can see the imperfections disguised at sea: the missing paint at waterline, the smudges of dock piles, the wavering steel plates. Its sheer size causes me to swallow my breaths. When I put out my hand, a phobia seizes me, and I retract, feeling that it might suddenly begin to pull away and draw me with it. It is like reaching for a living whale.

Then we are in a town again, wondering what to do with everything. Where should the kayaks go? The equipment? Who will go running down the street in neoprene-stockinged feet to call a friend who has agreed to put us up? Little we do at sea makes sense here. Other than a pair of jeans and a jacket, gear falls into a useless heap. After an hour of turmoil and shock, these questions resolve themselves, a kayak company having agreed to store the boats, and our good friend, Heidi, arrives, smiling, with a station wagon. We have a place to sleep, and once more we begin to dry.

JUNE 16

The tourist run in southeast Alaska kicks off in mid-May and runs steadily through mid-August, and merchants are out with their dip nets. Three new cruise ships line the Ketchikan waterfront, and together they appear like a great glacial face before town. The hulks are very much a business in and of themselves, but it is more amazing to realize that they are powered by free time. On a summer's day, tourists here can outnumber townsfolk four to one.

The *Sky Princess* weighs 46,000 gross tons, is 789 feet long, and can carry 1,200 passengers. It holds a fifth-mile jogging track, three pools, a health and beauty center, pizzeria, casino, and one of the largest showrooms afloat. Of the Princess fleet, it distinguishes itself as "understated elegance."

Our kayaks are each 17 feet, 11 inches long, 21½ inches at the widest beam, and weigh some 55 pounds empty, nearly 275 pounds fully loaded. Their single passengers are not passengers at all, but engines. Each kayak holds two weeks of fuel, camping equipment, and safety measures. They are smaller than lifeboats. On their hulls is the name *Mariner II*, a name they share with the first successful interplanetary spacecraft, the probe that discovered the solar wind on its trajectory toward the sun and the cloud encumbered globe of Venus.

At a cruise ship, I acquire a sample Inside Passage cruise itinerary:

Sun	Vancouver
Mon	Inside Passage Cruising
Tue	Juneau
Wed	Skagway
Thu	Glacier Bay Cruising
Fri	Sitka
Sat	Inside Passage Cruising
Sun	Vancouver

This afternoon Maren and I meet Ray Troll, the artist who creates the popular T-shirts we have seen all along the coast. Over a beer, he says he is heading to a symposium in Bozeman, Montana, "whose focus is how to make fish as popular as dinosaurs." He is cool and clever and tells of excursions to

Prince of Wales Island, speaking fondly of karsts and fossils, of the cold, dark underworld of deep-sea fish.

In his studio, after displaying a pickled ratfish in a jar, he retrieves some final pastel drawings. One of his best-known, "Spawn Till You Die," is a take on the Jolly Roger: a human skull crossed with salmon. Another, "Fabric of Life," is an intricate evolutionary procession from single-celled organisms to the automobile. He creates in the tradition of the natural-history diorama, scenes packed with sea life, organisms eating, competing, and dying. Each work depicts abundance and threat. No species ever seems to get its complete way, always a dark force lurks: overexploitation, overpopulation, or over-specialization. As one card notes: THERE IS NO FREE LUNCH.

"I have a seriograph called 'Preserve the Balance,'" he says. "But I always back up and think, 'Are things ever out of balance?'"

Downstairs from Ray's gallery is Marvin Oliver's gallery of Native arts. In the red-and-black formline prints, in the complex of ovoids, U forms, split U forms, and S forms that fuse human and nonhuman images, one can see a vision of the people, the relation of all life. However different their work, it is an understanding that Troll and these Native artists share.

JUNE 17

In Ketchikan the old codgers do not mingle among the slacks and matching sweatsuits that flood the docks. Perhaps they are infirm, housebound, true old-timers. Wherever they are, I miss them here among the hucksters, and their rough and stompy walks remain as memories from farther north.

Ketchikan to Portland Inlet

◆

Ketchikan falls away in spools of cable along shore, engine parts, fish processors, a single Coast Guard cutter, ships with the names *Polar Venture, St. Elias,* and *Glacier Bay,* and finishes as it began, with a flotilla of puttering boats trolling for salmon. To be under our own power, self-contained, heading southeast across the blue inlets of Revillagigedo Island is empowering. At first we loved the towns. They were warm respites from a life we did not yet know. But more and more they are fissures in our paddling lives, anomalies, and difficult. On the water there is no distinction between work and life, and the routine of camp and kayaking is nourishing and essential. All morning a grandness returns, the sky opens as the Alexander Archipelago that has sheltered us for two months drops to low islands and becomes the open waters of Dixon Entrance, the outer coast, the end of Alaska.

At the village of Saxman, just south of Ketchikan, we beach the kayaks and walk to the totem park. I recognize some totems from the familiar old photographs and sketches from Tongass and Village Islands and the Cape Fox village, made during the various turn-of-the-century expeditions. In the 1930s the original poles were gathered from these old villages by a Forest Service and Civilian Conservation Corps totem restoration project, brought to Saxman to be repaired and restored or replicated. Only in Ketchikan's Totem Heritage Center is there a complete collection of original poles. Some stand there paintless and cracked in a huddle. Others lie supine, the arms of their figures crossed, faces grimaced, flecks of pigment near the eyes, tagged as if in a morgue. These at Saxman, although repainted, hold their full colors: red, black, aqua, cedar. To us, the colors of sun, night, sea, and forest.

The totems, like their people, have left the smaller islands, gathering in towns. Saxman formed in the late 1800s, when the Tlingit villages of Cape Fox, Tongass, and others were abandoned, their residents seeking work in canneries. Beyond the growing centers of population, much of the coast carries fewer people than a century before.

The poles before us seem ancient, like standing stones, but even the originals are barely a century and a half old, perhaps carved when the first railroads were pushing across the continent. For one thing, even rot-resistant cedar does not last long in these moist environs. But the great poles were little known in earlier times. Unlike canoe carving, which was well established before Europeans arrived, the carving of free-standing totem poles peaked in the mid 1800s with the availability of European iron and steel tools. Before this time, with the exception of the iron found in shipwrecks that washed ashore, blades were fashioned mostly from jadeite or nephrite, shell, or beaver teeth. Carving was slow, and few sizable projects were undertaken beyond interior house posts. Metal blades, however, made wood carving swift and inexpensive. As wealth from the fur trade brought new status to chiefs and their clans, they wished to uplift these achievements. So totem poles grew in number, height, and complexity, works in their own right, independent of other structures. After their artistry and traditional stories, which are purely Native, these totem poles represent an alloy of Native and non-Native ways, a legacy personified in the figure atop one pole before us now who wears a stovepipe hat.

We return to the kayaks to find that ravens have discovered our lunch of bagels. One has made off with a bag of two, which it drags across the cobbles. Others roost boldly on the cockpit, combing and pecking until we are an arm length away. Ravens are always with us. Native lore and wisdom nods to their intelligence, and Native peoples all along this coast have long told of Raven's antics and power. The Tlingit speak of two ravens. Great Raven—also called Nass Raven, Yehl, or the Creator—lives above the Nass River where he governs the sun, the moon, and the stars. The other raven is his grandson, Scamp Raven, transformer and trickster, who loves to jab and jeer and fool. Sensing the presence of Scamp, we abandon salvage efforts and watch the heavy black birds hopping about, circling cream cheese, flying off with mouthfuls of dough, calling *ah-ho, ah-ho, ah-ho.*

JUNE 21

Summer solstice. Awake at 4:30 and paddling by 6:20 on this longest day. Orange jellyfish, as large as dinner plates, hover in the early shadows, and bark and spruce needles float by surface tension, completely dry, puckering the sheen. Toward Point Alava the shore regains a stunted and beaten outercoast appearance. Swells billow the surface, and beds of kelp, batches of greens, sway across the water.

Again a loon follows, yodeling. "The great northern diver," Maren calls out. She has studied loons in northern Minnesota and produces a remarkable loon call by cupping her hands and blowing between her thumbs. For a short time she carries a dialogue with the distant bird, whistling, *"Ooo-waaa-ooo."* The extra companionship is valuable to her as the horizon opens. Dixon Entrance is outer-coast paddling, the rival to these inside waters. Stretching before us, the land merely drops into the ocean. After traveling so long in the cover of high islands, the empty horizon is dizzying, like peering from a tall building across an unaccustomed expanse.

It is difficult to see the compass swivel north as we head into Misty Fiords National Monument, when the curve of Cape Fox seems so attainable on such a bright, clear day. Knowing that we are diverting four or five days off course. Knowing the weather may deteriorate. Knowing that we could be across this inlet in an hour and a half, hassle free. And our energy stalls. But Misty Fiords seems an important midpoint on this coast, its forest advanced thousands of years beyond that of Glacier Bay's, a century and a half behind the development of Puget Sound. And after the steel hulls of Ketchikan, a place that is green on the map and called a wilderness seems inviting.

The paddling up fiord is easy and smooth. Behind Rudyerd Island, the current floods near five knots, and we glide past the shoreline of whites and tans spattered with black lichen. Even in this national monument, the driftwood is cut, brought in by tides that know no boundaries. A floatplane flies over, full of tourists from Ketchikan. It sweeps broad, flat circles, tracing the inlet to the north, and with it, the influence of town never truly seems to leave. Turning a point, we flush seals off the rocks, sending them barking across the water.

All afternoon a storm's anvil cap smears overhead. Beyond the chattering riptide in Princess Bay, we paddle beneath the trees, along the cliffs. Without quite realizing it, we soon notice that shadows have vanished, and suddenly booms of thunder echo among the fiords. Behind, the thunderhead has billowed through the troposphere, and we power for camp.

A line of wind forms offshore. Just ahead of the gusts, we reach a cove and find feathers strewn over the water. A broad gravel beach at the head is too thick with alder, willow, and devil's club to penetrate. So, where boulders tumble from grass, we camp, ducking beneath the cedar, as clouds flood the inlet and summer's first storm debuts.

It is a terrific, crackling storm of severe gusts and torrential rains, and we watch the sky with delight until it slackens. When we emerge from the forest to resecure camp and kayaks, a noiseless wall of green and white plows by the entrance to our small cove. The vessel is so large for such a small channel that its sudden appearance is startling. In twenty minutes it returns, and the high rock walls are drenched with wake.

We go to sleep wondering if we have paced correctly. Can we afford this long side trip? Is it *worth* it? As we fall silent, a spruce needle drops onto the nylon and tumbles down the tent wall.

JUNE 22

Misty Fiords is a gray-green world of trudging clouds and solitary bird cries, quiet days pocked with raindrops. We meet gushing creeks around every point, rushes of sound and cool wind, and wherever there is a place to land, a river has broken the rock, pushing it flat, fanning the cobbles across the water.

This is my favorite paddling, the waters along cliffs, and I occasionally stop and finger the various rocks, the glacial striations that we have followed since the beginning. When it is raining, Maren tucks her ponytail under her cap. She has been first out of the tent these wet mornings while I lay crabby in my sleeping bag. There is no doubt we are a strong team, a strengthening team, that we each have our days, and today she was up early again and packing.

But I am eased into morning happiness now as we glide through these pools of deep solitude. Below, I can see the rocks descending through the water, walls of retreating caverns. I instinctively look at the sea as a surface, but today I see it as depths, as a floored entity, as the basin that holds it—which, after all, is land. Shapes from the bottom rise to within a foot of the surface. White quartz fractures the rock like cracks of lightning across a night sky. In other places the bands soften and ripple like ice cream.

An eagle feather I found in the cove last evening is the speckled brown and white of an immature bird, and I have it strapped to my chart case, covering Rudyerd Bay and Punch-bowl Lake like an approaching front.

When we reach Manzanita Bay, the place obtains more the feeling of a northern lake. Our bows send off symmetrical waves, cutting the world in two, as we paddle to camp across this stillness. Loons peer beneath the water, look up, then dive. Swimming with their wings, they pop again to the surface like balloons released from the bottom.

At last, evening's clouds are bright with sun. We stay near a Forest Service shelter, choosing to camp beneath an old cedar instead, our tent completely dry. Exploring near camp, I find the ribs of an old ship, a twenty-five-footer, gradually losing its third dimension, becoming more stain than form. When I return, I find Maren stretching in the tent. She has a knack of finding comfort nearly anywhere she goes, curling backbends over drift logs and collapsing on the warm beach rocks.

It has been a wet day, and we expend much energy to keep things dry. After the quarreling river otters have retired, I can hear the hinge of my jaw work. What I think to be the rumble of a cruise ship is blood flowing through my ears.

At last light, a kiss.

JUNE 23

We wake early to fog and decide to sleep in. Maren calls it a nap since it is consciously decided. Several hours later there is sun, and we chase the water as it leaks across the flats toward the abrupt eastern shore of deep bays—the fiords.

Today the world is revealed. After stopping for water at a stream flowing from a small delta of boulders, we paddle along granite shores to Rudyerd Bay, peering into the clear water. Rudyerd is stunning, with its two thousand-foot-high wall of polished granite and busy, with tour planes buzzing overhead like bees around a flower. The face is ominous.

Where streams empty, rock has peeled away and dropped to a colluvial shield of talus far below.

The beach at the head of Punchbowl Cove is crushed igneous rock, scoria, and above are the columns from an ancient basalt flow. It is marvelous, but we have at last found the bugs and must pace to keep them away as we eat, parading in circles with lentil chili, swatting at the air. Gnats patter the tent like rain. We find a mosquito head net on the beach, thin and nearly weightless, tumbling in a gust.

After dinner, we rejoice as terrestrial beings and climb through the old hemlock forest, stepping over the roots and over cones, through the rich red crumble of wood to Punchbowl Lake. When we near the high striated rock face, the air is ten degrees cooler, as if just freed from the glaciers.

Punchbowl is placid, a freshwater pool among cirques and knobs. And we embrace for a time before the mosquitoes become unbearable. Descending, it takes some careful work to place feet, to hop among the rocks and onto the pointed logs so as not to go cascading through the fern and devil's club. Often we slip on moss and lunge like dancers, arms extended and for an instant, poised.

To the north and west the inlet has a gentle curve and assumes the majestic haze so common in frontier paintings. A boat pulls up, a catamaran, and with it shouts and yelps. Then the *chank-chank-chank* of an anchor chain. Glaring at the boat, Maren says animals have to adjust to our schedule of a five-day work week and rambunctious weekends. "They are pleased when Monday comes," she says. "I know it."

JUNE 24

No-see-ums swarmed last night, and today blood is caked where their mouths rasped a layer of skin. Murrelets skittering across the water lead us from camp, and boaters snap our pictures as we paddle by. Morning light accents the grandeur of the place, and the shadows linger for half the morning on steeper westward faces until we turn toward the Pacific and leave the bay.

Tangles of bleached wood, the wreckage of avalanche chutes, heap beneath the steep slopes. Only shrubby willows and alders survive in the slide areas, a column of young forest growing at the angle of repose. When rocks steepen beyond this, there is only lichen, then sky.

By noon a wind builds from the southwest, but still it is clear. The shorelines are softening again, and looking to the opposite shore where we have paddled is like crawling into a half-lit memory. We carry a paddler's image of it and can remember every cove, every downed tree, every stopping place. But from this distance, the far shore is a smooth ribbon, only vaguely familiar, parallel stripes of green, white, and water.

At Winstanley Creek we meet some kayak rangers, and soon we have made camp together and are all climbing through the forest and muskeg to Winstanley Lake, fording streams and looking for chocolate lilies. At the lake we leap in for a frigid swim, paddling about in the upper layers of warmest water before sunning and reheating again as we descend to camp.

The two tents are pressed against the forest, just above high tide, but the tide will be retreating all night. It is good to have people alongside who are powering themselves, and after they try our spaghetti leather and have a laugh, Pat tells of his time as a kayak ranger. We discuss ANILCA, the Alaska National Interest Lands Conservation Act of 1980 that designated nearly 103 million acres of Alaska lands as national parks, monuments, refuges, wildernesses, and conservation areas. More than 5 million of these acres are in Tongass National Forest, which we have been paddling through for most of the journey. Misty Fiords, like Admiralty Island, was designated a national monument in 1978 by presidential proclamation, with most of their lands later achieving wilderness status under ANILCA.

ANILCA has many compromises built into it, Pat says, and he feels that managers should not build on compromises that pertain to wilderness. "Compromises promote deterioration of conditions and create confusion. Alaska wilderness has the opportunity to be that rare exception—big expedition quality wilderness—if we can allow it to exist on its own merit," he says, settling into a trough of rock. "That is, if we choose not to convert it into a huge theme park. It's easy to build and maintain facilities. We know we can do that. Resisting the urge is the real challenge for the future."

"So how do you go about managing a wilderness?" I ask. "It's something that by definition is unmanaged and perhaps unmanageable."

He nods as if he has already thought this through. "Managing wilderness is a process of restoration, patrolling, and monitoring conditions, so we can maintain the wild qualities. With many more visitors, it's more a job of managing the people than the areas." He says it is a question of using appropriate technology, to draw the line at motorized use. "The Wilderness Act states one should use the 'minimum tool' necessary to accomplish objectives. And to me a minimum tool is a kayak versus a powerboat. You could patrol the monument in half the time in powerboats, but you wouldn't see it in nearly as much detail. The areas I know best are the areas I have spent kayaking, canoeing, and hiking. For me it just keeps getting back to setting the kind of *example* that we should be setting as managers of the area.

"We just talked with people from New York. We walked up to Checats Lake and chatted quite a bit, and I was asking them about how they felt the wilderness was meeting their expectations. And their response actually surprised me. They said that in a lot of ways it did, but they thought there were too many flights on some days. At times they felt like they were in an airport. They weren't expecting to see tour ships at all. That isn't what somebody who just gets the idea to go to a wilderness area thinks about. They think about bears and wolves."

He smiles and pops a handful of gorp into his mouth. "I can remember thinking in those terms because I come from New York. My first perception of wild country was when I moved out west and began working in a wilderness. It was a pretty good size, a hundred thousand acres. To me it was astounding to think there was wild country like that. At that point, I was pretty much thinking that wilderness management meant building trails and building *things*. Then I began to realize that we're building ourselves out of a resource.

"I am not antitrail or anticabin. I think there is a place for that. I like the opportunity of being able to fly into a lake. But we have ninety-eight percent of the country developed for that purpose. Why encroach on that remaining two percent that is designated wilderness? Two percent is not a large percentage of land that some might say is being 'locked up.' I don't look at it as locking it up. We are not saying you can't go there or shouldn't go there. But if you do go there, be prepared, and consider that this is here for many reasons."

"Nights like these . . ." Maren says. And we gaze across the water before firing the stove for hot chocolate.

"This is my third year here," Pat continues. "We've gotten into the kayaks and canoes, the manual methods of doing things, a lot more. And we've set some management standards informally by that example. And that gives me a lot of ownership in Misty. I don't like the word 'magical,' but I guess that's what it is. It just has that allure to it. A lot of wild country. *A lot* of wild country."

A week's worth of whiskers shadows a broad grin. "One day I will probably come to the realization that I am too old for this hard-core backcountry heavy-duty wilderness stuff. I'm going to have to retreat to the trailed opportunity. Car camping or something. But because of the experience in the backcountry that I've gotten in my youth, I would never consider opposing the idea of preserving what's left. I think every generation of young people should have the opportunity to go out and get lost in the woods for two weeks so they can feel, if only for the sport of it, what our ancestors felt on a daily basis. To become familiar with our true ancestral home. To understand our insignificance in the world."

*   *   *

A quarter moon shines above the sun. At dusk the bugs dissipate, and a fog rolls off the sea. As we enter the tent, trees are still bright with afterglow, and somewhere near the end of wakefulness waves dump on the beach.

JUNE 27

Drizzle this morning and breezy. We are exhausted from a week of solid paddling and must break the steady routine before attempting any more of the outer waters. Like yesterday, the morning sky contains openings of blue and layers of wind, and after the calm days in Misty Fiords, we face a Dixon Entrance racing with cloud.

But not today. After a breakfast of Mueslix, I sleep for several hours, waking again at 2:30 for a lunch of macaroni and cheese, which Maren has steaming. My stomach is hollow, burning calories even by slumbering.

The day's excursion is to get water. This cove has two rivers that flow from lakes, and at its center a round evenly graded beach rises to a treeless knoll flowered with red snapdragons and the white shields of cow parsnip—"Indian celery," as it has been called. Peeled or boiled, then eaten, young cow parsnip stalks were in the diets of most every tribe along the coast. The Native village that was once here was nearly self-contained, with shelter, fresh water, a food supply. But even those within the frame of this cove relied on nutrients that had returned from the ocean in the form of salmon.

Two brown bears, yearlings, perhaps nearing a quarter ton each, forage among the rocks along the northern stream. So we head to the other, a fast-cutting river among the mosses. Balancing on slick stones, Maren dips our two ten-liter bags into the icy flow. Enough for a few days. We land on the village point again, on the broad midden beach that must have once held so many canoes, and step through the high grasses until they reach our shoulders.

The rest of the afternoon I sit and listen, pondering the

village site. The wind whistles from the south but barely ripples the inner waters. Outside, the surf shatters against rock. Maren envisions how the community must have lived here, the fires smoking, calls ricocheting among canoes, a family house on every beach and bay. Winter villages such as this most often commanded panoramic views of surrounding waters, where approaching canoes could easily be seen. A water path through the shoals marks the entrance to the inner bay, but from water level, at any angle, it is deceptive. Yesterday, while paddling through the maze, we had to stop, confused, ready to turn away.

Clouds dive into showers and rain. A loon circles, gliding in for a landing and then skidding across the water on its belly. If a city was abandoned, how long before it returned to field and forest? The kayaks rest across two logs, stern to bow. We sleep nested in a hollow among the roots of a giant cedar.

JUNE 28

Despite the early wind, we decide to leave, looking back at the placid village cove, then facing the chop.

The going is easy at first, skirting behind shoals, protected from the worst waves. But rounding a farther point, we are blasted with hard winds and reflection waves. We muscle into the wind and water, unsure of ourselves, inching along. One instant Maren's bow is in the air; then she disappears. It is all too much like Frederick Sound. Once we reach a small islet, the beach is blocked from wind only by a shoal that soon covers with the rising tide, and we know we cannot stay. The skies are the color of bruises. After mozzarella and chocolate, we continue.

Cloudburst! The low dark squalls deluge, spray misting the surface. Uprooted seaweed and shredded jellyfish wash onto my deck. We push around another point, but it is rough again, and we must find a camp, ducking behind the islands out of the waves. The southeast corner is an expansive and protected beach, but a fish buyer has tied up there with several fishing boats alongside. Although the generator drones away, no one is in sight. Finally, we paddle to a cove with an abandoned cannery, where we will sit out the growing storm.

It is a tough camp. There is no beach at high tide, so I must hack through alders to make a path into the forest and pitch the tent near the remains of an old cabin. An immense cedar stump, charred from logging days, rises behind camp. We have paddled between two abandoned sites today.

Maren cooks among the alders at shoreline, shuttling to and from a small berm where she has stashed the bear canisters. Another downpour washes the beach, and in fifteen minutes we collect enough water to sustain us for several more days. The rainwater is sweet, naturally distilled.

The evening is marked by bright holes in the storm and dense low fog. It has been a month since Wrangell. Too slow? Too much time in town? The detour into Misty too great? As winds press through the trees, we dream of a simple life, uncomplicated by such searchings among the tides. A life that is warm. We laugh about our cats, remember books, and recall summer memories. But I have always loved storms, especially those weathered in tents when gusts rattle and snap the walls.

It is nearly like becoming the storm itself, and often I poke my head out to breathe the turbulent air.

At night rain drums the tent, and it sounds like bad weather for tomorrow. Eagles chatter overhead. Earlier, we saw one carrying an eel to its nest. Maren sleeps supine, knees up, a way she's slept since childhood. The howl of the fish buyer's generator perforates the gusty wind, and raindrops gong scrap metal in the derelict cabin.

JUNE 29

Radio: *Security. Security. The marine forecast issued by the Pacific Weather Center of Environment Canada. . . . Synopsis: A nine eight four millibar low, two four zero miles west northwest of Langara, will move into the Alaska panhandle overnight. . . . Dixon Entrance East: Storm warning continued. Southeast gales four zero to storm force five zero easing to southerly two five to gales three five this evening. . . . Seas near three meters, building to four to five meters this evening. . . . Outlook: moderate westerlies.*

Eagles cry out through the storm, and Maren writes another newsletter, which she has adorned with lively drawings of bull kelp and sea stars folded into the lotus position. This she will send to our friends when we get to Prince Rupert. She has served as our faithful correspondent. From Ketchikan we got news that her audience greatly enjoys her tales from the coast and gathers to read them by candlelight.

The tent is so saturated and worn that drops seep through and pool beneath the sleeping bags and must be mopped every half hour. All day winds build in the trees, bending them like blades of grass. I listen to Ketchikan public radio: Count Basie's "Blue Devil Blues," Glenn Miller's "American Patrol. . . ." Jazz is city music and just doesn't work out here, so far from the sophistication and shiny brass. Boris Yeltsin has a sore throat. Then I hear the Nasdaq report and grimace, flinging the headphones into the corner.

Outside, swells penetrate the cove, and combing surf lathers the islands offshore. My grandfather Ricks, who died long before my birth, captured color footage during World War II of the battleship *New York* bashing through an ocean storm, inundated up to its big guns. It is a silent and choppy film that replays like a memory itself, a family treasure that had been lost throughout much of my youth until we discovered it atop a tall wardrobe in Grandmother's bedroom. Just sitting there. Until this day, those films were my only feel for what his eyes had seen.

JUNE 30

Fishing boats glide past the cove all morning, but finding it rough, they soon return. We, too, test the seas, each paddling an unloaded kayak into the open before reappearing with shaking heads. But as the fishing boats begin to stay out longer, we fall into our deliberation, negotiate another trip to the outside, and at 3 P.M. we decide to paddle.

We paddle for twelve miles without stopping, perhaps a mile offshore, in the heaving swells. When the swells strike shore, they burst into white clouds, and for an instant with each wave, we can peer through its translucent green body as it rises, curls, then shatters. We are glad to be far from this lethal breaker zone, but the exposure is equally as frightening. We do not know for sure if the storm has ended. Have we forced this too soon—and too late in the day? With each crest and trough, I reflect that each wave carries the combined energy of storms blowing across the oceans of the world.

It is consoling to see others on the water, a fleet of gillnetters setting their nets. They tell us that this has been the worst summer storm they have seen. And we paddle on with the murrelets, hoping to beat the growing threat of darkness. We are quiet, Maren paddling ahead, slowly but somehow confident. What darkness might bring on this sea is unthinkable.

The Tree Point lighthouse slips behind, and the weather seems as if it has finally broken. Blue and ruffled clouds hover across the great open, and we marvel at the distant islands now set out before us—the southern tip of Prince of Wales far to the west and to the south, Dundas, our first glimpse of British Columbia.

We paddle to a harbor and unload in the protection of an islet, the same refuge that Vancouver found on several occasions. The camp is a blessing, but the shore is ragged and rocky, and we must hike up boulders through brush to find level ground. As the first stars appear, we realize how long it has been since we have seen them, and there is a renewed sense of confidence that Dixon Entrance will be kind for one more day. The blue moon rises. The tide falls to a new low and begins to climb. Then as a late dinner comes to boil, a black bear steps onto the cobbles and strides away.

JULY 1

A glorious day! Sun fires the islets, and I imagine the great sails of Vancouver's ships billowing against the coastal trees. The bay is silvery and smooth, but already the northwesterly has drawn a dark line across the outer waters.

Paddling is like playing a game of chess. Days sum to strategy, playing tide against wind against endurance. The swells have all but dissipated, and the storm's wreckage floats all around. Salmon fingerlings wriggle in high pools of drying seawater. Driftwood is piled onto the rocks like kindling, and huge logs, full-grown trees, have been torn loose and toss in the waves. The coast here is severe, with pockets of beach shoved high against the forest. Clouds loft over Dundas Island, high tops smudged to the north, and we sail around Cape Fox with the current and the wind unimpeded.

By noon the tide is flooding, and we have crossed to a

small island and stand marveling at the even sweep and angle of the beach. It is a bright wind-whipping day, with a westerly blowing in from the horizon. The waves atomize as they hit the outer shoals, reducing to ripples that gradually subside to a flawless mirror inside the pocket where our pencil-thin kayaks are nosed ashore. A little more than a century ago this was a bustling village, and on a good day the beaches may have been strewn with dozens of the great cedar canoes.

Although I can see to the curve of Earth, this small crescent has perfect protection. To the north and east are narrow inlets and canals that can run like rivers in a strong tide, once buoying paddlers far inland. And this island is nestled at their confluence, at the meeting of inside and outside waters. We are near a region locally known as "four corners," which looks as much like a street plat as a crossroads of glacial fiords.

We are at a center.

I first learned of this island in downtown Seattle. There, in a tiny park in Pioneer Square, stands a totem pole whose predecessor was taken from this beach in 1899 by a group of Seattle businessmen touring southeast Alaska. It was an opulent pole, one of the few to honor a woman. When the tribe returned from fishing that day, an elderly woman who had stayed behind told them of the theft. By the time the businessmen were fined, however, the pole had already been erected in Pioneer Square, where it remained a landmark for nearly four decades. Then, damaged by fire and rot, the pole was removed and taken to Saxman to be replicated. And this second pole is the one I have strolled around many times, looking up at its curious procession of cedar faces: Raven holding the crescent moon, Frog, Mink, Killer Whale, Nass Raven.

Except for occasional visitors, the island is largely vacant, tribal land. I recall old photographs of this beach, the arc lined with high poles and long houses. In 1920 an anthropologist counted some 120 poles here. Now there are none. At least two Tlingit ḵwáans have occupied villages on these shores, one replacing the other when Haida invaded and displaced Tlingits living on southern Prince of Wales Island. On the northern shore, the United States established a fort to help govern the newly purchased Alaska territory. And the various stories of trading, thefts, and totems join the familiar legacy of explorers, scientists, missionaries, miners, and tourists who have journeyed to and lived among these and nearby shores. I lift a handful of beach. It shimmers with bits of shell and a thousand shards of rock. Like the geology of the coast, many peoples have come to these shores, collided, and overlaid the land. We linger until finally Maren pulls us away, and we catch the last of the flood into the canyons.

For the first hour we are swift, but the tide changes, a river suddenly against us. Within an hour, the canal is an ebb of white-water current peeling the kayaks from shore until finally we can ferry across to Wales Passage. And once we reach the shore, Maren shouts, "Yee-ha! Into Canada!"

The first strokes in British Columbia are calm and reassuring. In a day we have come from three-meter seas to this placid water, and the open sky of the Pacific has thinned to a blue seam between Earth's high walls. Glaciated hills—less extreme than Misty Fiords but majestic—frame our passage, and there is no thinking about currents or winds or waves in the late afternoon.

Just inside Portland Inlet, we camp at the foot of a roofless stone structure heading a bay and ponder our early-morning crossing. After listening to the weather, I turn off the radio and listen to the water. The tide will be high tonight, and already it gurgles near the grasses.

"Do you think we can make this?" I ask Maren.

She smiles. "I am beginning to think so."

THE CENTRAL
COAST

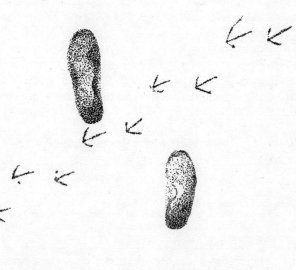

Crossing Portland Inlet

JULY 2

Last night winds and fog filled Wales Passage, coiling around the high rocks and blotting out the stars. After we bedded down, a strange whistle of wings sailed through the air, a low pass, a visit. The dweller of this stone building? A raven? Today my eye is swollen with no-see-um bites, and it tears in the morning breeze. This stone building is strange and alien in the environment, and looks like a sentry's quarters from some faraway castle. A forked tree grows from its eave like antlers, and a cornerstone reads, PROPERTY OF GOVERNMENT. Whether it is a former light station or Russian trading post, it is placed strategically on an isthmus where we, too, can see both the Portland Inlet and open Pacific.

By 7:00 A.M. whitecaps are already rolling in the cove, rolling from the east, and we are rushing, perhaps in vain, to ready the kayaks. This is a crossing we have had circled since first planning the trip: six miles exposed to the ocean, two and a half hours. As long as Aldrin and Armstrong spent on the moon, we will spend in this open blue.

We run the calculations: On an ebb tide, Portland Inlet is especially dangerous because the outgoing current meets the incoming Pacific swell, stacking up the waves along the entrance like ruffled feathers. With more than two hours of paddling time, we should leave somewhere near low tide, perhaps an hour before slack, so the current will be slowing as we leave shore. This will allow us to hit slack tide in midchannel and balance our westward ebb drift during the first hour with the eastward flood drift in the second hour, while minimizing the risk of the large seas at the inlet's entrance. But the wind is blowing from the east, which will steepen waves as the flood current surges west against the wind. It is probably blowing fifteen knots now, but it could build to a katabatic, an outbreak of interior air that would roar down the inlet. But that is not likely. The tide is also large, a -4.1 spring today, exposing the sheer bedrock walls some thirty feet. This large tide exacerbates factors, creating swifter currents, and hence steeper waves, against the swell and the wind. There are also virtually no landing places that we can see from our charts. The shore: vertical.

Just before eight o'clock we nose from the bay and turn into the wind. The waves are steep, but the kayak never smacks the water. We have not crossed anything this large with such uncertain starting conditions. We deliberate. Maren joins my kayak. "I feel OK," she says. I am a little surprised but concur, and we depart on this bright morning, paddling again into oblivion.

To the west, open ocean. To the east, up inlet, the high, pinnacled peaks of the interior, the Nass River, home of Yehl, the Great Raven, and the source of our morning wind. We are listening to the animals, to the trees, to the wind speaking. It seems strange, yet essential, our intimate counsel of the elements. There is little else that truly matters here. During the storm, Maren said she could hear the wind singing in the trees. She speaks of messages from animals. It is not some delirium or some New Age mania. If we reject the calls of birds, the whispers of winds, we will fall to error on the seas. The old stories—stories of Raven, Eagle, Thunderbird—somehow ring true. It is only a very small figurative step to believe that Thunderbird has a nest in the next cove, that the rush of wings last evening was Raven himself. I no longer believe these are mere myths but are the core of a people, guides for thought and action, the reality of living along this coast, among the tides, under your own power. In the canoeing days, if you did not learn to listen to your elders, to the creatures of the sky, water, and forest, you would certainly not live long. This is no leap for us to make. We have, in fact, jumped long ago.

After nearly three months of paddling, we are crossing from traditional Tlingit territory to that of the Tsimshian, and the land seems less angular and severe. While Portland Inlet forms a natural border, it is also a cultural and linguistic border. As we paddle, I try to imagine this inlet as the glacier it once was, as a formidable barrier of ice. Such visions have led to some recent thinking that the Pleistocene glaciers could have played a role in the formation of Native languages, that by isolating the peoples who already lived along the coast, the glaciers of the Wisconsinan advance could have helped create islands of new tongues, linguistic families that gradually expanded and diversified as the ice retreated.

From north to south along the Inside Passage, where once existed several ice-free areas there are five major linguistic families: the Na-Dene family (Tlingit, Eyak, and Athapaskan languages), Haida, Tsimshian (a family of Nass-Gitksan and Coast Tsimshian), Wakashan (Haisla, Heiltsuk-Oowekyala, Kwakwaka'wakw), and Salishan (a large family of twenty-three languages, sixteen of which were spoken on the northwest coast, including Comox, Sechelt, Squamish, Halkomelem, Straits, Nooksak, and Lushootseed, which covered most of Puget Sound country).

As we paddle across this inlet, I recall the Tlingit, who refer to the Nass River as their original homeland, which is far to the east now as I look to the great mountain spires. Again, the story of emerging from the interior does not mesh with a coastal-migration theory. Other Tlingit clans believe the Tsimshian Peninsula was once a homeland. Despite the many contradictions, it is interesting that several homelands are known here—the current Tlingit homeland of this coast and another of some farther time, perhaps of the interior, of farther south, perhaps of creation. And the mention of more than one homeland seems to direct the concept into a question that goes back to the peopling of the planet. Can we have more than one homeland? Perhaps those who ventured to the coast from that Tlingit homeland of the interior had originated elsewhere and carried stories of yet other, more distant, homelands, possibly of the lands of Asia.

Perhaps "homeland" is an idea that most strongly conveys where a people feel they are from, a place they are most connected to. Perhaps in its most true sense, homeland transcends the geography and sheer duration that a people live and have lived in a place and speaks to the kind of relationship a people have with their place—that in a homeland, people understand that they cannot be estranged from their country.

Gradually the open Pacific rolls away, and the winds diminish. An enormous floating tree, roots extending many feet higher than ourselves, is so dense and large that the slosh of waves fails to move it. The opposite shore sharpens into focus, and we follow a rock wall, finally within the comfortable zone near shore. Then we spy a beach, sandy and bright—the only beach visible for miles.

Paradise Passage pinches the current and we accelerate to perhaps ten knots with a tailwind. It is pure ease, the first time today that we can rest our paddles and coast. The current flows opposite to intuitive sense—flooding toward the ocean—so we are fortunate to have guessed correctly. There is so much beyond us every day. At its end, we spill into Work Channel and edge the shore, a wind and strong current suddenly streaming against us. Paradise ends, Work begins.

We pause at a small cove to gather water. The tide floods in fast. We move on but at last must wait for slack tide in a barely hospitable cove of boulders and kelp. The channel races. Where the current supersedes or equals the wind velocity, the water is glassy. Where the current is slower than the wind, the water is rippled. After an hour, the rapids die entirely.

We camp in a thin pass, pitching the tent on a carpet of moss just inside the forest and lining the bear canisters along the remains of an old log structure, perhaps a Hudson's Bay Company lookout or trapping shelter. Off the point, a small tidal stream empties into the sea, raising swells and whitecaps. As the tide drops, sea stars are stranded everywhere, three for each clam.

I sit on a high rock and watch the sunset over Dixon Entrance, this great length of shore we now know stretching into one view. So many have mistakenly called this our Alaska trip, but they are Americans and somehow do not see that British Columbia will be two-thirds of the journey. Abruptly, the tide turns in our narrow pass, a sudden wave of foam that pivots the bull kelp a half turn in the time it takes me to breathe twice.

Happy, I study pink clouds through the mosquito netting. Maren rustles in her sleeping bag. Solitary whistles of birds. Scuttling insects. A shudder of wind. Asleep.

Portland Inlet to Prince Rupert

JULY 3

Clouds circulate in the western sky as if caught in an eddy. The tide drops fast, nearly eighteen feet below the highest tides, and we carry gear over four distinct layers of intertidal life to the bottoms, stepping finally among the slick whips of bull kelp that hang limply on shore. Loading the kayaks, shoving bags into the hatches, and wading on unsure footings, we stand completely within the tide's range. My paddle, even when raised, does not span the distance between this low water and the highest mark.

A Zodiac approaches with two men in orange survival suits. Customs officials. They stop and cordially ask where we are going as we tromp in the seaweed. But seeing us skidding among the rocks and racing current, they must feel that we are little threat to national security, and they throttle on.

Around a point, headwinds grab and lift the water, which floods north now into Portland Inlet. Beaches are plentiful again, nearly continuous, and we land and change to our thin-bladed paddles for the push into Lax Kw' Alaams.

You can tell a community nears by what you find in the eddylines: Welch's grape juice cans, milk cartons, six pack rings, fishing lures, styrofoam cups, cans of WD-40, potato chip bags, shampoo bottles, logs, splinters, branches. Then you look up at the whirling weather, then down again at the face of Colonel Sanders bobbing in the waves.

The most prominent building in Lax Kw' Alaams is the church, a massive white red-roofed structure at town center, which gives the place the air of Winthrop's "city upon a hill." Although our chart still labels the community as Port Simpson, an update of the Hudson's Bay Company's "Fort Simpson" that was once here, the town is now known by its original Tsimshian name, Lax Kw' Alaams, and is the largest First Nations settlement on the British Columbia coast.

In the next two days we will paddle through Lax Kw' Alaams and Metlakatla, two towns that are intricately tied, profoundly separated. In 1857 William Duncan, an Anglican missionary, arrived in Port Simpson to work among the Tsimshian, and learning their language, he soon converted many. In 1862, he led a group to found a colony at the old village site of Metlakatla, some fifteen miles south. The community flourished, selling lumber and textiles, and emphasizing communal efforts, already a hallmark of Tsimshian culture. But when Duncan had a falling out with superiors, he led the community of about 830 to Annette Island near Ketchikan in 1887 and founded New Metlakatla. And what was once a single community was scattered among three.

We tie our kayaks to the dock. Fishermen are preparing for a big opening that will commence tonight at six o'clock. As we waddle ashore, a man in a van asks us if we need a ride. We hop in. He chauffeurs us to the village store and café, where we order two bacon burgers from a tiny, thin man with large round ears. The place is compact like a local grocery but stocked like a warehouse, cartons cut open and contents displayed. Hockey players skate across boxes of Wheaties. We are in Canada.

The grease tastes good. A group of local men gather for lunch; one is the fire chief. "We call my cousin Mousey," he quips, pointing to the man who scribbled our order. I smile, almost laugh. It is a perfect nickname. After lunch, when I say, "A wonderful burger!" Mousey looks stunned.

"You're wanted for murder?!"

Everyone is in tears.

The fire chief has opened the firehouse so that we can place a few phone calls. (There is only one other pay phone in town, at the fish plant.) Maren's parents tell us that my folks have been in an auto wreck, a bad one, one that sheared off the front end of their van, but that they are OK. We call, and they are recovering, having suffered relatively minor ankle and wrist injuries. "An old Buick's brakes went out, and it smacked us going sixty," Dad says. "If we would have been a few feet farther along . . ." It is a puzzling moment. We ask if we should fly to Illinois, but they wave the idea off, saying they need to rest. For months they have been worried about us, about our security. But how much more at risk are we among the tides and bears than on a busy street? This is a precious time to be afloat.

A stout and friendly man with bristly gray hair stops us in a dirt road near the old church and talks fondly of the building's renovation. He says that he found some of the rafters signed by old residents. "If they pledged a certain amount to help the church," he says, "then they could sign their names." This is not the original Duncan church, which has long since burned, but an old structure nonetheless, now roofed with red aluminum. The man says the city band still plays, mostly at funerals, and there is an old photo of the ensemble in the church. A gazebo overlooking the water was built exclusively for the band.

Near the church stands a paintless building with a broken stained-glass window and the shell of a bass drum lying in the grass. This was the Native church, run by the older generation, but as they have fallen into ill health, the man says, there is no one to keep it up.

We walk through the school and talk to two teachers, who pull up a Lax Kw' Alaams Web site chalked with historic photographs. They tell us of the computer programs designed to teach the Tsimshian language and that they live near the site of the Hudson's Bay Company fort that was once the center of town. They show us paintings that depict the town's former days, the fort's white walls, the longhouses spread across the beach. On every door is a Tsimshian word with an English translation, and above the main hallway is a sign:

We have the right to understand our past, succeed in our present and have hope for our future.
Hoyax dm waalm dm wilay goh La Waal ta gyigyet, dm wil da'axKqm dm aam qoh da Kum dzata dii LaKLeeKsm.

Maren says you can get to know a town by going to its school.

By afternoon the town looks forward to fishing. Fishing in the night. As we leave, people are abandoning other work and young men aboard the *Ocean Investor* shout to us. "Going to Seattle?"

"Yep," I volley.

"Seriously? I live in Victoria. What do ya do, just go up on shore and pitch a tent for the night?"

"Basically," Maren says.

"Sounds like a real trip. Can you get going pretty good in those? Can you roll 'em?"

Then spins the galaxy of questions we have heard so many times before.

Finally, someone aboard shouts, "We've got thirty tons of ice to shovel here."

"But no fish?" I shout back.

"We'll get fish tomorrow."

And we shove away for an evening paddle among the fishing boats and gentle lands of the Tsimshian Peninsula. A fish buyer is anchored behind islands waiting for the catch—forty-eight hours of sockeye. At the end of this hazy silver day, we find camp as the tide slips from beneath our kayaks like a carpet. In fifteen minutes it has retreated more than a hundred yards from our sterns. The tide is great, but the shore is gradual and smooth—the reverse of this morning's abrupt rock and kelp—and it is surprising how meaningful this is, how rich a variety it gives to the day.

Near camp I find a tray of rancid herring and toss it into the tide, fearing bears. Rapturous clouds and a rainy evening. We must be up early, 4:30, to load at high tide, otherwise we will be staying again at this drying bay. White lights sweep past, fishermen at work all night.

JULY 4

At 4:30 it is dark and pouring rain. Days are shortening, and we are a half day from the hot showers of Prince Rupert. As the tide leaks away, we must paddle a half mile from shore into the brunt of the wind, skirting each shoal before it dries. We round the points for punishing blasts of rain, and we have not been colder. When we approach Venn Passage, the tide is down, and we contemplate the silty dunes in a downpour, standing shin deep in eelgrass, eating Snickers. We break into shivers, and rather than waiting for the rising tide to navigate through the maze, we paddle the extra distance around the bars just to keep warm.

At Metlakatla we secure the kayaks to the ferry dock and wander into town, looking to reserve a room in Prince Rupert where another food shipment should be waiting. At the top of the dock is an arched sign: WELCOME TO METLAKATHLA. The town is spread across a hillside among intermittent pockets of flowers and fragrance. We stumble into the health clinic, dripping and hermetically sealed in Gore-Tex. Susie, the clinician, offers us hot coffee, a place to warm up, and a phone. "The elders are saying that it could be a cold winter. Last summer it was all sun. Now look at it." She tells us to look for the old canoe pullouts, rows of rocks pushed aside to smooth and protect a landing area. "Metlakathla. That's how it was originally spelled with an 'h.' Metlakathla. This is a beautiful place when the sun shines. Wild roses all over."

As Maren phones motels, I ask about the legacy of Reverend Duncan.

"You see, people left Lax Kw' Alaams to come here. Then when Duncan moved his work to Alaska, the community was again divided. Most left. Some stayed. We've got relatives at all three. Although we have conflict from community to community, in the worst of times—at a death or a disaster—we're very close. The differences go way back to those times."

A man enters with a minor cut to be attended, and she peels off a bloody handkerchief and guides him to an examination room. When they emerge, he is laughing, his finger now swollen with gauze. She takes us to a window and points between two islands. "That's where The Man Who Fell from Heaven is. Tide is rising, so you can get through. We can go through there with our speedboats, but you have to know where the rocks are and where they aren't. You won't have a problem." When I thank her for her time, she smiles. "Well, I've already called all the elders, and they are OK, so I just had to wait and see if anyone else needed me, such as you two."

High-powered skiffs roar past as we search for The Man Who Fell from Heaven. We don't know what he looks like, just a rough idea of where he is. After waiting for the tide to trickle across a rise of sand, meeting from both sides in sudsy shallows, we paddle across. A shabby man in overalls and a wide-open fly sees us looking and shouts, "On shore there! A flat rock! He fell from heaven, remember!"

Soon we find the large stone and kneel beside it as if it were a casualty. The petroglyph is striking: an imprint of a four-foot human etched into black rock and filled with rainwater reflecting sky. We have heard several stories about this person. One tells he was banished from his village to live on his own, and there he took a journey to heaven, where he tripped and fell back to Earth. When he returned to the village and told of his magical flight, villagers did not believe him until he showed them this impression. Then he was made a shaman. In Metlakatla we heard that, simply put, this is the rock of The Man Who Fell from Heaven. And if you lay in it, you will have a longer life, that the imprint of The Man Who Fell from Heaven will fit anyone.

Prince Rupert is veiled in mist. From across the channel, I radio the Prince Rupert Rowing and Yacht Club to reserve a berth for the kayaks. As we paddle, Prince Rupert emerges from the cloud, a steep, gridded city. Fishing boats gun past until we glide into port. "Can't trust 'em," says a woman from a sailboat. "You'll be OK, though. Most of the fishermen are out of town on the water for a few days. It's when they're here that you'll have problems. But take your compasses off."

Unloading, two kayakers paddle up who have abandoned their hopes of traveling the Inside Passage, having recently gotten off the ferry from Petersburg, where they bailed out, fatigued and half defeated. They latch onto us and seek our advice. While we fill up two wheelbarrows with gear, they pull a few Hefty bags from their kayaks. "Does your stuff stay dry?" they ask.

How does one answer this?

"We wanted to pack up and get away from it all," he goes on. "To be independent."

It is a wish I share, but we have learned that it is impossible. I look at our equipment. It is made in factories, the food, purchased in groceries and shipped to us by friends.

"You can never be truly on your own," I say.

These two need more help than anyone we have met. In a single afternoon they succumbed to hypothermia, paralytic shellfish poisoning, dehydration, and giardiasis.

"We spent a week and a half getting ready for this trip," one says. (By contrast, Maren and I prepared for months.) When their radio batteries went out—there are no recharging spots along the coast as they discovered—they could not get the weather reports and were caught on an exposed point in last week's powerful storm. They were eventually taken in and fed by a generous logging camp.

They thought the Inside Passage would be more like a river: You get in and paddle downstream. "I guess it's down-hill if you look at the globe," I say glibly. Still, they plan to paddle the remote upper British Columbia coast to Bella Bella, then ferry Queen Charlotte Sound to Port Hardy on Vancouver Island and paddle from there to Seattle. We see them later in town and all mention that we should get together, but we never do.

The taxi is crammed like a Shriners car with our bags of gear, and suddenly we have arrived in town—the familiar but half-forgotten hiss of tires on wet pavement, the sway of an automobile with bad shocks, the sudden lunges of stops and starts, the annoying wait at traffic lights. I can smell myself, the sweet and sour of human oils. When we reach the motel, the clerk says there are no waterfront rooms left. Smiling, Maren says that we would gladly accept a view of land.

Once in the room, we immediately flip a quarter for the hot shower. I win and strip down. I lessen the cold until the flow is nearly scalding, a hot jet sluicing away the strata of dirt from my body. I am a muddy hillside above a drain. Later, while Maren showers, I sit half wrapped in a towel, dazed, watching the Boston Pops Orchestra play "Stars and Stripes Forever" on TV, shedding a few silly tears, wiggling my toes, marveling at the ease of indoor living, the miraculous rebirth that occurs when I am warm and clean, my fingertips, drying, stretching, becoming taut.

JULY 5

We sleep in, a cozy morning in cotton sheets. Then more hot showers. Later we leave our room and explore the city. We learn from a statue in downtown that Charles Hayes, the founder of Prince Rupert, died on the *Titanic*. In Ketchikan we bought *The Shipping News* but have now shipped it home. By evening we possess the first genuine feeling that we can complete this journey.

JULY 7

We spend three days in Prince Rupert, wandering around town, eating eggs Benedict and fantastic Chinese food, gathering groceries and supplies, organizing charts, retrieving mail, preparing for the next most remote, mostly townless section between here and northern Vancouver Island. On our route, there is only the Heiltsuk town of Bella Bella some two weeks' distant.

Most notably, we do not meet many people here and lament the fact. It is a city, after all, and busy and self-absorbed with its own matters. Perhaps we are unperceptive from fatigue, from the blur of waves, but it seems more that our notion of time is completely unsynchronized with city life, out of phase. Mornings, I think about the tides, the weather. These are not concerns of the city, and so we are less able to see this place clearly. Days blend together. But like all places it does have moments and meanings, most notably when I realize what two and a half months on the water have meant.

Today, our final day in town, we walk several hours along the highway to Butze Rapids, a tidal rapids behind the city on the south of Kaien Island. We meander through new suburban split-levels and town homes to an industrial park where pulp smoke hangs over the Butze. The hard walk on asphalt and cement deadens our feet.

Rounding a curve of a cedar-chip trail, the highway sounds fall to the rumble of rapids. A smooth current folds over on itself in standing waves. Then roaring white. Then melting foam. We follow and refollow the water as it rushes through the narrows, and imagine going through ourselves. "Follow the V," Maren says. More than anything during our stay, this water has taken hold of us. And as we return to the motel, we see it marks a fundamental change: The currents and waves, once new, are now the familiar. In this first city on our voyage, we are most entranced with its water.

Prince Rupert to Porcher Island

As we slide the kayaks from the yacht club slip, two kayakers
paddle up. "That's Jack!" Maren shouts in disbelief. "I used
to work with him at King County."

"Hey!" he calls to us, beaming. "We'd given up looking
for you." He and his friend, Jim, are paddling north from
Olympia to Juneau, and we talk about the coast, about camping. "The southern end of Pitt is the pits," Jack chuckles.
When he asks if I have a GPS, if I would like to download
campsites, I shake my head.

We chat for a while, laughing, snapping each other's photo
for proof of the encounter, amazed that four kayaks could
possibly meet along this long and varied coast. The passage,
though, will bring people together.

The fog and drizzle have descended again, frosting my
growing beard with moisture. We maneuver from the city,
gliding beneath docks, among the puttering sterns of moored
boats, beneath the towering piles of a pier, and beneath countless fish pumps, their large silver tubing curled like sousa-
phones, waiting to disgorge the returning fleets. After passing
the Alaska ferry nearing departure, we follow the curve of

Kaien Island, encountering a massive concrete apron, a dock lined with rubber bumpers as large as tractor tires. Then the city gives way to open shores.

In and around Prince Rupert there are more known archaeological sites than anywhere in North America, many discovered as the city expands along the waterfront, building across the old beaches. Behind the structures of town, vapor rising from the forest mingles with the steam from the pulp mill in white columns that gradually fuse with the clouds.

As we paddle with the ebb between Digby and Kaien Islands, fishing boats power to an opening, leaving a bluish layer of diesel smoke along the water. They trail three parallel rows of steep waves that intersect with the wake of other fishing boats in a silvery diffraction pattern that we ride. A day of work.

As the channel broadens to Chatham Sound, we greet the tip of Prince Rupert: the great terminals of Ridley Island, monstrous structures reaching across the water like the arms of a mantis. Maren paddles far ahead, but I hold back, uneasy around them, as if at any moment they could rattle to life and walk the water. They mark the terminus of the railroad, the end of the line, where the interior of western Canada unloads itself into the Pacific in cones of grain, wood pulp, and coal. These structures embody the reason modern Prince Rupert exists at all: transport, in the grand tradition of moving goods between land and sea.

We round the point, and the coal loader inches from sight. The inlet to Porpoise Harbor, the river of Butze Rapids, is half ebbing, half flooding: slack. A school bus roars past. A floatplane overhead. Then Prince Rupert is gone.

Crossing the short distance between Lelu Island and Smith Island, clouds lower, and as we negotiate the steep shores of Smith, the fishing fleet swarms around the mouth of the Skeena River. There are more fishermen than we have yet seen at once, perhaps twenty-five gillnetters working in a square mile area, hauling in a few fish with each net, jockeying for position. Their boats are lobsterlike, spired with booms and antennae. We avoid some nets but must cross others, waving to the skippers, who, instead of screaming at us, simply pay no attention. Beneath the lines of floats, nets vanish into the water, and it is a wonder any salmon evade the invisible snares. Brushing the nets, weaving among the throbbing motors, the intermittent shouts, the drumming fingers of silent captains, we sense the salmon's alarm. A cove we had circled on southern Smith Island proves unfit for camping, logged and choked with anchored fishing boats. So we must paddle on.

And so Prince Rupert is not over. These fleets and the clear-cuts are its extensions, its transitory suburbs. The cities always overextend their bounds and are never as compact and self-contained as portrayed by maps. Just as there are no distinct borders around ecosystems, there are no such boundaries to our communities. Electricity for sodium-vapor streetlights circuits from turbines churning in a river or from burning coal, the strata of earlier life. In translating forests to clearcuts to wood pulp to paper, gillnets to grocery stores, a city's influence far exceeds its physical self. As we stream into Marcus Passage, with nearly five miles to Porcher Island, a fisherman hauls in a bloody salmon. It is the only fish in his whole net. He shakes it loose and continues working. By his listless manners, we can see that he is consumed with a disabling anger.

At midchannel the Skeena currents swirl and mix with the incoming tide, producing strips of current and swell around the numerous islands. Far ahead rises the high slope of Porcher. Like the Stikine, the Skeena belches out sediment that clogs the waters with shallows and large banks that bare at low tide. About halfway across a tide rip forms, slick folding waves, sometimes against us, sometimes at the beam. They unnerve us, never completely falling away until we pass Hanmer Island and out of the Skeena currents.

A black speck on the southern horizon materializes into a cruise ship, the *Spirit of '98*, a cheerful craft reminiscent of the old single-screw steamers that once plied these waters. It chugs from Grenville Channel, the trafficked and narrow passage between the mainland and the eastern shore of Pitt Island. Grenville is a highway of ferries, barges, and cruise ships and has virtually no landing sites along its rugged shores. So we will instead paddle down the western side of Pitt, following Principe Channel—much less trafficked, much more exposed.

On a finger of white sand, some twenty-five miles from Prince Rupert, we camp near a network of fallen trees that form a three-sided shelter with a sandy floor. As we cook macaroni and rehydrate spaghetti sauce, a small fishing boat races from a nearby anchorage, flushed like a startled heron. All evening cruise ships traverse the gap between the islands, each slipping from view in the time it takes to devour a cup of noodles.

The color of the animals—the orcas, the loons, the midnight-black ravens—are the colors of weather. A *khaaa* comes through the woods, and a northwestern crow flies from the forest. The familiar raven's croaking has been absent since Portland Inlet, and its absence is suddenly noticed. Surely they will return to our lives.

Porcher Island to Campania Island

We paddle through the slender, kelp-ridden passages surrounding Porcher Island, past the depths of Grenville toward the open sky of the outer coast. The northern British Columbia coast is one of narrow channels and swift currents, islands and sounds exposed to the open sea. Already it is much more intimate than southeast Alaska's Alexander Archipelago and its massive straits. Soon we will begin the joy of island hopping.

All afternoon we sneak along the coastline, following eddies against the oncoming flood, paddling farther from the mainland where the vapors condense and clouds bunch against the mountains. Ahead, the ceiling lifts to a brightness that we follow like a dawn.

Clear-cuts soar into the clouds, abrupt and razed to the dirt. There is no monkey business about it. The forest is filleted, innermost trees exposed from crown to trunk along the incisions. Peering up at this line, we see the cross layers of a living skin. The unwanted forest detritus—tangles of roots and branches—clots the shore where storms and tide eventually disperse it to the beaches as driftwood. Above, a jet's contrail bisects the sky. My bow divides my world. The cut tears the forest. We are mixed and confused and saddened, and float listlessly beneath the cut. After a brief squall, the sky lightens again, and the high mackerel clouds above reveal the true weather. Something blowing in, something blowing out.

At the mouth of Ogden Channel, the islands have shattered, broken by wind and weather into islets and chiseled coves. Again we are near the outside. To evade the building westerly winds, we turn into Petrel Channel. I mourn and dawdle at these intersections—practically a lunatic, looking the other way at the experience that will not be ours—before proceeding. River travel is much easier in this way; it is linear.

Around Caroline Point, a gillnetter nearly sweeps us into his net, throttling hard, wrapping the floats around us. It is frightful, then annoying, for he had plenty of time to react, to alter his course. But he did not. He blew no horn, simply kept coming, pressing to within fifteen yards of our sterns. Some of his crew bounce in a skiff, anchoring the net to a spike driven into a shoreline rock. Speed bumps.

We find camp in high grass at the head of a deep cove. Beaches are scarce now except this smooth pocket, and with a short carry it goes down as a good site. As the tide surrounds our dinner rock, a beautiful two-masted schooner anchors in the cove just off the terminus of a logging road. There is always such splendor amid such squalor. Every view has it. Looking up, the sky narrows, massing with thunderheads.

We are in shape but sore, more swollen-jointed than before, and this, too, will slow us from past days. In Prince Rupert, I awoke with a stiff neck and can hardly lay on my right side without pain shooting down my arm, a taut tendon from spine to elbow. My neck will not pivot to the left, a bruise from the kayak seat has darkened in the center of my back, each night my hands are palsied by strange twitches and cramps, and my right shoulder just does not work right. Maren's neck and shoulders have strengthened, but her middle finger has a strained tendon and snaps in and out of usefulness like a faulty transmission. In the mornings she shows me its crooked form. For several hours each day, she cannot straighten it. All joints grind in their sockets, pestles against stone. Engine troubles.

JULY 10

Shoreline bees are loudest this morning, droning like unsynchronized propellers. Centipedes ascend the tent.

Paddling from camp, we meet Kent and Joni, the couple who owns the sailboat, the *Grizzly Bear*. They contract with the Canadian Department of Fisheries, monitoring salmon in all the streams in this area, talking to the commercial fishermen, assessing how many fish are in the runs, how many are being caught, what size, and what kind. They built the *Grizzly Bear* themselves in Sidney, British Columbia, and live aboard. A bed of flowers laps over the window boxes. They spend two weeks out. One day in town, then out again. "We don't like towns," Joni says. "We get out as fast as we can."

They are friendly and helpful, talking over charts. "We have to check a fishing opening today; then we'll probably be back here again," Kent says, unfolding the coastal maps and leaning over the railing. "When the weather is like this, it'll blow thirty-five all afternoon. It will be clear but roaring."

As we depart, I look back to our tent site, a morning ritual. A black bear has ambled across the grass and paws through rocks.

The wind will keep us inside the islands today. Soon after reentering Petrel Channel, a southeasterly stirs it to a roar of whitecaps, and we buck on the swift and rolling water through the sunless afternoon. Petrel snakes eastward, then westward among the slopes. It is a channel most ships avoid. But from the far shore, a sailboat swings around and motors toward us. The *Grizzly Bear*. Maren laughs and says that to them we must appear more like an animal sighting, always afloat in the waves.

"Ho!" shouts Kent. I grab the inflatable skiff in tow, and we drift with the current. "Here," says Joni, handing over two jars of cooked salmon and a bag of salmon steaks. "Got these fresh from a fisherman this morning." And then they hand over another prize.

"Have you found any of these?" asks Kent, tossing me a green glass orb the size of an orange. It is a Japanese net float they found on the outside of Banks Island. The floats often break loose, drifting across the Pacific before being lifted by the winter storm waves into the forests. It is nicked by rocks but unbroken, airtight, a small bulb that has been awash for perhaps a decade, still carrying the breath of its creator.

Over the past year, they have also found two dead whales, two humpbacks, on outer coast of Banks. "One died of natural causes, one had swallowed a mass of black plastic. When we pulled on it, it just kept coming out, until we couldn't stand the reek anymore," Joni says. "It must have bypassed its baleen and gone straight down. Within a week the whale carcass was gone. Maggots. The sand was pulsing with them." Earlier today they found the corpse of a sea lion awash in the waves.

We talk about how this northern coast was more popu-lated in the first half of this century, how the more recent immigrants to the Canadian coast have returned to the cities. When we ask how long they have been living aboard, they smile. "Thirteen years today." They know all the inlets and creeks, where the salmon go. The old places. Then we say good-bye and push from the hull.

Camp is on a flat between a stream delta and an old cedar grove. No bears, although we expect them here, crowding around the stream as the salmon return. Kent said the salmon will start to run in three weeks, and for dinner we boil the salmon steaks, slurping up the fatty black skin. I rinse my hands in the tide to remove salmon oils from my fingernails. But after several washings I still smell of fish—a reminder why we have not fished while living in bear country.

The evening sky is pleasant and orange. My spirits have risen now that the rain has left for a few days, and I want to linger. The thought visits again: At fifteen miles a day we are traveling too fast, with too much direction. Only to be dropped here, to toy around. To go nowhere. I am sad in the mornings. There seems to be a strange sense of attachment to each campsite, however short the stay. Within a few hours, footholds are learned, the stable and the wobbly beach logs discerned, the sway of the ground beneath the sleeping bag becomes familiar, even comfortable. We sit and stare for hours at distant shorelines, learn their contours as seen from each vantage point. See the progression of grasses from the rocks into the forest floor. A drift log soon converts to a kitchen with pots and pans spread out along some of its length. Another serves as a superb drying rack. Another as a buttress and rest room. The unfamiliarity diminishes, the known increases, and suddenly we are snug and waiting for a storm to pin us there. They are ephemeral homes in the long string of moving days. We mold our lives among the curves of land like putty.

Twilight at eleven o'clock. The tide rises and quenches our small fire. The paddling, the hammering of tent stakes, the firing of a stove, the lugging of equipment are the meanings of our days. We are burning life lean and hot. If I give Maren one chore, I must cover one of hers. Together, we have forged a tight reciprocity, not as an ideal but as necessity.

On this journey we are together more than perhaps we have ever been, living almost seamlessly, and we have regained a deep comfort together, one that can exist in moments like this when we are embracing and looking out to sea and wordless. When underway, we may ride waves separately. Separately but similarly. We never exactly follow one another's path, yet we require each other to help pace ourselves. For a long time we stay with the floating embers, holding each other, staring out into the molten colors of evening, recharging for a day of new water.

JULY 12

Clouds speed over Pitt Island while Banks Island basks in sun. A strand of vapor dissipates, revealing a bowl of clear air and a forested peak. Cedars whistle with the northwest wind, and we use our wide paddles to take advantage of it, catching gusts in their cupped faces like sails.

After the distant village of Kitkatla days ago, there have been no towns, fishermen, or boat traffic in sight. Gusts stain the water, and red tide, driven into coves, coats our blades. The sun is a tarnished disk, and I can look directly at it without flinching.

We refill water pillows from a stream crashing over a pile of boulders. Like most streams on these islands, it drains a lake a short distance away. Salmon spawning grounds. On the chart they are fingers of water caught between hills. Many lakes form chains, linked by these small streams. At spawning time, the salmon pool at the river mouth, waiting for high tide to enter the familiar freshwater rush.

As we round Oar Point, following seas have quickened our pace, blowing us along shore so that again and again we must sweep and rudder, sweep and rudder. We see the high granite lobes of Campania Island towering to the south above the haze, and the grand scene magnifies as we round each subtle point of land. Soon the horizon of Hecate Strait opens through Otter Passage. On a clear day, Haida Gwaii, or the Queen Charlotte Islands, some seventy miles to the west, should be visible. Today they are lost in offshore fog. Then above us, a deer freezes on an outer rock, taut and alarmed by our sudden appearance, before bounding back into the forest darkness.

The southern side of Pitt is practically an outer coast. The water opens into Nepean Sound; the wind is stronger, the waves taller, big rollers toss the kayaks, and the shore is more ragged. The northern island is enviably sheltered from this northwesterly. We are nearing another crossroads, cornered by Banks, Pitt, the Estevan Group, and Campania.

For lunch Maren discovers a sheltered islet, its tiny harbor bottomed by sand and walled like a bastion. We eat on a warm rock, toasting in the sun as the tide seeps from the basin. The chocolate is melted, pancaked against the bags. Maren back bends over a rock, then lies on the incline, shielding her eyes from the midday glare. Her hair is thick and wild, a nimbus of gold tugged by the wind. To the west, Banks Island tapers to the sea, the Breaker Islands dribbling across Otter Passage like ellipses, a lapse in thought, before the Estevan commence their gentle rise.

By one o'clock we are ready to abort, but there are no landing places, and we must continue uneasy in the growing waves, pausing in the small respites behind rocks, scoping the revealed shore, then progressing. Suddenly, a brightness flashes in my periphery, and I turn to see two walls of rock close around a pocket of white sand. "Beach!" I shout, back-paddling to a stop. We enter the narrow channel single file, and inside, the wind and waves suddenly belong to another day. The beach is breathless and hot, an even grade of pulverized granite, grains swept between three loaves of rock like leaves gathered in the hollow of a tree.

As I set up the tent—now with a broken and bandaged pole—the alders rustle. I jump to my feet. Nothing. Then whatever it is moves again, fast, sprinting nimbly through the undergrowth. I rush to the open beach to see where it ran. Among the drift logs, a silver wolf stands, no more than thirty yards away. For the smallest moment we stare, silent. Then it lifts its head and howls, a deep growling howl amplified by the surrounding rocks. And howling and huffing, it disappears into the forest. Now we see that we have camped near its den, an opening in the base of a giant cedar strewn with fur balls, rolls of scat, and flakes of glossy hooves.

"We should move camp," Maren says, locking her arm in mine as we listen to the wolf. "We are in its home. It doesn't want tourists. It's telling us to go back where we came from, to leave this place alone."

"Yes, but where can we go?" I say. "It's late. It has already seen us." And there is nowhere else to go. The water is too rough. We must stay, invaders.

At 9 P.M., whitecaps still roll across Nepean Sound. To-morrow we face a short but exposed crossing of Otter Channel to Campania. Its swift currents must be crossed at slack tide. Slack comes about noon when the wind may be roaring.

Can we find camp at the end of Pitt? Or must we stay another
day among the wolves? For now the howling has quieted.

JULY 13

"Wolf pups!" Maren whispers into the tent, her voice soft
and astonished as I open my eyes. "Byron, wolf pups, on the
sand. Four. Dancing on the beach. Just now. Playing. Three
ran, but one stayed. We had a staring contest. It kept jumping,
afraid and puzzled, wanting to run. Then it would freeze, and
we'd stare again. Then it ran off to join the others. They were
frisky and full of fluff, silver and brown, with big ears and
paws, strong shoulders and narrow hips."

She is beaming.

On the beach is a chaos of paw prints. Small spots of
digging. The same maze of tracks we saw on the beach when
we arrived. "They must dance every morning," Maren says.
She is light-footed and efficient with common tasks, and the
rest of her morning fills with song. I regret not seeing them
but am joyful for her. All morning as we load, I linger quietly
along the edges of the beach away from camp, but they do
not return.

Another clear, blustery day with whitecaps stacking against
the flood. High cirrus quilt the sky, and the outer coast is a
blank of sea fog.

The ride from "wolf beach" to the end of Pitt Island is
fast and wild, following seas again, tugging and broaching the
kayaks parallel with the waves. As best we can, we paddle in
the lee of island and rocks. In midchannel, wind picks up the
sea and hurls it southeastward. Eagles alight from rocks and
hover above the water. We startle Barrow's Golden Eyes, and
they scuttle from leeward rocks into the open wind. "We are
disturbing this island," Maren says as we raft together. "We
shouldn't even be here. Why can't we just go where other

people go and leave these places alone? And I'm saying this from a kayak! We hardly stir the water."

The end of Pitt is treacherous, and we flounder through the reflection waves, pulling hard, each stroke as much a brace as forward power. Then the roar falls away as we round a point, and Campania Island's high land unfolds across the channel.

A half hour before slack tide, we halt off Pitt's southern shore at a perfect beach in a perfect cove. Among the grasses and cow parsnip, wild roses grow head high above the bleached midden and throughout the level expanses beneath the trees. It is an old site, perhaps a summer fish camp. They are luxurious in any weather.

Radio: *Synopsis: A ridge of high pressure extending southwestward from the Alaska panhandle will continue to build today and tonight. . . . Winds will increase from moderate to strong to gale force northwest this afternoon. . . .*

As slack approaches, we decide to cross to the eastern shore of Campania before the onset of high winds, agreeing that on the island's leeward side, we should make progress in calm waters. We slip into the blue wind. And we regret it.

The waves, initially small, grow as we leave the protection of Pitt. The crossing is heinous, and by the time we reach Campania, Maren is in screaming tears. "I just keep seeing Frederick Sound! Damn it! Why do we keep getting ourselves into this?!" I am silent but also shaken, and she knows this. We want out. Again we have reached our brink. But after a final push through a wall of high breakers, we are around the point and into glass. In a matter of yards the sea calms, and the day is again full of smiles and shaggy hills.

We lunch while standing on slabs of granite in shin-deep water. After filling the water bags at a stream, I probe for net floats. But I find these items instead: a rubber black-and-orange life raft shredded among the drift logs, its rusted cannister of compressed air attached; one hundred feet of orange cord; twenty-five feet of thick white-braided rope; an assortment of yellow and orange foam net floats; ovoid wooden net floats; a classic white life ring (no vessel name);

a Hamms beer can; various ropes hanging from trees like vines; a flashbulb floating in a stagnant pool of rainwater beneath a tree. The flashbulb is the old kind, with filaments like Einstein's hair inside its globe. Probably not used since the 1970s.

We unfold the maps to see what *Sailing Directions* says of Squally Channel. "High land here produces violent squalls, where nearby areas remain calm and windless." I look at Maren, who is enjoying a chocolate bar and keep this to myself. "Let's head for camp," I say.

Along Campania's rocky shore, the wind shifts, suddenly blasting from behind, suddenly a headwind. Gusts drop and spin from the high peaks, hammering the water. From here the whole island is brown, stripped of trees, with only a thin rank of green along shore. Above that, vegetation is stunted: occasional shore pines and muskeg.

Behind an islet, we make camp and unwind.

But night is uneasy. Trees creak and sway. Long insects traverse the tent's interior. For the first time the sky is cloudless into the night, and we have left off the rain fly. In moments of calm, we hear the gurgles of a nearby stream of mountain water. Smooth rocks shine in the woods. Another day has culminated in fear and joy. For the first time in a long time, we have the feeling of being remote, even alone. We are not really in the tide books anymore. The rest of the world has fallen away.

JULY 14

Radio: *Synopsis: A strong ridge of high pressure remains west of the Charlottes. Winds will increase today. Strong to gale-force northwesterlies will prevail over most waters. . . . Hecate Strait: Gale warning continued. Winds northwest from twenty-five to gales thirty-five knots easing to twenty to twenty-five overnight. Patchy fog, otherwise clear. Seas near two meters. . . .*

We spend a terrestrial day under bright skies.

In early afternoon I hike alone up the hill behind camp, leaving Maren to write, read, and relax—her three Rs. I want to climb to the top of Campania, to see both sides of an island, the inside and outside waters in a single vision. In a hundred yards I break from the forest into a sunny muskeg of red, orange, and pink mosses, sword ferns, sage, and shore pine that blankets the slopes up to the bald granite. Streams percolate through the deep sphagnum carpet. The soil is alkaline and saturated, spongy with millennia of decay. My boots are wet, but the ancient bog crunches as I hop across it.

I tie a pink bag to a tree along the forest edge to mark camp and begin to climb. In no more than a quarter mile the bag has nearly vanished. Using the islet near camp for reference, I take a compass bearing. Sixty degrees magnetic . . . fifty-eight. The ring of forest rarely exceeds one hundred yards of depth, a dark wall of pine. As I reach the first granite lobes, the island reveals itself: our turquoise beach—more an image from the Yucatán than from British Columbia—and beyond it, azure Caamaño Sound.

Keeping the bearing on camp, I follow dry streambeds to higher granite outcroppings, pausing on their blustery tops to look through the wind and breathe. Horseflies buzz in the slurry of my odor, and my head net haloes my head. I climb a new stream. It pauses in salty pools and disappears into the earth as the sinks of the Great Basin. Some five hundred feet above the sea I pause again, winded.

I am drenched with sweat. The northwest gale howls, pouring through a saddle in the rock not far above. The mud is cracked, the environment parched and desertlike, sparse and stubby with trees and grasses, lichen and moss, blueberry and huckleberry. Other than the intermittent shore pine, there is no forest to fight through, and the ascent is quick.

The Coast Range is spread across the eastern sky, snowy peaks trailing to the north and east. Shoals uncover as the tide drops. I cannot even comprehend how deep the ice must have been. At more than fifteen hundred feet above the sea, the polished granite still goes higher. I have not yet reached the cap of the Pleistocene ice.

Climbing a crevasse of granite, inching along its smooth and fissured surface, fingering the striations for grip, I press against the cool salt-and-pepper surface. Just short of requiring ropes and a belay, this climb demands that my arms and legs are fully extended, wrapping around the massif. As I creep along, the narrow shelves at last broaden and the curve of rock levels. The top has the loneliness of high rock, windswept, mostly barren except for splotches of lichen and a few trembling seedlings that push barely a foot high. Horseflies persist in the eddies behind my body, the northwesterly blowing nearly forty knots now. Overhead, a bowl of sky. Beneath, an eagle soars, climbing the wind, spiraling ever higher in broad, flat circles, nearly stalling each time it turns into the airstream.

And I can see both sides, the inside and outside waters. The west, across Estevan Sound, is stormy, the wind lifting the sea to a luminescent mist. Beyond the Estevans, a sliver of broad Hecate Strait. Big rollers, combing and reaching waves, cast shadows. With binoculars, I see them breaking far at sea. The inside waters are considerably calmer, intermittent squalls whisking the surface, whitecapping the water. The slopes of Princess Royal Island, where we will paddle when the wind dies, are smooth and green, forest broken only by sheer rock and long trailing chutes.

Below: the orange of muskeg, the two waters, flanks of oozing slopes. Has any human been where I now am? Strangely, I feel that I am the first. I sit on the high rock, my hands cool against the stone. The sensation is comforting, hand against rock, and the rock carries a chill as if it had never quite warmed since the ice inundated even this highest stone.

My descent is fast and furious, tearing through the underbrush, scraping through the shore pines, skirting rocks and rushing through trees, sponging across the steep moss between rocks as if it were shin-deep snow. It is good to be bipedal again, clambering around looking for footing rather than paddle placement against the waves. I have lost some agility and occasionally falter, knees buckling before recovering. And suddenly my mosquito net is gone. I stop, catching my breath, then retrace my steps, climbing nearly a quarter mile to the base of the high granite, but it is nowhere.

In less than a half hour I am at the forest wall again, retrieving the pink bag, deep in skunk cabbage and on to the brightness of shore. Maren is pink and nude, balancing on a large drift log, just finishing a sun shower. Reheating the water to a tolerable coolness in the slant of late afternoon rays, I also shower, and wash my clothes in our cook pot, then wear them dry in the last sun, following mink tracks across the white sand.

By evening the wind has risen to a strong gale. As we say good night with a gentle hand clasp and begin the fall to quiet breaths, I retrace my steps among the upper slopes, looking for the head net. Atop Campania was the one place I did not see human presence, did not feel it. It seemed untouched, like so few places. Even the remote shores are littered with engine parts, cans, hopeless tangles of rope—everywhere the presence of a larger society awash in the tides. On Campania, for an instant, I had escaped that. Now the high rocks, where I felt so alone, shoulder the burden of a modern human presence—filaments of head net caught somewhere among the high snags. Tonight it seems one of the greatest losses of my recent life.

The tent fibrillates in Campania's rushing breeze. Still no rainfly. There will be no rain.

Crossing Caamaño Sound

Yesterday we paddled to the end of Campania in the faltering gale, and this morning it is calm. We are awake early for the crossing to Princess Royal Island. Not far from the Campania shore, swells, three feet from crest to trough, press in from Hecate Strait and mix with the ebb, producing a manageable but complex and uneasy pattern that nudges the kayak and unexpectedly drops from beneath it, leaving the bow to smack against the hollows. From here to Bella Bella, we must cross three small sounds—Caamaño, Laredo, and Milbanke—that open to the ocean. The scale is less ominous than southeast Alaska, but the exposure, at times, is greater. The population is considerably less. We still parallel the heavily traveled Inside Passage route that snakes through Grenville Channel to Princess Royal Channel on the island's eastern side. In Milbanke Sound, we will intersect this route and enter the main highway once again.

A slight westerly ripples the surface, and a squall squats above Whale Channel, sunbeams penetrating to a line of gold on the water. The small boat that stopped last night at our solitary beach, thinking us shipwrecked, is anchored at the end of Campania and motors away as we pass the cove. The ebb flows at about three knots and drags us south toward Laredo Channel, a passage to Laredo Sound. For two hours we paddle through the humbling current, which is swift yet soundless. Behind, in a clearing, the peaks of Campania Island rise above the shoals and shores. The passage opens and closes as we progress. Islands eclipse each other like planets, then slip behind.

The shores of Princess Royal Island are dusky. Soft cumulus blot out all but its lowest flanks, yet above we see only blue. To the north unstable air builds into thunderheads above Pitt Island, but here it is calm. Against the open of Hecate Strait, the southern tip of Campania is illuminated against the dark cloud. It is the last image I carry of Campania, that magical island, still so remote—a final brightness as the clouds reform and send columns of sun out to sea.

After drifting several miles south with the ebb, we stop at a beach behind Druckers Islands. Outside the shoal ocean swell sucks at the rocks. Still, there is no one, and it all feels wonderful. As the tide rises again, we push over bull kelp that is tangled in a heap, and herons vault into flight.

The forest on Princess Royal is old, not the muskeg of northern Campania. On the outskirts of Chapple Inlet, a small clear-cut descends to the water. It is nothing massive, but it stands out, the first cutting we have seen in several days. But now I am taken that the forest is here, how we have become accustomed, in only a few days, to the green and white spires, the living and the dead trees of healthy forest.

At Surf Inlet a sea fog forms and tide rips chatter. The currents are swift enough to spin the kayaks forty-five degrees to the right or left, and by the time we round Johnstone Point, we must wait on a rocky isthmus for three hours for the tide to slacken. We fashion a small dry dock from drift limbs and slide the kayaks high above the rising water. In the past, when a visiting chief arrived by canoe, the Kwakiutl of the northern shore of Vancouver Island would sometimes kill slaves on the beach and use their dead bodies as such rollers.

At high tide we paddle again, and for the next eight miles we battle the rising westerly, searching for camp.

Cruise ships pass again in Laredo Channel. The place names have swayed to Spanish—Caamaño, Campania, Laredo—and recall the several Spanish expeditions that once sailed these waters. We bypass two small inlets, eyeing a cove farther south. When we scoot onto the beach, the tide is sinking away, dropping from the boulders to a fine sand. I must hack through the salal to step ashore, as there is nowhere to camp in the open. By our tent, vertebrae lie in a heap, the wreckage of a bear skeleton scattered by the tide. Lodged among the cobbles are ribs and more vertebrae, a jawbone with a loose but inextractable fang. The bear must have washed ashore or been killed or eaten. The sweet stink of low tide does not leave this beach.

Minks scream all night. Maren's clothes are dotted with blood from insect bites. My paddling jacket is caked with salt. Suddenly, at sunset, this otherwise unflattering camp becomes fantastic—flaming cirrus silhouetting the cedars, shadows against the evening fire—foretelling a change of weather.

Laredo Channel to Ivory Island

JULY 17

For the first hour and a half, we ride a speedy current down Laredo Channel, floating some seven miles in little more than an hour. But after a few gradual swells at slack, the current changes almost immediately, a line of chattery black water racing toward us, the kelp sweeping around, the boiling eddies near shore becoming the only navigable paths. Then we break into the big openness of Laredo Sound, and the day sizzles with rain.

Laredo stretches somewhere near the general division between the Coastal Tsimshian and the Heiltsuk peoples—what some anthropologists have drawn as the division between the northern maritime and the southern maritime environs. And in the past days, as when we paddled from Tlingit to Tsimshian country, the shores have become subtly different than before. Seaworms now dangle from the undersides of rocks. Abundant bull kelp now contends with spiny perennial kelp. Salal now flourishes—for several nights I have had to trim it back just to penetrate the forest. And beaches are again few along these smooth but steep shores. The forest is high, a tangle of old trees that occasionally gives way to stunted trees and muskeg. Then a salmon leaps from the water, the first we've seen. The run is no more than a week away.

There seems a kind of connection between the larger traditional cultural and language areas and these subtle environmental changes, as if somehow they have developed together. We shall see how well this idea holds. For now, the link is a meaningful one.

In the center of the sound, among three islets, we rest at a low-tide beach at the mouth of Laredo Inlet. It is a fantastic place, and we receive it as a gift. Among the thick hills of Princess Royal Island, lives the endangered Kermode bear, a ghostly bear known as the spirit bear, often white like a polar bear, yet a subspecies of black bear. Perhaps its coat had evolved during a cryogenic life among the ice sheets. Scanning with binoculars, we see none. They live far at the head of the inlets, walled by rounded peaks whose angles were eased by the great ice.

We camp on a cobbled beach. The horn of Swindle Island that juts into midsound seems void of camping. But during a dinner of lentil stew, as the tide drops, what looked like rock uncovers to perfect beach. We sour, then recover. Here, salal is dense, and I must pitch the tent directly on its soft bed. There is no snapping their nimble stems. In the morning, when the tent is gone, they will rise again, slowly, like children wakened from bed.

Maren and I trade massages. She rubs my shoulder with her thumbs, then with the point of an elbow, and says it feels like a bundle of cables.

JULY 18

The two-mile backtrack to Wilby Point is difficult, sweeping and C-stroking with strange beam seas that slap the sides of our kayaks, and around Wilby swells pulsate fast and steep. It is not a good start. We paddle together but do not talk much. Trees become torqued and tortured. At this low tide the land seems more severe, pressing like stiff arms against the water as if we are deliberately being kept at a distance from the forest. Driftwood is cast high on these headlands, splinters and kindling piled as they ride the huge storm waves to shore.

Then, on an exposed islet, a fluttering tent and green and yellow kayaks. Afraid this is a tour group, we hesitate, but finally, since we have seen no one else for days, we approach, rounding a rock on opposite sides like an invading party trying to confuse its prey. It is obvious that they, too, think that we are a tour group infesting their campsite. But seeing that there are only two of us, they line the shore in smiles.

They are two couples, Jody and Nick, Barb and Steve, from Vancouver on a three-week paddling trip, and Maren and I stand ankle deep in the water, coming to know them well in the time it takes the tide to rise a foot. At one point Maren grips Jody and says that every morning she has been afraid until a few days ago. Now, she says, that fear has gone.

As the conversation turns to coves and camps, Nick asks if we saw the Stadium. "It's mentioned in a brochure—an old potlatch site," he says.

"I can't believe that's in a brochure," Maren says.

"Yeah. Klemtu is really pushing tourism now. When we got off the ferry, there was a big banner up, and people were there to greet us, give us advice. It's one of the friendliest towns we've been to. The new ferry, the *Discovery Coast*, just started visiting the area this year from Port Hardy, so it's all a new thing."

Jody, who works for a non-profit environmental group, describes a map that shows the original extent of old-growth forest, plus another map that shows its current status: occasionally cut in southeast Alaska, virtually untouched along these shores of central British Columbia, and decimated from Vancouver Island down. She tells of two more maps that show the numbers of Native languages once spoken along the coast and their current status. There is nearly a perfect correlation between lost forests and lost languages. We are in the last and richest stretch of the coast. "When we showed the maps to some First Nations elders," Jody says, "their eyes welled with tears."

We stand talking on the beach until the tide inundates the shore, then paddle away. They hope to round the outside of Price Island, and we see them return slowly to their gray tents in the wind. There exists a camaraderie, an empathy, among paddlers, one that must have been a bond for people who first lived along this coast, one that grew from living within the wind and waves and seeking refuge so often among the shores. And in a short noon together, we have shared this without words.

The small islands break the sea's torment. Quiet trees line the rivers, while those a quarter mile away are bent and erratic with wind. Entering Higgins Passage, we maintain the lakelike solace. Higgins is slender and precarious with peninsulas, islets, and unmarked rock. Birds are everywhere. From water level the channel is tough to discern, and feeling lost, we follow a chain of powerboats into the narrows. But gliding through shallows just above the rocks, we soon cut away to the solitary coves and passages. After the summit, the channel straightens and widens toward Milbanke Sound. Birds swoop down—surf scoters, gulls. Maren spots two red-faced birds walking from the forest. When they see us, they leap into flight, screeching. The elusive sandhill crane. Fish are jumping and Maren is relaxed, leaning back, afloat on the water. "This is really wild country," she says.

The central British Columbia coast is mostly crown land, wild because there has not yet been the need to use it, but most of it is in no way protected. The people from Vancouver said that this part of the coast is destined to be logged, that a new forest plan already has it subdivided into plots of "to-be-forested" land. Many people argue that ecotourism is a way to sustain the biodiversity and economies here, while logging and mining proponents see the land as a way to profit quickly. Still, the coast is dotted with boom-and-bust notions and will again see the foibles of scheming and market predictions, short-lived demands, and shorter-lived enterprises.

Rain tonight; squalls working up the thin channel. Camp

is beneath a red cedar among a maze of mink trails. On shore, a cedar drift log with a diameter that outspans my height has been chainsawed, and all evening the sweetness of cut wood wafts through camp. We make a modest fire—our first since Pitt Island—and warm by the flames tearing in the wind. Maren smiles.

"Happy anniversary," she says.

JULY 19

When the sun begins to die, days will be like this. We do not need to have the discussion about paddling. There will be no paddling. Waves and whitecaps fill the passage, and ocean swells from Milbanke Sound have penetrated the inlet, rolling westward in foaming bursts that spray into the forest. The sky lowers, then raises as the squalls pass through, the variations in atmospheric pressure visible among the clouds.

Radio: *This is Comox Coast Guard Radio continuous marine broadcast, using transmit facilities at Cape Lazo, Texada Island, and Alert Bay on VHF channel weather one; Calvert Island and Port Hardy on channel weather two; Holberg and Sonora Island on channel two one bravo. Break.*

It is refreshing to hear of new places now within radio range, the names of places farther south. We are moving along.

Deep booms echo across the water, distant blasting or cannon fire. After several minutes the faint drone of a motor arrives, and a tiny open hull bucking the swell roostertails into Higgins Passage.

Radio: *Marine forecast issued by the Pacific Weather Center of Environment Canada at one one four five Pacific Daylight Time, Friday, July one nine, 1996, for the period ending noon Saturday, with an outlook for the following two four hours. Synopsis: A trough of low pressure will remain stationary in a north to south line through the Charlottes and will weaken today. A ridge of high pressure over the U.S. coast will build slowly north-*

ward onto the B.C. south coast on Saturday. Moderate to locally strong south to southeast winds will gradually ease to light to moderate by tomorrow morning as the trough weakens and the ridge begins to affect the region. . . .

Greens pale to grays. Our biodegradable dish soap has turned milky again, as it does when the weather cools. Gather rain with the tarp. Many hemlock needles afloat. Iridescent abalone shells decorate the beach. Find deer vertebrae from just above the hips, and I insert my finger into the spinal tube. It is smooth, like hand-polished wood.

Radio: *Sea state values are combined wind-wave and swell height. . . . Central Coast from McInnes Island to Pine Island: Winds southeasterly one zero to two zero knots easing to five to one five Saturday morning. A few showers. Seas near one meter. Outlook: Light to moderate southwesterlies. . . .*

Bulbs of moss festoon a dying cedar behind the tent, its branches a mass of arthritic knuckles clutching the air. In the old forest the ages live together, and relationships among its species are its truest wealth. At the height of winter, storms blast these islands, leveling groves of centuries-old trees like kingpins. The felling gust—the likes of which have not occurred where they stand for hundreds of years—may hit suddenly from a passing squall that leaves a clear sky by evening. Or perhaps their fate will arrive as an advancing line of chain saws or a freak forest fire. Only cedar glows on these cloudy days.

Radio: *Lighthouse reports filed at one three four zero Pacific daylight time: Boat Bluff . . . McInnes Island . . . Ivory Island: Overcast, visibility one five, light rain shower, winds southeast one four estimated. Sea: one-foot chop, low southwesterly swell.* Then Dryad Point, Addenbrooke Island, Egg Island, Pine Island, Scarlet Point, Chatham Point, Cape Scott, Quatsino . . . These distant rocks, points, and islands are familiar now, mere names slowly converting to places. Ivory Island is about a day's paddle away in Milbanke Sound. While many lighthouses are now automated, Ivory remains staffed, a working relic.

Radio: *Automated reports filed at one five three five Pacific daylight time. . . . Ocean Buoy reports filed at one four five five. . . . West Sea Otter . . .*

Colonies of gulls and grebes float and fish along the shoal of rocks. Our point uncovers at low tide, revealing an anvil shape of granite and kelp. A dead bird bobs offshore. Now the sky is completely white; a squall of mist and wind approach like a wall of snow. When it overtakes us, birds suspend fishing and perch on the leeward side of the rocks in a dark seaweed. Clouds race across flanks of smooth-wooded mountains. Maren wonders how the Vancouver friends are doing on the outside of Price Island in such weather.

Radio: *Security: Advisory for Hecate Strait: A large deadhead approximately three feet in diameter with two feet showing out of the water is reported, approximately five nautical miles southwest of Seal Rocks. . . .*

Last night our fire cracked the granite beach stones, cleaving off chunks with peppered undersides. The rock is fresh, undirtied by weather and lichen, and glimmers in its first exposure to light. It is rough, the only face of stone we have felt that has been untouched by glaciers.

Squadrons of sandpipers across the channel fly in precision. White bellies flash suddenly beneath the brown backs as they track along the forest, adjusting their course in unison.

Because we still listen to this radio we must mistrust ourselves with reading the weather. If the batteries go, how confident and courageous would we be?

Radio: *The three seven-foot sailing vessel* High Hopes *was reported disabled with engine problems. Position: tied to a mooring buoy in Thurston Harbor with two people on board. Vessel has white hull with green trim. The* High Hopes *requests a tow into Queen Charlotte City. Mariners are requested to advise if they are able to assist this vessel.*

This is Comox Coast Guard Radio continuous . . .

JULY 21

Late yesterday afternoon the Vancouver people joined us, having aborted the outer coast of Price, and we talked around the fire in lively, rollicking conversations that headed in all directions. This morning when the sky clears, we paddle together, a flotilla of six kayaks streaming across the mercurous waters of Milbanke Sound, a nothingness, an endless glare of sky and water and the unnerving groundswell of ocean power.

Crossing the shipping lane of Milbanke Sound can be treacherous. The trench of Finlayson Channel, the inlet at the top of Milbanke Sound, is the main highway on the Inside Passage. And as we have seen so many cruise ships, I again imagine looking up to discover a prow suddenly looming above. As we pull from Jorkins Point, a distant ship, dark smoke puffing from its single stack, steams toward us, but we cross well ahead of it.

Clear-cuts slice above Moss Passage and Mathieson Channel, and booms thunder across the water: blasting, the construction of logging roads. "There are plans for logging all of this," the Vancouver friends each say at one time or another. "That's why we're here. It won't be like this very long."

With company and conversation, the day passes quickly; eighteen miles and we make camp behind Ivory Island on a spit of beach that is only inches above highest tide. It is not often that we meet people with whom a connection is so strongly and so genuinely established in a matter of days. We enjoy this easy relationship: There is a dependence here on one another that bonds—much like that in the smaller coastal towns. A clear night descends, Venus and stars. Distant airplanes. Across the small channel, a white navigational light flashes on the back side of Ivory. Summer is a month old, and in this month we have paddled from Misty Fiords and survived open Dixon Entrance and nearly half of this most remote British Columbia coast. By the map, the distance seems considerable, and since Prince Rupert, our course has straightened from the wild zagging among the large islands of southeast Alaska to an efficient yet wavering line.

As the tide rises, swells slap nearby rocks, and Maren says she expects another dream of inundating tides.

JULY 22

The tide reached within ten feet of the tent, and the morning is bright with planes of fog rising from outer islands. A parade of gleaming ships bends around Ivory, plying north into Finlayson Channel or south into Seaforth Channel, toward Bella Bella. After breakfast, Maren and I head for Ivory and part with the Vancouver friends, who will paddle south across Seaforth and into the salt lagoons of Athlone and Dufferin Islands. After two recent rest days of stormy weather, the diversion to Ivory seems foolish on this clear, windless morning—a deliberate slowing for unknown prospects—and we float offshore, idle and unsure before crossing.

The fish are jumping all over now. Maren calls them toaster fish because they eject from beneath the waves. To the south, into the sun, a long low craft with some ten people aboard projects the sleek upswept silhouette of a cedar canoe. The vision is ghostly but real and lingers until we can see someone bend and tug at a motor.

We first saw the Ivory light station from the ferry, a jewel among the rocks. On the backside of the island, we bypass a red-and-white boathouse and continue to the lighthouse side, hoping to meet someone or find an obvious landing.

In a growing swell exposed to Milbanke Sound stands the Ivory light station, brilliant white and red against the blue zenith. I approach a man in a skiff reeling in a sockeye. "Are they taking visitors?" I ask.

"Aye," he says, flopping the salmon aboard. "I'm Rene, principal keeper. Come up for a cup of tea? Go 'round to the boathouse and walk across the island. I'll meet you."

Signs say: BOARDWALK CONDEMNED. DO NOT USE. It is five feet and five planks wide with red and black tarpaper shingles nailed for friction steps every half stride. From the boathouse, the boardwalk twists and turns, pitches and yaws, as if buckled by earthquakes, by sinking, or by rot into waves and troughs like the sea itself. Some of the boards have collapsed or broken through in foot-sized holes. The quiet center of Ivory is overgrown with moss and mottled by shade and sun. Waves of skunk cabbage and sword fern lap over the boardwalk's sides. The heart of Ivory is a bog, an old cedar stand, never cut and seemingly so distant from the raging ocean.

Gradually, as we approach the light station, the trees diminish to stunted and flagged spindles, the day again bright and blustery. The light station is on Robb Point, an islet bridged to Ivory at all but the highest tides. After climbing across the rocks where the boardwalk has been washed away, an immaculate white railing lines a new level boardwalk, which meanders past the bright helipad, lettered with brilliant lighthouse white: IVORY ISLAND.

When we arrive at the light station, Rene is working the smokehouse. "Our first batch of the year," he says, opening the door and feeding us a chip of smoked salmon. "Caught yesterday." Dressed in comfortable clothes that suit any work, he is immediately likable. We tour the grounds, including the vegetable garden surrounded by the foundation of the original lighthouse and covered with plastic to protect rows of zucchini, lettuce, and broccoli from furious winds. From the immaculate boardwalks to the smartly painted homes, it is apparent that Rene takes great pride in his tasks. "Maintenance and upkeep are top priorities," he says.

"This is a good day," he notes as we peer over the seawall at the surf below. "On Christmas Day in 1982, at four in the morning, a wave crashed through the window of the lightkeeper's home, waking them up, filling their home with seawater. Since then, on the twelfth of April 1996, a wave came in over the breakwater and around the house but not inside."

We are among the buildings when he stops. "Ivory's been here since 1898. We're trying to make it a century of staffed light station service. But that might be difficult, eh?" As we sip hot tea in the kitchen, news of a reduction radio meeting crackles over the air. "Light stations are being destaffed every month," Rene says. "Maybe tomorrow it will be us. I doubt it, but it could be." As a precaution for now, his wife, Sherrill, has begun part-time work at a bank in Bella Bella, continuing her career in bank management. And then Rene signals to a man who has been speaking the weather report into the phone to join us. "Chris, this is Maren and Byron. They are kayakers."

Chris's eyes widen as he shakes Maren's hand. And when he turns to me, I am astonished. "Stirling!" we both say. "Stirling, Scotland!" Ten years ago he and I studied and traveled in Scotland, to Loch Ness and the highlands. Now we meet again here, in the remote fiords of British Columbia, on this tiny island accessible mostly by helicopter. We quickly fall into a conversation about each other, about the coast, about Scotland. Chris is from Nova Scotia and has worked in light stations there, most often in solitude as a final keeper to the stations being destaffed and transferring to Ivory two and a half years ago. He has just been married, and Seana, his wife of two weeks, has gone for a run around the island. "She'll be back soon," he says. "And glad to have visitors."

I shake my head in amazement as Maren and I set up a spartan home in the boathouse, draping wet clothes from the rafters, spreading sleeping bags upon the planked floor. Then we head back to the light station and meet Seana, delightfully spoken and athletic, who grew up rowing dories in Nova Scotia. As Maren and Seana settle into conversations about fitness and marriage, Chris and I parade the grounds. The lawns are cropped close and manicured; it is as if we are walking a polished ship.

Dutiful and imaginative, Chris has an unswerving penchant for lighthouses. Their home—one of the light station's buildings—is decorated with pictures of lights, of waves breaking across lights, an architect's drawing of the Cape Hatteras Light, an old manual foghorn—the kind that rattles windowpanes—books and reminiscences on lighthouses. As we head outside he hands me a copy of his book, *Vanishing Lights*. "I am a member of one of the last generations to be able to work as lightkeepers, and this is about my experience in the final era of life with the lights.

"Like everything they're becoming automated. All but one in the United States, the Boston Harbor Light, are automated, and that one is just for tourists. In Canada, lights are being automated fast. Nova Scotia is losing staffed lights quickly. So I got the opportunity to move here. Along the BC coast we still have staffed lights. And Ivory's view is most grand."

Chris remains curious and engaged with his work, just as he was as a history major when I knew him in Scotland. Here he has learned mostly everything on the job, from plumbing repair to sight-reading the clouds for the detailed aviation weather. We talk of lightkeeper duties, of weather reports every three hours, of search and rescue. As we stroll past the light structure, he calls it a monstrosity—a radio tower with a bulb on top. Nothing like the cylindrical tower with the massive Fresnel lens he has worked at before.

Standing against the seawall, he fixes a gaze across Milbanke Sound. "Visibility I gave as greater than one five this morning. McInnes is approximately fifteen statute miles west of us. You can see beyond McInnes, so I gave one five plus. And wind [at that time] was west at seven knots. I gave a one foot chop. Since there are troughs between the main swells, it is more than rippled. I always go a little bit higher. A low southwest swell. And it's fourteen degrees Celsius on the nose."

"A summer day."

"Summer day. The second one of the year. Seems like it, anyway."

He points out Skinner Rock and Rat Rocks and a cruise ship turning north. "Sometimes you can see people hanging over the railings, the flashbulbs going off," he says.

We watch the cruise ship as it squeezes into the narrow mouth of Finlayson Channel, two sailboats bobbing in its wake. "I'm a land dweller by virtue of how much time we spend on land, but we are physically in the middle of the sea. With the support we provide to aviators and mariners, secondary search and rescue, you feel like you're part of the whole thing.

"I think it's important. It's something I feel more strongly here than I did on the lights at home. There's more interaction with the marine public, whether it be the pleasure boaters or the tugs wanting to know if it's good out here. If they're in by Dryad and they want to go on the outside, and they call and say, 'Has your wind gone down yet?' that's more than navigation."

I bring up GPS.

"It's pretty difficult up here . . . because every thing is 'inside.' I guess GPS is accurate enough to do that. But until GPS happened, really, you couldn't do it. You still needed the lights and the horns."

As we climb to the light tower, he tells of the lights of the Inside Passage, of the first light station built in 1860 on Fisgard Island near Victoria. How Race Rocks in Strait of Juan de Fuca went up a short time later, and that the bulk of the north coast lights were established during the gold rush days of the Klondike, when so many streamed north.

"This is a DCB 10 Crouse-Hinds, circa 1957," he says, pointing to the rotating beacon. "It works on the same principle as the old Fresnel lens. Two lenses giving a flash every five seconds."

The day is blue, and we stand atop the red tower looking across the Pacific. Life here is lived in primary colors, in the phenomenon of light. "This is a pretty romantic life you have going," I say.

"It's not romantic at all," he replies. "It's practical. You live here, and you maintain it as you would your own home. And also I think, especially in the old days, the Coast Guard expected a pretty high standard. It doesn't seem they are too concerned about it anymore, but people keep the standard up, anyway. Personal pride. You've got the time to do it, so why not?"

"So what's the job here?"

"The lightkeeping instructions say that we are keeping the station in a state of readiness at all times. They don't say for what, but what they mean is that you will be ready to fight a fire at the station or launch the boat or deal with a ship or a helicopter. And that's what we do. We're always ready for something or other. As ready as you can be.

"We do the routine maintenance. We check the main light twice a month. We check all batteries in the foghorn emitters. All that stuff. Oil changes for the generators every five thousand hours. They change the engines out every fifteen thousand, actually fly them out. That's roughly every two years. They drop a long line in."

We descend the light's metal ladder, and I follow Chris to the generator house, the gardens, the cistern. "This is a pretty high standard of living for a place like this," he says. "If you took away the generators and took away the government support and took away everything we have here, we'd be homesteading like every other fishing or logging camp. It's pretty urban, in a way. We're burning fossil fuels that provide us with all the amenities of town. The keepers up around Green Island near Prince Rupert have cell phones. The keeper at Bonilla is on the Internet, e-mail and the whole thing from a light station sixty miles from Rupert in the middle of Hecate Strait. It's pretty wild, but it's pretty urban. And these are the most remote lights in Canada."

Another cruise ship bends around the island, heading north.

"They always call it a constant parade of traffic," Chris says. "You can't feel isolated with that."

After a dinner of salmon and fresh greens, all four of us climb above the red rooftops up to the light and look out over the railing on the open waters of Milbanke Sound. As the light rotates, I feel its warmth sweep across my shoulders. We are at a beacon, a strategic turning point on the Inside Passage, once more at a meeting of waters: the ocean, the inner channels. Chris and I are astounded by this coincidence, extending our friendship from the glacial fiords of Scotland to these of the Northwest coast. This passage seems as much about connections and intersections as it is about broken islands and varied cultures. Like so many places we have been, Ivory is a window to the greater continuities of life.

The boathouse is on the dark side of the island, where total blackness is interrupted only by stars and the intermittent flash of a single white navigation light. At twilight it pops on like a streetlamp. As I stare now into the spangled night, a satellite sweeps through the dark band of the Milky Way, speeding toward Cassiopeia. What can it be processing so high? The locations of ships along this coast? The GPS is the nemesis of the staffed lights, and the sighting of this small bead of distant metal, like the sighting of a comet, seems to mark a change.

Gusts of night air seep through cracks of the boathouse, brushing cool and fresh across my face. There was a time before the lights, when nights were dark and canoes, not cruise ships, plied these waters.

JULY 23

This morning Maren stuns me with one sentence, saying, "You have become the man you were meant to be."

Clear. Chris and Seana invite us to breakfast, and we cross the island to join them for a cup of Lighthouse Tea brought from Nova Scotia. In a day the boardwalk has grown to a treasure. Once used as a road for a small tractor that hauled supplies between the skiff at the boathouse and the home, it is now barely a footpath and carries, in each soft step, the feel of every country lane I ever strode.

While I am away, Maren sees two orca thrashing and playing in the shallows near the boathouse.

Watson, Sherlock, and Skeena are the light station dogs. Watson, a black-and-white spaniel, just had tendon surgery in Prince Rupert and limps around, staying mostly indoors. Sherlock, a floppy beagle, is low and solid. Skeena, a smallish German shepherd with an appetite for sticks, can imitate a foghorn. She is relentless and frisky, and Chris must often tell her to "Take Five," her command to relax—which she does, sprawled on the lawn, gnawing sticks.

Maren and Seana swim in the frigid sea while I relax in the boathouse and Chris prepares the afternoon's weather report. We meet before dinner by Chris and Seana's. Today a reduction conference on the radio announced government plans for the future. Light keepers listened to their radios, learning if their station will be made redundant. This time none are scheduled for immediate closure, but the main talk among keepers is when they will be let go, when their light stations will be automated.

It is amazing that this is happening right as we are here, as though the coast is at a teetering point. "The government only sees the money spent," Rene says, leveling his ball cap, "not the money saved by lightkeepers who save people and assist with rescues so the big helicopters don't have to get started on a search and rescue for a cost of about $100,000 at a time."

We sip a home brew—an India pale ale—cellar cool on this hot afternoon, watching a tug towing an empty log barge work north to the Prince Rupert pulp and paper mill, where it will reload and return. "There's talk that destaffed light stations could be used for scientific observation: orca and birds," Chris says. "They could be made into bed-and-breakfast inns. But the bottom line is that all parties except the government want to keep them staffed to help the marine community."

After dinner Chris and Seana show their wedding album, only two weeks old: June 29, 1996. "Look at the beach," Seana laughs. "You can see the tide advancing in all of the pictures." The newness of relationship and the excitement of Ivory radiates from them. "I got a leave of absence from my job and decided to come out here. Why not? It's the best honeymoon we could think of. A full year."

Their light year.

Late in the boathouse, after we have said our good-byes and as Maren and I sit at the picnic table, marveling at the community that this seemingly vacant coast has brought to us, I have a vision of Ivory's last moments as a tended light. The last weather report. The final duties. The departing chopper. As it thumps away, that last keeper looks back at the shrinking cluster of buildings, then suddenly looks away, the mindless light left blinking, charged by the sun, radioing weather like a probe on Mars. The keeper speeds to a new life, across an unknown blue.

It is another clear, windy night, and I go to consider the planets, the creamy distant worlds perhaps swept by glaciers of methane or ammonium. As I gaze upward, it is there again: a satellite tumbling soundlessly through our galaxy and into the bright field of Cassiopeia.

Ivory Island to Bella Bella

JULY 24

We leave Ivory Island early and paddle east along Seaforth Channel, toward Bella Bella. It is a day of transition and of many images. On a promontory, two figures lean from the forest—memorial poles. The totems are askew and rotting, hairy with moss. Shocks of sword ferns sprout from their heads. From their silent point, they have an unobstructed view of Milbanke Sound, the Ivory light, and Price Island, distant now on this tranquil day.

Although a cruise ship passed some fifteen minutes before, when we reach the middle of Seaforth Channel, its foamy slipstream still boils. Its wake arrived earlier, five waves four feet high. Ahead, Dufferin Island is lined with beaches. Since Campania, the outer islands have been much lower than islands closer in, and for the first time since the Portland Inlet we can see the mainland snow peaks from the water. As we cross, the swell diminishes, and the ship's blue hull, already miles away, takes a mighty turn south down Lama Passage, toward Bella Bella.

Four cruise ships clamor by as we paddle east along Dufferin and Horsfall Islands. After traveling a rural route for several weeks, we have suddenly merged onto the freeway. By the time we reach Campbell Island, the first floatplanes, a twin-engine Beechcraft and a single-engine Cessna, sink to a runway among the hills. Into town again.

Past Dryad Point Light, Bella Bella opens on a broad beach. In recent summers members of many Northwest tribes have landed here after canoeing the old paddle route through the Inside Passage—much as we will—crossing Queen Charlotte Strait at the northern tip of Vancouver Island and continuing up the coast of mainland British Columbia to this beach. Above the arc of pebbles, Bella Bella, also known by its Heiltsuk name, Waglisla, or "the place of many small rivers," spreads across the gentle hill, a townscape of low homes spiked by a hospital and a new school. A small skiff zips about, running between Bella Bella and villages on the eastern shore.

We land near the Bella Bella Band Store, the best-stocked supermarket on this section of the coast, looking for Frank Brown, whom I radioed from Ivory Island. He helped organize the carving of a cedar canoe here and paddled it with a group of fellow Heiltsuk people to Expo '86 in Vancouver. This paddle helped to ignite the canoe resurgence among the First Nations of the coast, and after paddling so far ourselves, we thought we should compare craft. When we mention Frank's name, several people speak of the paddle. "Three weeks from here to Vancouver," one man says. "You'll find Frank a mile south in McLoughlin Bay."

As we veer into the bay, we see the cedar canoe tied to a dock. It is the first time I have seen one afloat—the upswept bow and stern, painted with the four clans of the Heiltsuk: raven, eagle, killer whale, and wolf. Near the fish processing plant's manufactured beach of purple urchin spines, Frank has built a longhouse, what the Heiltsuk call a big house, which serves as a museum and interpretive center. There is a birthday party at the beach, and young girls with bright life jackets swim out to greet us, squealing and dog paddling in the shallows. "The Kayakers! The Kayakers! Capital T! Capital K! The Kayakers!" A young man with close dark hair rises from a lawn chair and walks out along the dock. It is Frank, and his family and friends welcome us for a salmon dinner already in progress.

"They're a little excited," he says, laughing at the kids. "Pitch your tent and come eat."

JULY 25

The ferry arrives at 6:15 A.M., the flat-nosed *Discovery Coast* up from Port Hardy that we heard about in Laredo Sound. This is its initial year of service, bringing tourists to this relatively remote central coast for the first time in large numbers. There are many paddlers here now, and we have already been called "hippie kayakers." After the ferry noses ashore, a couple of paddlers assemble an old Klepper on the beach.

It is a busy morning for Frank and his wife, Kathy. Their enterprise, SeeQuest Adventures, caters to this new ferry service, providing nature and cultural tours for passengers. Frank waits at the dock in a fleece jacket to lead a group on a tour into the forest. After the walk, some will return to the ferry for the ride to nearby Shearwater. Others will paddle the three miles to Shearwater in the cedar canoe, then rejoin the ferry. "This is a new thing," Frank said to me this morning. "Some of our people are wary of the increased tourism in the area. But it's a way we can share our culture. The Heiltsuk have always adapted. Always been traders, working between the northern and southern tribes, the people of the interior over the old 'grease trail.' It's my tradition. The project has been approved by the Heiltsuk Band Council."

Frank is determined. He went to college in Vancouver and studied outdoor recreation management, and after organizing the paddle to Vancouver's Expo '86 at age nineteen, he continued the work with the paddle from Vancouver to Seattle in 1989, when he challenged the maritime indigenous nations to paddle to Bella Bella, which culminated here in 1993 with the arrival of twenty-one ocean-going canoes from thirty Native nations.

We follow Frank on his nature walk, then assemble around the canoe. It is heavy in the water, its hull nearly two inches thick. Granite blocks serve as ballast, and a dozen paddles line the canoe, their long leaflike blades resting against red benches. The paddles are rough-hewn, some painted, some plain, none yet with the hand polish that develops with years of use. It is not difficult to see the canoe as the living tree it once was. At the knees of the bow paddler, the cross section of tree is exposed, the concentric rings of sapwood and heartwood. Before carving, the canoe log is set in the water to see how it rights itself, with the heaviest side forming the hull.

Along its length, beneath the black paint and throughout the interior, are the scalelike rows of adze marks, the thousands of human strokes that have shaped this craft. After the introduction of plank boats, the old canoes, which had to be maintained and kept moist to prevent them from cracking, fell into disuse. Indeed, while this canoe was steaming, slowly being spread, it split, and Frank says his heart sank when he felt the wood go. But the crack was repaired, and now the hull is wrapped in a layer of protective fiberglass.

With each person who boards, the canoe sinks a little more in the water, then gains stability. "Once we get going, we'll adjust the rocks for balance," says Frank's assistant, Duane.

Within minutes, as we set out to cross the short distance to Denny Island, this crew of novices somehow paddles in unison. After months of paddling a kayak, I find reaching over the gunnel with a canoe paddle awkward, and my blade splashes ineffectively through the water. I must slow and steady my strokes to keep cadence with the group. In the kayak I am used to negotiating each wave, pausing if I wish, leaning and sweeping on my own accord. The canoe dampens smaller waves, and there is a presence that adds a dimension to paddling, a coordination of efforts through which paddling decisions must be made. Two seats ahead, Maren paddles steady. A person shifts their weight, and the canoe rolls to the side. Others compensate, and we roll dangerously to the opposite direction. "Shift the rocks, eh, Duane?" Frank instructs.

As we settle into the paddle, Frank begins his stories. "In '86 there were thirteen of us who went to Vancouver in this canoe. Most sites on our trip were ancestral canoe landing sites. And there was a lot of protocol when going to another village. You would announce who you were and that you had peaceful intentions, and ask for permission to come ashore. Their chiefs would acknowledge the courtesy that was bestowed upon them for the request for landing, and they would welcome you. I heard that when one of the tribes was paddling through, one community said, 'We have mixed feelings about inviting you ashore because our elders recall when the tribal wars were still happening, that one of their uncles was killed by your people.' So it was not that long ago."

The canoe was carved from a seven-ton red-cedar log. Although it is hollowed, it does not *feel* hollow, as our kayaks do. It is a noticeable mass, with the hull of red cedar between me and the water. We are riding within a living being, a creature of the forest.

"It took our carvers about six months to carve," Frank says. "It was the first canoe carved in our village for one hundred years. They would take a couple of chops at it then stare for a while because you can't put wood back on. Our elder and head carver passed away just as the project began, so we almost lost the art of canoe carving."

For a while we hear only the steady slosh of strokes.

"Paddling down to Vancouver was like opening an old box of treasures," Frank remembers. "We were able to view the land through the eyes of our ancestors. They were a hearty bunch. Now we are softer. An age of instant gratification." He digs a few strokes and pries the large rudder blade to avoid some rocks. A few people shift in their seats, and the canoe rolls again to one side, then gently back to level. "The canoe takes everybody. It's communal. If a person is tired or a person is mad or sad in the canoe, you feel it, these feelings are transferred. I think canoe travel is where that tradition of looking beyond yourself came from."

As the ferry blasts its five-minute warning horn, we nudge to the Shearwater dock, where canoe passengers shed life vests and snap final pictures. When the tourists have gone, Frank tosses a rope over the canoe's bow and attaches it to the motorboat that Kathy shuttled over. "Hop in the canoe," he says. As he engages the motor, the canoe rises. At nearly fifteen knots—probably as fast as a cedar canoe has ever traveled on water—the craft is amazingly stable, cutting through wave crests and boat wake as if this versatile craft was somehow prepared for this as well, all that time ago.

Tendrils of fog seep to the water at dusk. Beneath a waxing gibbous moon, I sit on the urchin beach in the sodium vapor haze of the fish plant. The speaker on a late ferry booms across the water. Then comes an odd gull call. A car horn. A chain saw. Bella Bella is emerging, changing, like so many places we have been. Frank says that nine forest companies are working in the area, and the surrounding hills are slated to be carved into quadrants for logging. That one day Bella Bella looked behind, and a clear-cut was gnawing over the hill, which required some fighting to stop it before it surrounded their reservoir, contaminating the village's water supply.

A car crunches to a stop, and two young men walk onto the dock and peer at the old canoe. "They paddled all the way to Expo in this," one says.

The other kneels and knocks against its side. "Skims in the water, eh?"

JULY 26

The morning is foggy, and Frank and I sit on an old drift log outside the fish plant overlooking the ferry dock. "You see this new dock?" he says. "Modern. Steel. Concrete. Dreams of access. That's what built it. Dreams of access."

He quiets for a while. "We are in an interesting time and

a very difficult time because we need to be able to sustain community and diversify the local employment and economic opportunities for the band membership. And what I'm doing with the SeeQuest Adventures is attempting to demonstrate the economic and employment viability of Native heritage and ecotourism business.

"Importantly, in this budding industry, we're not just sitting back and watching it all happen and getting left on the beach, which unfortunately happened in many cases. This is kind of like the calm before the storm . . . and now the development is going to come. We should have an opportunity on influencing how that development takes shape so that it doesn't damage our community, or we minimize the damage and try to maximize the benefits—if any benefits come."

He is passionate and thoughtful about his work and his words. Several times since last evening he has spoken of his connection to this area.

"How does the idea of the Heiltsuk homeland figure into the thinking?" I ask.

"Homeland to me is a very important concept. It's even more important than a concept, really; it's a part of myself as a Heiltsuk person. We have ten thousand years of history in the central coast. The oldest known archaeological site on the entire coast is over at Namu, a Heiltsuk village site. And with the years and years of continuous habitation, a very intimate relationship has developed between this Heiltsuk traditional territory, our homeland, and the people who have found sustenance from its resources. And we would like to be able to sustain our community.

"You think about the names and the lineages of the people, specifically the chiefs' names . . . and it goes back hundreds and sometimes thousands of years, back to first-generation stories, when the Creator put our ancestors down here. And that's a big part of what a homeland means: People can trace their lineage back all throughout the millennia."

"A richness of tradition and time."

He nods. "One of the most important gifts that can come out of the homelands of indigenous people is cultural diversity. Every tribe along this coast has a piece of the knowledge. There are pockets of ancestral knowledge maintained through the communal fashion, through oral history. And if things are meant to be, you will make the connections to those people. And if they feel comfortable, they will share with you, and you'll be able to piece it together and come up with something very needed in society today."

He looks off across the channel again. "There have to be alternatives to the way humanity is going. One of the problems we have along this coast is that the various resource interests are all managed as separate entities. The forests are managed by the Ministry of Forests. The fishery is managed by the Department of Fisheries and Oceans. And that whole scientific process is very important, but everything is more interconnected than this. When you ask about the homeland, that's what I mean. We cannot segregate ourselves from the resources the way we have been and expect it to work."

As we talk, the sky clears, and it is blue again. "So where are we now?" I ask, hoping not to initiate the abysmal talk of environmental and cultural plight.

"I really believe that we have to take the best of both worlds," Frank says. "But if we abandon our heritage, then we are poorer people. The canoe was abandoned. It became an object of curio, a museum piece, and canoes were pulled up on the beach and rotted. And so now we have carved a canoe. And there were doubters. . . . I spent three years organizing it, but ultimately it was the people that breathed life into it. We paddled down the coast, and I think that inspired the coastal tribes, and it just really never stopped.

"The beauty of the canoe is that it's something that ties our whole community together, not just the Heiltsuk, but the Haida, the Tlingit, the Tsimshian, the Kwakwaka'wakw, the Makah, and Coast Salish. . . . It's a common heritage. All along this coast, it's this waterway that ties us together, this inland sea. There's a long history of voyaging up and down it. And if it's not in our oral tradition, it's in our DNA."

"So, the canoe has come again," I say. "What does it bring to this coast?"

"I really believe in the healing power of Nature. It can heal a sick soul. It can ease a restless mind and a restless heart because the Earth is a living being, a living entity. It has an ability to absorb and sustain and nurture. I guess that's why we call her Mother Earth. And I have felt that, and I really wanted to be able to share that with other people. That's why we made the challenge in 1989 in Seattle. We wanted to invite people to paddle here, so they could go through that healing journey themselves.

"It's a real treasure and a legacy we've been given, but it's something that we have to go out and find. Someday you and I will be old men, if we're lucky, and we'll have all the aches and pains of the old men. But the things that will continue to make our hearts warm are the memories of these wonderful days sitting on the beach and feeling the warm breeze blowing against our faces. These are precious memories. You have to go out and make them. You have to go out and create them. That's about all I have to share, really."

As Maren and I paddle from McLoughlin Bay, a cruise ship plows by, the closest we've been to one since Ketchikan. From fifty yards, its flared bow nearly filling the channel. Passengers line the decks, sunning beneath the strings of lights that illuminate nighttime galas. The glint of video cams and binoculars flash in the sun. A volleyball game is going on, the white ball arcing high in the netted pen. And long after the ship has passed, a blue curl of smoke hangs in the valley. When the wake rips along shore, the cedar canoe, tied along the dock, bucks and pitches as wildly as a steer.

Near Napier Point, we look back to Bella Bella spread across the hill. Suddenly, another cruise ship pours overhead, so close that we can smell the café. The thing is ferocious and quakes the water. When it has gone, we cross to Denny Island, and I glance once more toward Bella Bella, the ship eclipsing the town entirely.

We follow the old canoe route along Lama Passage as it bends eastward into the high peaks of King Island, then south along Fisher Channel, down to Namu. To go outside here, among the small islets west of Hunter Island, is tempting—surely beautiful and surely adventurous—but the late-summer sea fog has returned. We are traveling south, after all, and will see the outer coast soon enough in Queen Charlotte Sound.

The afternoon is thick with haze as a low pressure rides over the Charlottes. As we enter Fisher Channel, a tug and its barge round Kaiete Point, pulling north. The barge is immense—stacks of containers and miscellaneous plastic-wrapped cartons. Wedged in among the mass are sailboats, pickup trucks, and cars, stacked like playthings in a box. "Headed for Bartlett Cove," Maren says.

"Kaiete" is a hereditary chief's name of the Heiltsuk, one of two names that came to the Heiltsuk from the Tlingit three hundred years ago as a way of designating and maintaining a community standing of a boy and a girl, each half Tlingit, half Heiltsuk, who were born in the north and who had returned to Heiltsuk country. Today, Frank's uncle, Carmen Humchitt, carries the name Kaiete. The girl was named Gomdamach, referring to the labret worn in the lower lip of a high-ranking woman, and it is the name of Frank's grandmother, which will one day be passed along to his eldest sister. Names as much as waterways tie the Native peoples together, to their past. Each family holds its names as property, an instant genealogy that can be traced far back. And here, this point of land enters into the lineage of land and people intertwined.

The First Nations people of British Columbia have never signed a treaty with the government relinquishing their land rights, and recently their claims to the land, which were simply ignored when British Columbia joined Canada, are being recognized as valid, that the oral history is legitimate evidence to confirm aboriginal title and rights. As the high courts of British Columbia are upholding, "homeland" is not just a philosophical ideal but one grounded in history and fact.

Just around Kaiete Point we pause in the shelter of Pointer Island. Among its rocks are the cylindrical feet of a helipad, the foundation of a disassembled light station. The nautical chart has its FOG SIG crossed out. The former station has been replaced by a solar light, a white candlelike structure that charges by day, then flashes after sunset. The ruins are incomplete, as if half the station were washed clean away by a storm. I cannot imagine Ivory Island meeting a similar fate. Maren and I agree that it will be some time before the pavement of the helipad crumbles to sand.

The evening is long and luxurious. With a growing breeze, we find a shell beach among islands on the west side of Fisher Channel and prepare for tomorrow's crossing to the mainland that we have not touched since Metlakatla. As the mountains blue with nightfall, fog reforms. The tide floods to our stove as we eat spaghetti. Again, we have made a home on an isthmus of land, the tent pitched on the two yards of grass between beaches.

Crossing Fisher Channel

JULY 27

A liquid day. Although there is a light wind, the fog takes all depth from the sky until burning away by noon, when the winds rise. We must compromise: paddle with poor visibility or wind—a compromise we would rather not make. Maren says that perhaps we do not have to. We could wait. But with the weather pattern settling in now, we could wait days or indefinitely. Since we can paddle along shore before crossing Fisher Channel, we reluctantly pack and head south.

Fog conceals the commonplace. We have lost most of our sight, and other senses gradually sharpen. The air shakes with noise—always engines—and water flutters with wave and wake, disturbances from distant craft. We respond like eardrums, paddling to the water's beat, the cadence of paddles.

For a time we have the comfort of a shoreline, and fog veils the reality of the steep eastern slopes, the channel's breadth. Behind an island a tug nuzzles its barge, curled like a sleeping animal. In a half hour the tug's deep-throated voice arrives, long before its shadow. Soon a troller hammers past close to shore, orange scotchman dangling like suns from its deck. Past five hundred yards the world stops. Compass: due S.

After a long and hesitant pause on a beach of severe rock, waiting for the fog to rise, we decide to cross, anyway. Paddling one hundred yards from shore, we stop, sprinters setting in the starting blocks. "Let's do this quickly," Maren says. "I want to get out of here."

We can see the other side, truncated at the first row of trees, and about a mile up and down the channel. Then an earshattering roar splinters the air, a black spider dropping from the sky—a helicopter with an orange rescue body case and a life raft hanging from a runner, racing beneath the ceiling, its propwash depressing the water. Then it is gone.

"Do you think the fog is breaking up?" Maren says, watching the brightening sky.

"Looking better," I say. We listen to the drone of the barge fade and begin paddling in the stratum of clear air toward the eastern shore, the silver band of driftwood.

"Look for the Fog Rocks light!" I shout. "That's when we can ease up. The end of the shipping lane. Can you believe these names?"

"Names have reasons," Maren says.

We are too low to be picked up on radar, and the shipping lane is less than a mile wide. Twenty minutes of risk. The fog thins but rises no higher as we paddle, dipping in the milky sea, following each other's prints across the emptiness. Halfway, we spot a speck on the northern horizon.

"There's one," I say. "Let's go!"

The black speck grows but remains comfortably distant. The Fog Rocks are visible but dim, and their single automated light is extinguished. Near the rocks, a whale suddenly surfaces, blows, then, raising its flukes, dives deep. I slow and turn to wait for Maren, who is not far behind. And then I see the horror. Although she is more than safe—only thirty yards from me—the looming bow of a cruise ship has broken through the fog. The ship is decapitated, its bridge and upper decks consumed in cloud, the white hull curling over green water.

It makes no sound, blows no foghorn. It could not have been that speck. It came too close too quickly. Had we hesitated . . . From its belly issues a blast, the deep harmonics of a foghorn, so loud that it nearly ripples the surface. When the blast ends, it resonates across the water and among the canyon walls like the final chord of a great organ reverberating among the vastness of a cathedral. Then it bellows again. "Too close," Maren says, paddling up. "Way too close."

I nod. I cannot tell if she is mad at me, at us, or just angry that we tried the stupid thing. I am certainly all three. "We were probably in greater danger just then than anywhere else, and we didn't even know it."

"That's how danger works," she says.

I scan the water, looking for the whale, but it has not resurfaced, and we paddle on. By now we can pick out individual trees on the eastern shore. A horn sounds again, a minor chord. And as we look behind, a new hull has emerged, deckless, slipping north. We can do nothing but float and watch, trembling as a second angled bow crashes through the water, crumbling gray into white, the blue steel, the foamy churn of propellers.

"We're lucky skunks," I say, smiling nervously. "I don't like this freeway travel."

"And we've still got to cross Burke Inlet today," Maren says. "I don't know if I can do it after this."

Reaching the calm of the Kisameet Islands, we scare a flock of Barrow's Golden Eyes, and they flop along the water ahead of us, never quite gaining the air before skidding behind a rock. When we overtake them again, they startle and flap along the surface, and we play tag with them for nearly a mile down behind Kipling Island. Tufts of grass sprouting from fissures in the rocks have the appearance of flames shooting from the stone. Two eagles swoop, searching for salmon. Near Burke Inlet, the fog has lifted to a height of two trees, and the shore is glowing.

After pausing at a tiny beach, snacking in our precrossing way, discussing the route, the pace, the potential landing sites, we set out. A small barge pulls from the mouth, turning north, having made its delivery to Bella Coola, the small community at the head of the inlet. It is up there, too, north among the shores of Dean Channel, that an exhausted Alexander Mackenzie wandered from river and forest to the tidewater to eventually etch his name on a rock: MACKENZIE, 1793, ACROSS CANADA. I imagine him seeing the tide slowly rise or slowly sink, realizing that his westward journey west had at last reached an end. But Mackenzie showed no excitement in his journal. Perhaps he had realized that after making some celestial observations to prove his location to the scientific age, his arduous journey was only half complete. He then had to return.

Soon the fog dissolves, the high mountains reappearing and then sun. Green returns to the hills, and we can see up the inlet and ahead to the islands. Rounding the next point, Namu is a clear cluster of silver roofs tucked in the back of a bay. It is an old cannery town rolling with boardwalks and ascending hills and stilted across the water on pilings. We have heard that the café is a good one and plan to stop for a hot lunch, but as we near, the village seems vacant.

A man appears atop the dock. "If you're looking for somebody, there's nobody here," he says and walks away.

We climb the ramp and peer in a window of a building. It is a machine shop, stocked with tools, drill presses, welding masks, sheet metal, miscellaneous pipes and parts. The man is not here. Grass has sprouted in the cracks of the pavement, like an abandoned airfield. Heaps of twisted metal lie in the alleys between the green industrial buildings. In the stillness of bright sun, the place seems all the more deserted. A sign on the door to the power plant: DANGER ASBESTOS.

Namu is half derelict, half intact, habitable yet uninhabited. In the barbershop prices are written on a marker board: CUTS $15, COLORS $35, PERMS $40, HIGHLIGHTS $35. CASH ONLY PLEASE. Half-empty shelves in the grocery hold bags of Alpo, candies, and faded magazines. The post office is closed. The café, newly painted in pleasant but misplaced Caribbean pink and aqua, is also unoccupied, its gleaming roof lettered NAMU, a menu posted over the grill, mugs on a table. Up the hill, porches peel away from a row of ill-kept homes. In the settlement's center is a maintained quarters, the largest, the yard freshly mowed. Still no one.

At the kayaks a man stumbles from a moored boat, shading his eyes like a just-surfaced mole. He tells us that Namu closed several years ago, and when the cannery quit, people just dropped life and left. "I think it's beautiful here," he says. "You better talk to Gerry and Chris, though. They run the place, a lodge out of the main building up there. They're on the other side, around there." He points around the machine shop and power plant. Paddling around the immense pilings, we see the rest of Namu along a magnificent boardwalk. Large frame buildings, all painted in the uniform red-and-white of a company town, back the walkway, which planks the entire shore like a train trestle, crossing a creek and fronting some row houses before the thick forest ensues.

"Welcome to Namu; I'm Gerry!" shouts a voice from atop an old vessel named the *Blue Fjord*. "Where you headed?"

We tell him about the journey.

"Enjoy the sun!" he replies. "Just make yourself comfortable. That's what Namu is about, eh? Comfort."

We tie up on a floating dock and explore the boardwalk. The large building must have been the dormitory. The rooms are gutted, painted a pallid yellow, and scrawled with graffiti. Shards of broken glass crunch underfoot as we step among the wreckage. At a large windowless building Maren peeks her head into the dark doorway. "There's a gymnasium in here," she says, leading us in. "Look at this!" The air is cool like a cave. Adjusting to the darkness, I see it, too—a full basketball court, a wooden floor. And next to the court, a bowling alley.

The boardwalk follows Namu Creek a quarter mile to Namu Lake, a tranquil mirror amid the uncut hills, a plentiful supply of fresh water. It is not surprising that humans have lived here for nearly ten thousand years, the longest such legacy that has been time dated on the coast. Like so many favored living sites, it is guarded from weather by three or more islands. At low tide, a fish trap is bared, a subtle arc of stones piled centuries ago.

Paint peels from the buildings like flaking skin. The large dormitory is labled THE EDGEWATER, after the Edgewater Inn on the Seattle waterfront. Another: NAMU HILTON CONVENTION AND VISITOR CENTRE. Paralleling the boardwalk is a wooden pipe constructed of planks tightly wound with wire in the likeness of a barrel. Once it carried water from the lake.

Gerry comes down to say hello. "If you need some dog food, we've got that. Kit Kats, too, from 1991." He laughs, immediately witty, the kind of person who can spark conversation with anyone, from fishermen to physicists. He explains that BC Packers, the fish-packing company, finally left Namu in 1991, and it was purchased by a new owner. He helps Chris, who runs the fishing lodge, and together they look after the place in summer. "Our cook, Niki, is coming in on the ferry today. There's no dock here, so I've got to go out and meet it. Don't let me miss it."

"Is that your boat?" I ask, pointing to the *Blue Fjord*.

"No, that's Michael and Judy. They'll be here tonight. Full of tourists. Should be a fun time. You're welcome, eh?" When we ask about the Namu site, he says Chris's father, Dr. Roy Carlson of Simon Fraser University, was one of the archaeologists who led the excavation in 1977 and 1978. The discovery was made where an old dormitory was torn down, uncovering a shell midden and some cultural remains. "There's no museum, though, just a filled-in pit."

After pitching a crude, tentless camp on the dock, we stroll around the boardwalk again. Gerry and Chris have gone to meet the *Discovery Coast*, stopped in Namu Harbor, and are now fishing for dinner. The boardwalk flexes in places, and we must pick a safe path through the rot and holes. The cove before the river is bounded with "no fishing" markers and flopping with sockeye—continuous silver flashes leaping from the water—returning to spawn in Namu Lake. For millennia the salmon have drawn people here: Native peoples, then the cannery, now the fishing lodge. Occasional fishermen troll in the harbor but catch nothing.

By the Namu Hilton, an old man stares at the dilapidated structure.

"Amazing," I say.

"I used to work here," he says softly. "This was the mess hall. My mother started working in Namu when she was fifteen. I started working here when I was eighteen. See those buildings over there?" He points at the derelict row houses beyond the creek. "That's where we lived. 'Indian town.' The second home . . . my daughter was born there. She even has Namu on her birth certificate." He studies the collapsing "Namu Hilton Convention and Visitor Centre." "My, it's a mess now. Look at it. I haven't been back for five years. But I always like to stop in Namu. We had such good times. There was a dance every Saturday in the gym. A band. My brother played saxophone in there. We'd have basketball tournaments. There were so many people here."

"What was the town like then?" I ask.

"I lived where the Natives lived. I'm from Bella Bella. Then down on the beach, that's where the Japanese lived. The dorm over there"—he gestures toward "The Edgewater"—"that was where the white people lived, the college students who came up here for the summer. The homes are where the managers lived. They were white, too. Beyond them was where the Chinamen lived. Then the Métis. Across this bridge here we had a red line painted. You couldn't cross that line after seven o'clock. It was there to keep us separated. Keep us outta trouble. There were so many different groups here all at once. And there were fights. Right near the bridge there was the jail." He chuckles. "I never spent time there, though."

The encounter is like meeting a ghost. No one has seen a boat either dock or depart. We snapped his picture when he crossed the bridge and half wonder if his stooped image will develop.

The archaeological site, long emptied and abandoned, is nothing more than a rectangular pit covered with cedar branches. It has a commanding view of the bay, high above the river, and one can imagine a life here, beneath old cedars and surrounded with the sweetness of ripening thimbleberries.

*   *   *

We cluster around the *Blue Fjord* in the evening. Maren converses with the Germans on board, two pairs of mothers and daughters, some single women, and an old man with his grown son.

"Beautiful vessel," I say to Michael, the captain.

"She's the old courthouse ship for this area at one time. Offenders from Namu and elsewhere have been locked in here while waiting trial. We've converted the old courtroom to bunkrooms, but she still has charm—the rails, the back covered deck. We run whale-watching charters up and down the coast, mostly in Johnstone Strait. You'll be going through there."

"Eventually."

"It's gorgeous. We work with the scientists around Robson Bight, know them all. The whales know us, too. One time A-30 broke from the pod and sped right toward us then sat there spy hopping. She must know the sound of our motor. We see her nearly every time." When describing the whale behavior, he is animated and excited, slicing through the air with his arms.

Chris, Gerry, and Niki soon return with a pail of prawns. "Let's get these on the bar-bee," Gerry says with an Australian accent. And we reach into the squirming tub. "Here," he says, taking my hand. "Dig your thumb behind their head and twist." Prawn brains spurt; then they tense and muscles twitch. In ten minutes we fill two dozen skewers.

At dinner, I cannot stop eating Tator Tots, popping nearly a dozen down before the salmon and prawns are ready. Down the table, Maren seems to look up from her plate only to laugh and jab in punchlines of her own. As the feeding frenzy subsides, Judy sings and strums the ukulele, and we leaf through the *Blue Fjord* songbook, singing every tune. During a chorus of "Fishin' Blues," we dedicate a new verse. "That's bee-eau-tiful," Gerry says, laughing and clapping. "I'm a-goin' fishing/everybody wishin'/that they were hangin' out in Namu."

Namu to Shelter Bay

JULY 28

When we awake, the *Blue Fjord* has gone. We delay leaving
until the fog lifts and spend a pleasant morning of coffee and
conversation with Gerry and Niki in the main lodge. Niki has
a bowl of kingfisher feathers. "Poor fellow," she says. "Flew
into the window."

More fishing boats are anchored in the harbor today, and
our friends prepare for their lodge guests, as human habitation
at Namu continues in three- to five-day fishing charters. As
we ready the kayaks, a boatload of men land an immaculate
wooden dinghy. They are starchy, wearing collared shirts and
slacks, completely misdressed for the place. As we squeeze
into the kayaks, one man pops his head from a first-floor
window of "The Edgewater." "Hey! Here it is! This is where
I lived!"

Then we are headed south once more. At Namu, where
Hunter Island arcs westward and NOAA has found room to
stamp a compass rose on the chart, Fisher Channel broadens
into Fitz Hugh Sound, which in some two days' time will
open to Queen Charlotte Sound, the exposed Pacific once
again. There is no fog as we paddle from Namu, gliding along

the Esso fuel dock, past the broad beach where cannery workers once swam. Soon the shore steepens, and every cove is claimed by gillnetters watching a clock, waiting for the start of another opening. Blotches of neon orange paint, modern-day pictographs, mark favorite net sites. At noon, the engines gun.

During a break in last night's singing, when conversation had drifted to the controversies about salmon fishing rights of the United States and Canada, Gerry had advanced the notion that the coastal river fisheries could be managed at each river, rather than at sea. "That way you would know where the fish came from. There wouldn't be any discussion about whose salmon they were. The fish would come to a river, and that would be the answer. People would just have to wait for them to return like they used to." All afternoon sockeye and coho leap from the sea, their entire bodies exposed before flopping sideways into the water. Restless energy. They are nearing home.

Inside Koeye Point, along the beach at the mouth of the Koeye River, we stop to lunch. We had heard about the development here, a small logging operation and a new wilderness lodge carved into it. But it is worse than we have imagined because the river mouth is so beautiful. The lodge is a cheap structure made to look elegant, which casts it even cheaper. We have also heard it was built without the proper paperwork, and the government has shut it down, at least temporarily. The ruin, the resources, the waste. Why not have built it at Namu five miles north, where development already exists?

Leaving the bay, we see the distant but definable flips of kayak paddles, and a single kayaker soon greets us. He is in a bright-red boat and thumbing coordinates into a GPS as if it were a video game. "I just came through Hakai Passage. Going to catch the ferry in Namu tomorrow. Do you have one of these things?" he says, holding the pocket-sized GPS.

"Not this trip," I say.

"No? You never get lost in the fog?"

"We try not to paddle in fog," I say, looking to Maren. "This is a busy place."

"When you have a two-week vacation, you can't help it," he responds, then disappears up the Koeye. Across the sound, sea fog obscures Hakai Passage. It is late July, and we are concerned about Kelp Head and Cape Caution, the two major points we must round in passing through Queen Charlotte Sound. Already this coast gains the familiar gnawed appearance of exposure and open sea. Two crossings approach— Rivers Inlet and Smith Sound—and we must meet them both in good weather. The milky stare of fog through Hakai is unsettling, but we must move on.

In haste, we bypass several white beaches pooled around small islands where we should have stopped, and when night is near, we find ourselves campless, the shore nothing but escarpments. In a deep cove where a pod of sailboats are anchored, a man and woman from a single-master, the *Segue*, tell us of a nice beach at low tide now behind an islet. It is a peculiar islet, half treeless and grassy as if shaved, half forested with a singular towering spruce. But like every other islet here it juts fifteen feet above the water in a dome of rock. The cavity on its back side is the small beach rapidly submerging with tide. It is a wonderful landing site, but the ascent to land is hideous, a climb over boulders some twenty feet high to a tier in the forest. We hoist everything, kayaks included, up the near-vertical incline, nesting them in a hollow. The camp evolves into a four-tiered town house—kitchen in the intertidal zone, kayaks on level two, miscellaneous bags and bear canisters on level three, and our bivouac bags—the first time we have used them—beneath the spruce on the island's summit.

As the waxing gibbous moon rises, we lie gazing up through the spiral of branches, cocooned in our bags. All night needles flutter down. The thud of falling cones. A vole scampers. Without the cover of the tent, I wake intermittently to check for rain, but the night is silent and bright, the round moon shining through the boughs. Breezes carry the clinking of halyards, and the tree, combing the air, seems to breathe.

JULY 29

Shreds of fog linger among the passages of Fish Egg Inlet, but otherwise it is clear. Last night's camp would have been unimaginable at the start of our trip. Now it seems routine, even easy, and we are sad to leave this site, this tree. In the early brassy light, we have discovered a clear-cut on one side of the bay, and as we pull from shore against the flooding tide, we see that an adjacent cove serves as a log storage area, stocked like a tinderbox with freshly cut trees. "They are coming," Maren says. The spruce, nearly five feet in diameter, is several hundred years old. Nothing grows beneath it, and we undoubtedly are not the first to sleep in its cover. How long will it remain? What a strange island. Why is it half shaven, half creeping with low vine? An old cut? A homestead? A burial? And why was this solitary giant spared among its peers atop this prairielike nub?

On the water, our narrow tracks dull the otherwise flashing mirror of the passage. Soon we notice small patches of tangle, the knobs of bedrock exposed like a spine, the first fresh clear-cuts in days. As we weave among the lowlands and islets, a razed hill passes before a forested slope, devastation in every glance.

This morning we are seeking fresh water. It has been more than a week since we had to gather water in a tarp. Before that, there was a stream north of Higgins Passage. We filled the water pillows from hoses at Ivory Island, Bella Bella, and Namu, and in this short distance of coast, the once gushing streams have nearly dried. So watering is a daily priority. Where some streams are marked, none exist, and we must prowl for them in other ways. This morning we spot one easily—the trough in the forest, the concave arc of the shore, a light-green lichen, the fresh runoff drawing fish and a frenzy of feeding birds and seals to its mouth.

By the end of Convoy Passage we first sense the ocean swell. To the west, Cape Calvert—the southern tip of Calvert Island—drops abruptly with a nose at the bottom. Wake from the large ships plying up Fitz Hugh Sound races shoreward as low-period sea waves, breaking the sea's regular tempo, crashing in sets of five to seven on shore.

Around a point we see the hazy shadow of Kelp Head, and beyond it, the fainter and flatter Cape Caution, the battered points laid out like carrots dangled before us. The *Discovery Coast* exits the channel and plods north, running its circuit like a jogger, its presence somehow both expected and surprising. As the ebb gains momentum, the water glazes over. A small fleet of sport-fishing boats trolling in aimless circles catch the sun like silver fish. Beyond them, across the water, are pockets of white beach.

Nearing shore, we must weave among the fishing boats. Each trails two or three lines, taut across the water like freshly spun web. The boats are filled with men, with big hats and cotton shirts with collars, perhaps a capless visor. Occasional whoops come when a catch is made or lost. There must be about two dozen boats total, pacing through the flopping fish.

The beach, a smooth sheen of white with a view across the Pacific and many miles inland, seems to mock last evening's stair climb. It is one of the finest beaches we have seen, and we stop early without debate. Tomorrow we cross Rivers Inlet and begin to negotiate the open waters of Kelp Head and Cape Caution. A rest will be good.

As the tide drains away, I climb to an outer shoal to explore the hulk of a shipwreck, its spars and ribs buckled over the rocks. It must have been at least fifty feet long, judging by the large timbers, an older boat, a seiner, perhaps, cast among the rocks like any driftwood by the indifferent tide. To the south lie the expansive beaches that we will see over the next days.

Dark clouds convene at sunset, and I snap on the rain fly. Fog builds over Kelp Head. A single sport-fishing boat ventures close, then, as if alarmed by our presence, speeds back to the others.

We ignite a fire on the sand in the eddy of a rock. It burns hot, sending sparks whirling into the night, and we stare long into its heart. When I return from collecting driftwood, Maren has scrawled I LOVE BYRON with a stick in the sand. Dry cedar tossed on the fire instantly crackles into flame. We hold each other, holding tight, comfortable in one another's silence, a stillness between us that is stunning when we open to it, a gift that is received again on this long voyage. In the night wind we sit staring across to the open horizon of ocean from a beach that unbelievably still exists this late in this century.

JULY 30

This morning, the fire is a black stain in the sand trailing sweeps of charcoal that run like watercolors with the receding tide. Today we slowly move into traditional Kwakwaka'wakw territory, the outer heads of the mainland, the beaches. Again, so subtly a different region. Astonishingly, the archipelago of cloud I saw last night is still above, and as we set out among the small islets, the lofty networks of billowing cloud and blue strangely resemble the coast ahead. I can clearly make out the bulges of Kelp Head and Cape Caution, the rift of Smith Sound, in the stratocumulus. The images are almost exact, down to the islets, reflections above the actual land forms. To the south, a large cumulonimbus forms Vancouver Island, and between it and a fragmented cloud mass to the east is a narrowing split of sky—Queen Charlotte Strait.

Rationally, I dismiss these patterns: clouds blowing across a random sky. But I am moved by the uncanny correlation in a deeper way that I cannot fully articulate. In my heart it becomes a sign, the raw feeling that we will proceed safely through this treacherous area of open surf and gray headlands. After watching the suction and swirls of my paddle for perhaps a mile, I am moved most of all by the thought that we are here and are—at least once in a lifetime—able to see the land, sea, and sky unfold in the direction we are headed.

Rivers Inlet is a quiet, billowing sea. The swell is low and dizzying. At one meter tall it's not dangerous but unnerving, the power that is out there, surging toward land. We spend so much energy contemplating the hazards of the open ocean that we are suddenly across, greeted by a second swarm of sport-fishing boats trolling along the cliffs. Without a landing site, however, we must paddle to the expansive beaches nearer the headland before going ashore. All morning the broad beaches of Kelp Head have shone bright against the forest. They are the largest beaches we have seen, fine sand, between a half mile and a mile long. Waiting offshore, we monitor the steep silvery curl of crashing waves. Surf.

"I'll go in first," I say. "Remember to brace against the wave if you twist sideways."

Timing the waves, I wait just outside the breaker zone for a lull, then paddle hard. But I have chosen incorrectly. The backwash is so great that I cannot move ahead; a big wave is coming in, and I am pulled backward into high, turning foam. Instantly, I am hurling toward the beach, skidding sideways, leaning against the wave. Then I hit sand, which flops the kayak on its side, flooding it with seawater. I squirm onto the beach, drenched.

"Nice!" shouts Maren from outside the breakers.

"All right. *You* try."

She does, timing it expertly, scooting ashore and hopping free, radiant. Dry.

Within an hour we are paddling again, and the afternoon blow, a stiff northwesterly, is well underway. Although Kelp Head is only two miles wide, it seems longer, with wind waves stacking on swells and hitting us from the beam and from behind, shattering on the granite. We rise and sink from sight. Spray bathes the shore, and every few strokes a breaker slaps my hull. We steer into the narrow pass between Tie Island and Extended Point, hoping to take a shortcut, but the waves steepen, and we must rudder. Then comes the blast of a whale, unbelievably close to the rocks. Is it grounded? Injured? It occupies the only passage, and it seems as if we may skim right over it. It blows again. A gray. We are flying. Somehow, at the last moment, it sinks away, and with the wind howling near thirty knots, we round the point and into dampening waves, behind Shield Island and into the respite of a deep cove. The beach marked as a dotted line is a pile of rocks. Anchored in mid cove is a familiar craft—the *Segue*, the sailboat we saw two days ago.

"You're making good time!" shouts a man in dazzling clothes, who introduces himself as Tony. "Why don't you come for dinner? I'll bring you the solar shower."

Bushwhacking uphill, Maren finds camp on a high bluff, and assembles a tent pad out of the foundation of an all but nonexistent cabin, piecing bleached plywood together, pulling rusty nails. The view is spectacular, looking east up Smith Sound to the peaks of the interior. As I bathe, the rock I stand on breaks in half, slashing my foot. It is not a deep gash, but it is an irksome one. Injured while showering. I am out of practice, perhaps. More than anything, our feet suffer the abuses, and they are most vital yet most exposed, constantly wet in neoprene. This could prove complicated if it does not close in a few days. I bend over the foot as the flap of skin fills with blood.

Aboard the *Segue*, dinner is plentiful and fresh: crab cakes, yams, potatoes, beans. Tony's wife, Jane, a teacher, reads Paul Theroux and talks often of exotic travels. Tony, a superior yachtsman, tells of racing days and various voyages, the yacht club in Vancouver, and the finer points of navigation and tactics. "I hope you will be done by the end of August," he says. "That's always stormy. The seasons have to reorganize. At the yacht club we don't even plan to travel then."

It is a pleasant evening, one we can relax and enjoy away from camp chores. With Kelp Head behind, once we round Cape Caution and obtain the shelter of Vancouver Island, we will enter the final third, the home stretch—down the narrows of Johnstone Strait, the Discovery Islands, the Gulf Islands, the San Juans, and home to Puget Sound. In musical terms, "segue" means a transition or to continue without pause, and this idea carries into the evening a meaning for us all its own.

As Tony putters us through the blackness, landing the dinghy among the low-tide cobbles, the moon rises, and at camp it shines round and full over Smith Sound. The sky is cloudless. If I stand strategically, I can frame the moon in spruce boughs—one of my favorite scenes. And after a time, the glare is so bright I must look away.

AUGUST 1

We paddled little yesterday, crossing only Smith Sound before collapsing on this expansive orange beach. Early this morning a wolf visited the sand, leaving arcs of paw prints that melt away where the latest high tide has swept the beach completely smooth. With their padded centers and splayed claw marks, the prints form squares like the fiery stars of Pegasus.

At 4:00 A.M. it was sprinkling, and now, looking out to the Pacific, a purple storm cell has touched the water. We are nervous about Cape Caution. The name is enough. Vancouver, who named this point, nearly foundered his ship, the *Discovery*, on a rock some fifteen miles southeast of here in August 1792. Perhaps the ships whose tatters lie along the past beaches met their fate by similar mistakes. The abundance of wreckage along these crenellated shores far exceeds idle coincidence. For two nights we have been with them. It is enough to make us cautious, indeed. Will we round Cape Caution before the storm moves onto land?

As we approach the cape, the already sparse trees shrink, flagged beyond recognition by winter's hurricane-force winds. The sea is metallic, heaving with swell. Knotted bull kelp seems to tie stray rocks to shore. Everything is in tranquil motion—rising, falling, sloshing, slopping, swaying, fanning in the sea.

A whale blows. This is the quiet water in which one expects something from the deep to erupt suddenly, that a leviathan will suddenly hurl its bulk into the air and crash down, shattering the seamless horizon. Then it breathes again, a dusty jet melting away, the rubbery mass sinking in the same place beneath a curl of water, asleep.

Broad beaches open and close, nested behind arms of rock, in sight for less than a minute as we skirt among the shoals.

Fishing boats, white against the rolling slate, troll past us. At the head of one of the beaches, an entire barge rests in the forest, set down among cedar and spruce by an unthinkable wave.

Approaching Cape Caution, the sea ripples in an odd and unpredictable way, and a fog descends until we can see no farther than ten yards. For the next two hours we are blind again and must make our way by sound, listening to the way water meets the varying shore, comparing the sound with the chart, then listening again.

A whale we never see parallels us on the ocean side for several miles, its breaths exploding through the surface, marking our seaward boundary. We look at the compass, then study the chart to see if it all makes sense. Beaches roar, waves toppling and rolling along the surface in a lethal line of breakers as if we are approaching a waterfall. As beach changes to rocky headland, the waves hush and steepen. But most of the shores are bouldered, peppered with crashing surf and pockets of sudden and dark silence, where from the white air a boulder slips past like an asteroid. Then the breath of a whale.

As the fog rises, we hear distant engines and foghorns from the west, and a floatplane roars overhead, tracking the coast. At last the sky opens to an expansive beach with ranks of waves tumbling across the shallows. This beach is wild, one of the longest on the coast, and our footprints seem to be the first on Earth.

The sky purples again at sunset, a complete cycle. We have shaken the habit of our other lives, the arbitrary clockwork of society, and live now with the tides, with light and darkness in a freedom that we gained simply through embarking on this journey. Will we see another full moon before reaching the endless bright of Puget Sound? Every contemporary traveler in the wilds must wrestle with this thought, this other life.

Tomorrow we play the chess game of getting in position to cross Queen Charlotte Strait and the mouth of Nakwakto Rapids, one of the swiftest tidal currents in the world. Near last light, the northern tip of Vancouver Island uncloaks, its mountainous outline billowing like the shadow of an approaching front.

AUGUST 2

As the low-pressure center dissipates, the clouds tear apart and rise. The water ahead is gray; beyond, where there is sun, a line of blue. Waves roar across the flat sand, two and three rollers at a time, following each other in, and we launch straight into the surf. In a mile we are huddled in a cove, clutching whips of bull kelp, waiting for slack at Nakwakto.

Swells pile to towering hummocks where the surging ebb meets the incoming swell at Nakwakto's Outer Narrows in Slingsby Channel. Nakwakto is the only exit to many miles of inland fiords, and with such a volume of water to exchange, the tidal current can reach sixteen knots of thunder and spray. Like tidal rapids up and down the coast, the Nakwakto is known as a prime fishing ground, and this was home to the Nakwoktak band of the Kwakwaka'wakw, who had dwellings and fish camps throughout the area. The rapids guarded their villages from all but the Haida and Tsimshian invaders—and the lethal waves of smallpox that ravaged the coast in the early and mid-1800s.

Although we are only crossing its mouth, we must still wait for slack, which lasts for only about six minutes here. Fifteen minutes from slack ebb, the water has changed little. Nakwakto is the first of the many tidal torrents we will face inside Vancouver Island, and we see that this final segment, too, will have its perils.

Sensing the calming water, we let go of the kelp and paddle into the open. Eerily, there is no sound, no rush of water, and crossing is like riding the wind. Troughs are cavernous, and the watery walls appear as if they could curve and topple at any moment. But they do not. Looking ahead is like peering through a tube. At the crests, we can see deep into the channel at the heart of Nakwakto, where the full strength of the current wraps around Turret Rock. Then we drop back into the cavern.

In ten minutes the water flattens, the sea wind subsides, and we are across and paddling down the shores of Bramham Island. Behind us, the sea just beyond Nakwakto remains confused and steep. A solitary troller waits in Miles Inlet. The shore is fractured, as though it has been reset and bonded by a mason, and tiny coves burrow into otherwise inaccessible walls. These cuts are no more than two meters wide, stuffed with cobblestones, boulders, and driftwood. At high tide they flood completely. Gradually, the swell diminishes as Queen Charlotte Sound gives way to Queen Charlotte Strait. At last we are within the growing protection of Vancouver Island.

A blue tarp breaks the accustomed forest green, and a skiff motors near an island and circles a gray whale. Someone waves and invites us for tea in their makeshift camp in Skull Cove. At the entrance, these whale researchers have built a humanlike figure from balanced stones. This Inuit symbol carries the same meaning as it does in the high Arctic, signaling with outstretched arms that this place is safe for people. Over steaming teacups and crackers, they tell us of their research on gray whales and their new ecotourism business along this remote area of coast. When we ask about camp possibilities, they suggest Shelter Bay. "You'll find a 'Club Med' beach there," the director says.

The rest of the day is serene. Inside the Southgate Group—a collection of pleasant, low islands—we grab hold of a log raft tied to a cliff. The logs are skinned and battered, bound with thick steel cable, tagged like the totem poles in the Ketchikan museum, like animals to be set free for tracking. Some logs are splotched with blue and green paint. Many are large, a few feet in diameter, while others are mere spindles. All are freshly cut, the bark still raw and red, but no cuts are in sight. Perhaps the raft has been helicoptered from an interior operation or simply stashed between tug runs. Past the raft, brilliant orange lichen drips from the rocks. It is so bright that it seems as if Earth has split open to its molten interior.

The beach in Shelter Bay is powdery, like volcanic ash. It is an ecotourism site, used by at least two kayak companies that are just beginning to lead kayaking tours here. Tent sites are plantless, and a crude table has been fashioned from boards and driftwood. To us, the camping is easy, even luxurious, but dirty. Nearby, a stranded floating home has been gutted, and styrofoam particles from its floats are strewn about the forest like snowflakes. After dinner, a deer mouse hops into one of our empty bear canisters, shuffling and jumping but unable to scamper up the slick walls. Luckily, it did not find the granola.

We ponder the weather and pray for a clear, calm crossing. In midbay, a single motorboat spins around its anchor. They have been out for six weeks and have had trouble finding fuel on the north coast. The owner explains, "We stopped in Namu, but it was closed, so we had to buy gas from some Indians in Bella Bella and limp up to Klemtu on two gallons, where there was the first real fuel dock. It can get dangerous up there. We're going to power over to Port Hardy tomorrow."

"So are we," I say.

"Ha! Boy, in those? How long will that take?"

"A day or two if the weather is good. You?"

"Oh, two or three hours."

While checking the tide table, my headlamp flickers to the sickly yellow of drained batteries. All evening, as the tide sinks, the powerboater checks the depth beneath his craft. At one point he sees me watching and gives a thumbs up. "Still four feet!"

Crossing Queen Charlotte Strait

All night we smelled sulfur, and at low tide this morning it leaks in yellowish stains from the beach, the sand gassy, like rising dough.

Fog banks again. We paddle past a barnlike fish farm to the Wallace Islands and dawdle, waiting for the fog to lift. Crossing Queen Charlotte Strait—or "the straits," as it is known here—involves several small crossings, using the strings of islands as stepping stones, and sprinting across the lengthy and trafficked channels to rest among the island medians.

The Alaska State Ferry speeds past our opening in the rocks, slipping north in Richards Channel. It is the *Columbia* again, our ship. Every corner brings us full circle, and often we feel as though we are at once at the beginning, the middle, and near the end of this journey. From the forest, a raven calls *klok*, *ah-ho*, *klok*, the voice echoing like water drops in a cave. We have not heard this familiar bird for many weeks, perhaps since Alaska.

As distant islands materialize, we nose into Richards, leery of a repeat of Fisher Channel. Two sailboats, old underpowered schooners, motor against the tide. We wait for them, hovering just outside the shipping lane, scanning for traffic. We look for distant specks and spot one, very distant. There always seems to be at least one. And passing to the stern of the slow boats, we begin the dash to the Millar Group, still shadows in the haze.

The sailboats are extravagant, the mobile homes of the Inside Passage, full of stereos, books, wet bars, kitchens, full beds, and showers. They skirt from anchorage to anchorage, where they stop and drop the hook in deep, soft-bottomed coves that have become the coastal equivalent of RV parks. When possible, we avoid "good anchorages." When the sail-boats pass, the people wave, and one white-bearded man lingers on deck, giving a brief salute before turning to work the halyard. The dusky distant speck has now materialized into a black-hulled seiner pushing up white waves around its bow.

Once we leave the Millar Group, a tug parade routes down Richards Channel, and the little-traveled Ripple Passage is a relief. Rafts of gulls twirl in the eddy lines.

Gradually, the innermost stirrings of Queen Charlotte Sound, the shudders of ocean swell dissipate—the last we will feel of the open Pacific. It is a joyous moment, for suddenly it seems as if we are so close to making it, the two outer waters now behind us. White feathers spatter the sea and float unwet on the surface tension. Maren sings. We are back inside.

In the middle of Ripple Passage, we gauge our headway to the Walker and Deserters Groups partially by the regular floatplanes that rumble overhead, old Grummans that cater to resorts in Smith and Rivers Inlets. Where before they routed ahead of us on their half-hourly shuttles, they now track behind, angling above the water toward the broad beaches of Cape Caution. Clouds descend over Vancouver Island. When we were aboard the ferry, this shore was boiling with surf, and I was restless and slowly sickened. It was our first confrontation with the power of the sea. And still we are obsessed with its ways, wanting to know exactly where we are, how far from land, and how fast we are approaching it. Always we are plotting direction with our senses, discerning where the current is flowing, speculating when the wind might revive, anticipating how each paddle stroke will thrust us.

We stop for lunch in an uninhabited cove in the Walker Group, the middle islands, standing on cobbles covered by seaweed, moss padding the kayaks. By afternoon the water has surprisingly calmed, and we continue across Gordon Channel, across the turning tide. Waiting for a cruise ship, we paddle to the edge of the shipping lane. Although the traffic has cleared, the current is fast, and the tide drags us sideways into lumpy water. Maren leads our weave among the rips to Bell Island, at last bumping onto a beach of unusually smooth cobbles.

Fatigued, wanting to cross the last channel to Vancouver Island, and unsure whether to continue to Port Hardy, we try to reserve a room in town using the VHF. After several tries, we contact the Cape Caution marine operator, who patches us to the Port Hardy Chamber of Commerce reservation service. As we muddle through the awkward transmission of stutters and delays, the weather deteriorates, fog forming to the south and drizzle falling from the north. When I finally reach the customer-service representative, a dorsal fin rips across the bay. "Orca!" I shout into the radio.

Silence. Finally: "Your credit-card number, please."

"Sorry. We are in kayaks. I just saw an orca."

Silence. Then muffled background chatter: "He's in a kayak. . . . I don't know. 'Orca' was the last thing I heard."

"Hello. I'm here."

Silence. Then: "Your credit-card number, please."

The orca surfaces again; one of nearly ten whales, moving south with the tide along the coast. It registers that these smooth stones on Bell Island are a prelude to the rubbing beaches at Robson Bight where the whales brush against those smooth stones, loosening parasites or perhaps simply enjoying a massage.

Soon the orcas are gone, and we have a bed-and-breakfast booked in Port Hardy for two nights, starting tomorrow. The drizzle descends. One more crossing: Goletas Channel. Heard

Island is clear-cut, and clear-cuts line Vancouver Island. Trails are hacked through the salal, and floating cabins dot almost every cove. We examine another fish farm, the whole operation—nets with fish flapping about like kids in a crowded pool—floats on oil drums. Two luckless fishermen drift nearby, spinning in the current that will shoot us across to Vancouver Island.

The drizzle that has been advancing down Vancouver Island, blotting out the hills, at last deluges. What we had thought to be a barge is actually a pod of floating buildings, a fishing lodge. Paddling to the dock, we are greeted by Lyle, a jovial man who invites us to stay for dinner. "You must try Lyle's red sauce," he says. "You simply must try Lyle's red sauce. There is no not trying Lyle's red sauce." The skiff that was near the fish farm pulls in. "We've caught three so far," Lyle says. "Tonight we feast!"

Dinner is a luscious spread of grilled salmon, turkey salad, Romaine lettuce, fresh Parmesan, cracked-wheat rolls, and tortellini bathed in Lyle's red sauce. Snickers for dessert. The reception is tremendous after the long paddle but a shock, as well. It is so easy. Despite the lack of television and phones, this rustic lodge has running water, hot showers, a complete kitchen, and a sturdy roof. They are a group of university alums and staff on an annual retreat. Only one woman is among them. "I'm sure you'll want this," she says, handing Maren her blow-dryer. Maren smirks, hesitates, then extends her hand.

Despite these jolts from our routine, we celebrate, for we are extremely lucky. Again we have met the right people, paddling as if directed to their dock from across this vast water.

An older man who has explored the Queen Charlottes in a small boat talks over dinner of his dream to travel the southern coast of South America. "It's the mirror of this coast," he says. "Similar latitudes, broken and carved by glaciers into beautiful islands." He carries a dignity with his age and wants to hear of our inner experiences. The global perspective he brings to the table is elegant, and as he talks, I imagine the polar caps growing, inundating the farthest reaches of land, then sucking back, the extremes of the continents revealed, scarred and smoothed and new. He seems to have lived his years in reverence.

Other conversations swell with discussion about the scenery, more talk of wild things than we have heard in wilder places. Books stack the coffee table: *The Last of the Arctic, Wild Animals, The World Beneath the Sea*. It all signals a reduction. With this crossing, something has come to a close, an elemental wildness that exists across the murky waters of Queen Charlotte Strait. From here we face a gradual, perhaps sudden, reentry to the cities, to the lives there that we can hardly remember. Today we brushed the first few molecules of this great atmosphere, deflecting the first frictions of society and stress. Even at this fringe, there is an intensity that we have been away from.

So we are here at last, Vancouver Island, paddling from months of dark nights on remote beaches to a well-furnished floating resort, welcomed among people who have taken the better part of a week to relax and get away from it all.

AUGUST 4

The fishermen are up and grumbling at 5:00 A.M., but we sleep. Fog and drizzle cloak the strait, and we are glad to have made it across yesterday. When islands are visible, they are fuzzy, as if we are peering through a frosted pane. We say good-bye after a lengthy and filling breakfast, then paddle the few uneventful miles into Port Hardy, landing on a beach that surrounds the chamber of commerce office. Our bed-and-breakfast is ready. And after loading the kayaks and gear into the innkeeper's pickup truck and riding in the back, parading through the streets like brightly dressed clowns, we arrive.

Waiting for the shower, I switch on the radio. The AM band is all murmurs, whistles, and static. The FM receives a strong signal from a weather station, and somewhere near the middle of the dial blares a talk show, Canadian Public Radio. This second station is a significant find, one that takes a few moments to register. This is the first time we have received more than one radio station. We are within range of something distant, something large. Twisting the knob a quarter turn brings the strongest signal yet: "Good times and great oldies serving northern Vancouver Island. That was the Stones with a classic from '64, 'Time Is on My Side.' "

GOING INSIDE

Port Hardy to Alder Bay

AUGUST 7

For two days we run errands, receiving our final food shipment, changing charts for the journey down the inside of Vancouver Island to southern Puget Sound, and finally mailing home winter clothes we have now carried into August. After the thrill of first phone messages and showers, town is annoying. The days seem fragmented and inessential, and Port Hardy greets us in a few irregular parcels, sights, comments, and conversations.

Today, on the final morning, as I prepare my toast, I reach past the Fruit Whirles for the honey. The jar's label reads: FIREWEED HONEY—ANOTHER FINE CLEARCUT PRODUCT. The back of the label declares: "North Island Citizens for Shared Resources promotes the balanced use of resources by advocating the preservation of special places, and protecting the working forest." When I ask a tablemate what makes a place special, I am soon told a philosophy about logging. "Look, trees are going to die eventually. Why not cut them down?"

When the pickup truck delivers us to the beach, someone says to our host, "I thought you didn't like them people, kayakers." The last impression of town is a sign above the toilet in a unisex rest room: THE DISCOLORATION OF THE WATER IS DUE TO WEATHER CONDITIONS AND IS NOT HARMFUL TO YOUR HEALTH. Then we step from the manicured lawn and onto the beach.

Rhinocerous Auklets pop up, then dive again, flicking their tails. Admiring the small tuft on their beak, Maren says that they are wearing spectacles. By the opposite shore of Hardy Bay, the water is murky, an olive color, but clearing. A skiff crosses our path, twin 225 horses foaming, its bow completely free of the water, the aquatic equivalent of a monster truck.

The first week of August is nearly gone. On this misty day we feel behind. Tomorrow, we hope to meet Maren's sister Laura in Alder Bay, and Maren's energy has received a boost.

Shedding layers in town was good. Without the bulk of heavy clothes, a large knife, vise grips, and a few collected rocks, the kayak is noticeably more responsive. We retained the hatchet, the bow saw, and the lawn clippers for the cruder camps; it is hard to know how difficult or easy camping will be ahead. At some point, we must begin to stay in parks.

It has been days since we have been away from engines, and rounding Dillon Point, I can at last hear the footsteps of Maren's kayak, her paddles dipping through the water. As we pole through a thick kelp bed, the morning fog lifts, and the expanse of Queen Charlotte Strait obtains a peaceful brilliancy.

The salmon leap high and often. Once, I come within a foot of grabbing one from the air. Suddenly Port Hardy seems long ago, so quickly gone behind this thumb of land. Ahead is Fort Rupert, the first time we have paddled through two communities in a single day since Bartlett Cove and Gustavus. Yet for some reason Fort Rupert looks strange, lacking a presence on the water. There is no dock, no wharf. The sweeping pebble-and-cobble beach curves unobstructed behind the islands of Beaver Harbor, silvered at its upper reaches by drift logs. It is little different than many of our beach camps, and the town greets us like it has greeted visitors for centuries: as paddlers.

While Maren stays with our kayaks to move them out across the flats with the ebbing tide, I climb a few streets to the Copper Maker gallery and find a carver at work. He glances up and smiles when I enter, then quietly goes back to his mask. In brisk strokes he shaves cedar away. One side of the mask is completely painted, while the face he works is only roughly tooled. As if reading braille, he fingers both sides, comparing depths and curves; then without further measure, he takes wood from the unpainted hollow of an eye. With each thunk of steel against cedar, the yellow wood flies like sparks, showering him with his element. The air is sweet, as if strolling through a forest, and the floor is soft with cedar chips. For a half hour I watch him shape the piece, his tools polished to a keen silver by the soft, straight grain.

He is an artisan of the old ways, and it is thrilling to see something being made by hand, to observe a human touch turned to force and then to form. The strokes are large and confident, and I wince, believing he will misstrike and irreparably gouge the wood. But he does not. His technique is brawny yet exact, nothing like timid etchings made with a pen knife. Then he quiets, puts his adze on the floor, and lifts the dancer's mask high.

"Say hello to Raven," he says.

When I return to the kayaks, I see that Maren has anchored them with stones ten feet from shore and gone to walk near the big house, the traditional long house of the Kwakiutl. From among the beach grasses, I glimpse her strolling along the high cedar walls and carvings. At my feet, clam shells overturned like washbasins still hold tidewater on the dry shore. Laundry from shorefront homes snaps in the breeze, near satellite dishes. The scene is at once contemporary and ancient. The new homes, the big house, the open beach, the Inside Passage.

The day now bright and blue, we paddle to the edge of town, landing on a beach of polished stones that shine even when dry. Behind the shorefront homes, in a small glade of amber grass and thimbleberries, stands a tower about twenty-five feet high constructed of flat, dark stones, the hearth of the Hudson's Bay fort that gave the town its current name. The berries are ripe and juicy, and we eat many. Behind the chimney stand more buildings, unpainted, weathered, and barnlike, and one can still envision the old fort surrounded by the community.

Much has descended on this place. In 1888 anthropologist Franz Boas met a local man, George Hunt, and started a relationship with the Kwakiutl here that lasted four decades. Near the turn of the century, photographer and filmmaker Edward S. Curtis relied on George Hunt's knowledge of Kwakiutl culture for filming *In the Land of the War Canoes* on these beaches and the shores of nearby islands or across the straits in Blunden Harbor. But Hunt, who had grown up in Fort Rupert and knew the Kwakiutl language and ways, was of Tlingit and English ancestry. His mother was a Tlingit noblewoman who had married Robert Hunt, a Hudson's Bay employee. And it was George Hunt's mother who commissioned a large totem pole that once stood before a house here. It replicated a family pole, one that had been stolen from her island village in Alaska by a group of Seattle businessmen in 1899.

Embedded in the beach is the skeleton of a car chassis— engine, drive train, four brittle tires. As we paddle away, images mix like a tide rip: cedar and the totem pole, the small island in Alaska and this beach in Kwakiutl country, a family's long collaboration with Boas and Curtis, now a car sunken among these glossy stones, the prelude to the great rubbing beaches of Robson Bight, the meeting place of orcas—and our intersection with it all. Again we are at a nexus, where our lives as paddlers have mingled with these many lives and places. Day after day we have joined the web of connections along this passage, this broken coast made one by water.

All afternoon we paddle with a tailwind along the pebbled and cobbled shores of polished black rock. The land is low— the recognizable footpad of ice. On Malcolm Island a light station stands like a grain silo in the evening sun. Malcolm is flat and sandy, and its only town, Sointula, glistens in the first darkness.

We make camp on a sand spit near the Cluxewe River. An immense stump washed from the river seems now to be planted in the littoral zone, and the rising tide reduces it to a wooden island. Down the beach, a mobile-home park glows with campfires and an overhang of smoke. A white cruise ship passes near, a plume of yellow exhaust blowing ahead of its bow as the northwesterly whitecaps the strait all evening.

AUGUST 8

Beaches stretch as far as we can see, and Maren is excited about meeting Laura. For a time we hover off a point in the channel between Port McNeill, the timber capital of northern Vancouver Island, and Sointula, an old Finnish utopian community, marveling at the irony of it all. Then we paddle on among the half-logged islands toward the shining antennae of Alert Bay.

Today, we were woken by the scream of auto tires racing along Highway 19, which runs nearly the length of Vancouver Island. The forest now is uniform, second growth replanted like hybrid corn. Has been since Port Hardy. Below this forest line, along the margins of towns, the beaches are manicured, boulders pushed aside like canoe pulls sans canoes. Some homes are truly giants, new homes on this old coast. Twenty-eight windows on one, forty-four on another. We can look across the water and see the movement of cars, the flash of windshields and chrome work. "How much utopia and industry look alike," I had said to Maren as we floated between Port McNeill and Sointula. We both feel inundated—the towns, the logging. Cables and shipping lanes now crisscross the chart. Gray roadways, disguised as topographic lines, snake along shore. But still we paddle, the bow parting the world ahead, the blade grabbing the water pulling us along. Near Port NcNeill a black bear crawls from the forest, bringing broad smiles to both of us.

In several miles, the shore drops to the Nimpkish delta,

the river flowing from a magnificent estuary. The water is shallow, so we must walk our kayaks over a gravel bar. As the river current meets the opposing tide, ripples break upon themselves, standing waves about a foot high, lapping at the bow, nudging us seaward. The estuary is rich in salmon, and a fishing eagle startles as we pass too near, breaching the mysterious threshold between species, the distance of uncertainty and caution. We hover there ourselves, ready to alight, to turn north again and flee to Cape Caution.

Ahead is Alder Bay and the campground where we are to meet Laura. It is remarkable that such a rendezvous is possible, given the unpredictability of our days, the tides, the winds. Arranging the meeting from Port Hardy was difficult, not knowing if we would plan the meeting for a day too late, a day too early.

Like any village we have paddled toward, the campground grows before us for some time, its graded lanes ascending from the beach, its boxy mobile homes. Usually Maren loves to talk about villages and developments as we approach them, assessing them as a planner, searching for their community center, remarking on mistakes made in creating and utilizing open space, pleased or displeased that they have contained or not contained the sprawl, or whether their natural waterfront is or is not intact. But here she is squinting, looking for her sister. And finally a figure rises from a beach log and walks slowly toward the water, the form materializing as Laura. Maren whistles and begins to sing as she races far ahead. By the time I nose ashore, they are hugging and crying with joy.

We show Laura our gear, the bear canisters, and go about our chores. Several times she tugs on my beard and laughs. After tasting the spaghetti leather, she suggests eating in town the next evening. We agree that Alder Bay is an appropriate name for a campground in a clear-cut, for the alders are often the first trees to reclaim the treeless expanses. The campground is a city of ephemeral homes with a town commons of an ice, bait, and registration station. It seems to replay the whole history of so many coastal towns on a weekly basis: booming every summer Friday, busting on Monday. At dinner we astound Laura by telling her that this is our first camp with a picnic table.

While Maren and Laura catch up, I walk the grounds and gather names.

Mobile homes: The Elite, Vacationer, Pace Arrow, Frontier, Prowler, Cascade, Coronado, Easy Ride, Triple E, Aristocrat, Mallard, Millennium, Timberline, Tockwood, Encore, Holiday Rambler (Endeavor model), Sportscoach, Okanagan, Brave, Itasca, Corsair, Vogue, Vanguard, Southwind, Establishment, Sunrise, Sprite, Komfort, Western Wilderness, Chinook, Senior Country Cruiser, Slumber Queen.

Boats: Invader, Trophy, Ocean Sport, Islander, Starcraft, Polaris, Explorer.

They are portable utopias, the names echoing Captain Cook's ship, the *Endeavor* and Captain Vancouver's ships, the *Resolution* and the *Discovery*. We have entered the Leisure Belt.

It is strange to be camping amid so many people. Sport fishermen carry beheaded salmon. A dozen kayakers return in bright boats from a guided trip to see the orcas in Johnstone Strait. Septuagenarians stroll about with Thermoses of tea and coffee. Young bucks puff on cigars around a fire and urinate on the wheels of their boat trailer. By the fish-cleaning facility, scales silver the dock, and a cache of halibut carcasses lap in the waves. Salmon heads have been haphazardly severed by the weekend fishermen, leaving hunks of good red meat for the gulls.

Laura and Maren are engulfed in conversation until we must sleep. All night the headlights of late campers sweep past. Shadows lurch in half-lit trailers. Gravel crunches beneath tires. No darkness tonight, but the tide reaches high and, as predicted, falls away.

AUGUST 9

Although the antennae of Alert Bay shine above the fog, I cannot see the world's tallest totem pole. I paddle early and alone to bean-shaped Cormorant Island and stride in neoprene boots along Alert Bay's waterfront to the U'Mista Cultural Center to see the potlatch collection. When potlatches were outlawed in 1884, they and winter ceremonies went underground. In 1921, despite the government ban, a potlatch was held on nearby Village Island, and many involved were arrested, the regalia—the coppers, masks, and rattles—confiscated and scattered among museums and private collections. The law was repealed in 1951, and U'Mista has repatriated the lost items with great success. As I stroll the gallery, the old masks are displayed on poles, unenclosed, so the spirits freely visit.

At Alder Bay, fascinated with utopian Sointula, we break the paddling routine to take the ferry to Malcolm Island with Laura. A woman on the ferry strikes up a conversation, and we slip, perhaps in apologizing for my haggard beard, and tell her of the journey. "Up here it's muscles and brawn," she responds. "People fishing and logging. But where you're heading on the Sunshine Coast, it's artsy-fartsy easy life. You can even swim in the water it's so warm."

Walking off the ferry, a teenager waits for her mother. "Need help?" she asks boldly. "I'm a local."

"What should we see in this utopian town?" I ask.

"Utopia. Yeah, people still talk about it, try to keep that thing going, but it isn't working very well. Everyone's gone fishing so much. We have to make money. That's what takes utopia away, the moneymaking."

We stop for orange juice in the grocery. On a window is painted: THE SOINTULA COOPERATIVE STORE ASSOCIATION WELCOMES VISITORS TO MALCOLM ISLAND. OUR STORES ARE OWNED BY THE RESIDENTS OF THE ISLAND.

We wander through town. "Sointula" is Finnish for "harmony"—an inspiration for Laura, who is a jazz pianist and composer. The homes are colorful, neat, sturdy square frames

with an air of efficiency. On a glade overlooking Cormorant
Channel, we pause in the cemetery and ramble among the
stones reading names: Jarvis, Helmi, Sundstrom, Salmi, Han-
nukainen, Siider, Jakola, Wirkki. Many lived into the early
1920s. Some graves have sunken into the ground, with bushes
now prying through their headstones; others are mounds of
fresh rock. Bees visit tall daisies among the graves. This is the
most tranquil spot in town and abides with the spirit that the
founders carried with them across the North Atlantic.

A clomping horse and a girl on bicycle follow us back to
the landing. Waiting for the ferry, we enjoy hot tea and scones
and ask the shopkeeper about Sointula. "This is absolute
Eden," she says, leaning over the counter with a dishrag. "I
just moved here from Vancouver. I never want to move, ever
never ever. It's a utopia, yes. When I got here, people sat me
down and told me what it's like to be a fisherman's wife.
Things happen erratically, here and there, you go when you
go."

Her husband chuckles, having just returned from a month
of fishing in Prince Rupert.

"I've been in town two months," she continues. "Spot,
the town dog, will walk you home; people wave . . . not at
all like the city, where you have to look down. I want to live
here the rest of my life."

"Have you been here in winter?" Maren asks.

"Winter? Yeah, we just get six months of rain. But I
love rain."

Her husband sits quietly until we inquire about the orcas.

"We have orcas, about thirty of them. They drive salmon
into nets. We like them around, except when we're diving.
When I go down to unwrap our end line from the prop, I
don't have the courage to look behind."

Alder Bay to Refuge Cove

AUGUST 10

Saying a long good-bye to Laura, we leave Alder Bay in the fog. Today we must cross Johnstone Strait and expect another meeting with the orcas. Within a few miles, broad Queen Charlotte Strait thins to Johnstone Strait, a slender channel that separates Vancouver Island from the high mainland, a dip between the mountainous bulks that once flowed with Pleistocene ice. As we paddle, the morning cloud lifts, and we are surrounded once more by salmon trollers.

In Telegraph Cove, a notch on the south side of Beaver Cove, we rest. The settlement is built around waterfront warehouses and boardwalks, and serves as the base for the most experienced whale watching group in Robson Bight, which is a few miles south in Johnstone Strait. "Except for the people and the parking lot, this sure looks like Namu," Maren says. Not more than a minute later, the *Blue Fjord* noses to dock.

"Hey! Hey! You two! You're already down here, eh?" shouts Michael, rushing a passenger to the airport. "Small coast."

It is like waving to neighbors.

When Michael returns, he kneels and points at the chart. "Here's what we were talking about in Namu. The orcas run a circuit here through Johnstone Strait, Blackney Pass, Blackfish Sound," he says as his finger circumnavigates Hanson, Swanson, and West Cracroft Islands. "So there's quite an alliance among the researchers and professional whale watchers. It's reciprocal. We need the whales for business. The researchers need us to help them track the whales for their studies. We talk on the VHF, on the whale channel. They take our observations seriously. Right now they are doing some research, measuring stress on the whales, changes in breathing rates, as boats get within a hundred meters. There are boats all over now. We've been doing this for ten years. It didn't used to be like that."

Then he recalls more recent encounters: "A-30 turned from the pod and came straight for us. Then a big blast of air out of nowhere . . ." His voice rises and falls with each surface and dive. In Namu, he handed me a business card, a picture of a humpback alongside the *Blue Fjord*. It showed a decisive moment. While Judy took the helm, Michael had jumped into the water with the whale and freed it from a heavy rope that bound its pectoral fins.

"We're going to a reunion with the orca research teams tomorrow. See you there?"

As we leave, they also depart. Ten minutes earlier or later, and we would have missed them.

Telegraph Cove is a built-up historic place where the telegraph line used to run through. Not more than a decade ago it was a quiet town of pile buildings and boardwalks, a dormant sawmill, and a few boats. Now the boardwalk is lined with gift shops and T-shirts emblazoned with orcas, posters of every kind of whale and dolphin. Stuffed orcas in three sizes. Whale dolls. The south side of the cove looks like a quarry. A shopkeeper says that condos are going in and that a golf course is slated for somewhere uphill. Telegraph Cove is what Namu was: a working place, then a quiet place. But it is a decade and a half beyond Namu now. And we are thankful that there are no roads to Namu just yet.

There has long been talk of a coastal highway, a ribbon of road that would cut along the shores and span the inlets to southeast Alaska. But such a project is expensive and impractical. The coast is the highway, the opponents say. Let it remain so.

As we paddle into Johnstone, two squadrons of Canada geese circle from the cove heading south. The air is cool, and for the first time in several days high clouds streak the sky, announcing rain. A stubby craft buzzes past, WHALE WATCH BY ZODIAC lettered on the hull, loaded with a foursome eager for encounter. Then we are on our own again.

Robson Bight is restricted, a patrolled ecological reserve, and people are strongly discouraged to enter reserve waters. Heavy fines slap those who set foot ashore, except commercial fishermen, who are currently exempt from reserve restrictions. We must reach the east side of Johnstone Strait and depart shore where a camp of kayakers, a tour group, is held up in a bay. Their boats are the larger tandem kayaks, bright colors lining the beach like a tray of pastels.

The islands ahead are light-brown volcanic rock and scoured bedrock, not the sands of Malcolm and Cormorant Islands, which are merely glacial deposits. The water is choppy, and a distinct current races near the Hanson Island shore. High on a cliff an orange tarp and a gray dome tent flap in the breeze. We cross directly to it and for a moment float beneath. A figure leans over the cliff and stares through binoculars, talking into a radio.

As we edge Hanson Island, a flotilla of kayaks rounds the bend. Another tour group, perhaps twenty tandem kayaks. The scene resembles the great hunting fleets of Russian-led baidarkas that pushed across the Gulf of Alaska in search of sea otter pelts. But these are ecotourists in search of whales, looking to shoot with ungainly reflex cameras. "You better hurry if you want to cross Blackney Passage," says the scruffy guide. "Tide's about slack now." And they paddle on. As a whole, their cadence is irregular, unpracticed, and they ride stiff and erect across the rolling carpet of sea. Their shortcomings are all the more noticeable against the striking ease of Maren's strokes, a motion of the full body, energy from the torso traveling into arm to paddle to water.

Robson Bight unfurls across the strait, a subtle indentation at the mouth of the Tsitka River backed by a steep, crevassed forest with a high peak and a single cap of snow. South and north: clear-cuts. Robson Bight is the last uncut river estuary on the eastern coast of Vancouver Island. It, too, was destined for logging, until a film crew captured footage of an orca's birth and showed it to the world. Then the bight was protected as a sanctuary in 1982, an ecological reserve for orcas and their habitat, with additions for buffer lands designated in 1988 and 1989. Orcas are found in all the world's oceans, but many congregate here, older whales bringing their calves to this shore, making an annual pilgrimage to these rubbing beaches of Robson Bight.

We tune to the whale channel: "You've got some fairly major boat traffic inside the reserve down there."

"Looks busy. Warden 1 will be underway about now."

In Blackney Passage the current is rumpled and flooding fast, some five knots, boiling. We hesitate, assessing conditions. This will never abate. Just as we dig the first strokes, the bow of a cruise ship plows from behind Hanson Island, and we backpaddle to a stop. The looming blue-and-white craft we last saw emerging from the fog in Fisher Channel now heads south. In less than two minutes it is through the narrow pass, rumbling. Always the rumbling. Then, pumping with adrenaline, we dash across in its wake, fighting an unpredictable current, constantly looking over our shoulders.

We paddle directly to another tarp just above high tide, a whale research observation post. The cruise ship hovers in midstrait. "Whale watching," says a bearded man, stepping from beneath the tarp. "At least it lets us know where the whales are. There are four times as many cruise ships as there were just a few years ago. And everything is happening because of the whales. They have brought us all here."

He climbs closer to the water and straddles a boulder. We

sit in the kayaks as if in a floating classroom. "How do we know when they are bothered?" I ask.

"Many people see the percussive behavior—the tail and fluke flaps—as neat behavior, and it draws them closer. It is actually a distress signal, a warning. The biggest problem are the sport fishermen. They don't know how to behave around whales. People don't think motors affect the whales because the whales keep coming back, but it's more complicated. And the reserve . . . Well, obviously the whales enter and leave the reserve. It's only a part of their whole circuit. So are they protected anywhere else? It's impossible to draw boundaries. Their whole area is their sanctuary. No one really knows what they do when they go out to sea."

This researcher, too, speaks of the cooperative effort between the whale-watching groups and the scientists. The other researcher soon leans over the railing, smiling. She is a volunteer for the summer, traveling from Japan to spend time with the whales. Their outpost is a small wooden deck with a video camera on a tripod. "We have underwater video cameras for close passes," he says. "Hydrophones are all over. This whole strait is wired like a recording studio."

As we listen, a kayaker joins us. He is from England and says he paddled from Sidney, British Columbia, in seven days. Now he's going to take his time on the way back and spend ten days. We feel like slugs. He listens to our conversation for a few minutes, then says he must get going and sprints off, scooping strongly through the water. Eventually, we push from shore.

We first see the orcas behind the Sophia Islands, two plumes of mist, the black blades of dorsal fins. The whales work along shore toward us, coming fast, water billowing ahead of their shadowy backs. Perhaps sensing us, they peel from shore and continue, swimming at nearly ten knots. Although no incidents between kayakers and orcas have been reported, paddling so close to these swift and cunning mammals is fascinating yet unsettling. They have an intelligence that we do not comprehend, an agility in water we can never match, a self-assuredness here that, even after months in the kayaks, Maren and I do not truly possess. They could upset our craft just as they would ram a two thousand-pound stellar sea lion, knocking it senseless before devouring it. They have been known to speed directly at a boat, then an instant before impact, dive, resurfacing immediately behind the craft. Their dorsal fin can exceed the height of a human. To them, we are low in the water and slothful. "I'm sure they're talking about us," Maren says. The thought is chilling. The whales continue north, diving, exploding mist into the air, giving us a wide berth.

After passing another cliff-top observation post, we discover a tent city of tarps and gumdrop domes, the base camp for the Robson Bight warden patrol. Tenting on a nearby beach, we spend the evening listening to the nearly constant parade of tugs and looking across to Robson Bight. Johnstone Strait is the main shipping route here, and it should prove our busiest sea yet.

Sunset progresses through colors of a star swelling to a red giant, then fires an islet in brilliant tones. For the past two days there has been a magnificent burst of light at this time, when the sun shines clearly beneath a low cloud before sinking away.

AUGUST 11

We awake to the breath of orcas. The exhalations come as hollow blasts across the water and stir us from solid sleep. Four or five breaths burst at once, a family threading through the kelp along shore. In the thin clearing beneath the fog, the glossy fins rise. The tallest fin of the dominant male is high enough that during one surfacing it slices into the low cloud. As they round a point, the breath subsides to a stillness we have not known since Cape Caution. There are no ships in this early hour, and we can hear the din of mosquitoes. Then the rustle of rocks. Down the beach, a large black bear paces, but finding nothing beneath the stones, it returns to the forest.

Last night we heard explosions in the strait, gunshots. And at the research camp, we learn that some crewmembers from the seiner had been throwing seal-scare bombs into the water from a ten-foot skiff and firing rifles. "For fun," the research members say, enraged.

A BC Parks official and the police are on site and have filed charges. "Some fishermen on a wild night out," they say. Dave Briggs, the research veteran of more than a decade who heads the cliff observation post, radioed them in.

"Those fishermen came from that seiner sitting in the preserve," says a researcher. "Since the fishermen are regulated under the Department of Fisheries, a national entity, we can't kick them out of the reserve, which is a provincial entity. It makes no sense at all."

The bay here is a seasonal shantytown of researchers and wardens responsible for patrolling the Robson Bight preserve and dispatching warden boats to keep vessels from the restricted area. The community assembles in summer when the whales return, usually in June, although this year it was mid-July. "Who knows why they were late," the research manager says with radio in hand, busy sending the morning patrol crews out. "They spend ninety percent of their lives underwater. How do you research an animal that you can only see ten percent of the time? We know so little."

Hearing there is a good vantage point from the cliff to see the bight, we first try to hike the few miles via a rough and overgrown trail. But we encounter a black-bear sow with cubs, so I paddle to the cliff while Maren opts to stay at the base camp with the crew, savoring another day on land.

I drag the kayak ashore beneath the observation station and climb a steep trail, pulling myself up by an old fishing rope tied among the trees to some two hundred feet above the water. On the radio, the cliff is known as Eagle Eye, and the view across the silvery strait is commanding. Robson Bight is dark with trees against the surrounding lighter second growth. We are up with the winds, where ravens twirl in updrafts. The post is a hodgepodge, manufactured from driftwood nailed into crude huts with the ubiquitous blue tarp completing three sides of each shelter. Hot chocolate and coffee circulates among the researchers. Solar panels power microphones, amplifiers, and radios. In the blue light beneath a tarp, three observers on duty peer through 10 x 50 spotting scopes and jot down data points.

"Here's what we're looking for," one says, handing me a data sheet. A grid divides the strait into various observation zones with a key on top:

CFV: Commercial Fishing Vessel; CCV: Commercial Charter Vessel; COL: Commercial Ocean Liner; GPV: Government Patrol Vessel; TUG: Tugboat with/without Barge; RKG: Recreational Kayak Group; RPV: Recreational Power Vessel (big or small); RSV: Recreational Sailing Vessel; PRV: Photographer/Research Vessel; CAR: Self-propelled Cargo Vessel.

"That's what comes through here. We're tracking traffic."

The whale identification method is handy but arbitrary, full of names like C-2 and I-11, and among the talk of RSVs and RKGs I fail to follow even basic conversations. More notably than anything else, perhaps, the legacy of orca research in Johnstone Strait has focused on identifying the genealogies and social organization of the whales by photographing their dorsals and the distinctive saddle patches at the base of the fins. It seems nearly the work of anthropologists, this research that dares to recognize another species in terms of families and individuals.

The banter among researchers and whale watchers braids into the wind.

Radio: *Sending warden boats after the white boat. GPV Warden 1 clear.*

Dave pulls the binoculars from his eyes, exposing two circles of untanned skin. He is a gentle man, excited about his work, and has been here every summer for thirteen years, often unpaid. He lives in a tent with an orange tarp drawn taut over it and rarely descends from the cliff. Someone has said he has been down only once so far this year.

"Is that still the same cruise ship?" he says. "It's been sitting there a while."

"OK, you've seen enough," another researcher taunts the vessel. "Let's move. Give 'em some room."

One researcher gathers data for his work at the University of British Columbia. As Michael mentioned in Telegraph Cove, the research uses the time between blows as a measure of stress in an attempt to determine the limit at which boats begin to upset the whales. "The guidelines are apparently arbitrary," the researcher says. "One hundred meters. Well, we think that sounds right, but no one has tested it before." When he wants to track a whale, he flushes the ninety-horse outboard into the strait and measures the whale's breathing rate.

When I observe a pod, he overhears me say, "Orcas."

He drops his binoculars. "They really shouldn't be called 'orcas,' you know. Orca is part of their scientific name, *Orcinus orca*. We don't call humpbacks, *Megaptera novaeangliae*, do we?"

A clear day, clouds rising above the strait. Word comes that W-2 has been spotted and is headed our way. "He's a pretty rare old man," Dave says into the radio. "It would make a great track. Can we stay another hour? We're salivating."

Radio: *I've got them moving in midstrait. W pod pretty close together—everybody! I'm doing fifteen knots trying to keep up.*

They are close. W-2 is an old patriarch who rarely visits these waters, perhaps three days a year. The older whales (a cow may live for seventy-five years, bulls for fifty) are especially valuable to the project because they usually exhibit stronger responses than younger whales. They remember a time when it was quieter, and it is believed that they direct many group decisions.

"Still waiting for W-2," Dave says into the radio. As we canvass the strait with binoculars, he tells a story of a man who used to sit on his porch not far from here and shoot at the whales. "The young whales swim right past that point, but the older whales don't go there. They veer away. It seems that the old whales remember the atrocities done to them and their kin in the past, the shootings, the days of live capture. And they stay away from places where this has been done. It's not verified scientifically, but it makes sense."

We get word that W-2 has slowed, staying up near Big Bay, and after lingering for another half hour, the tracking is called off. "What a long day for such a short day," says the researcher, and they descend the cliff and pile in the orange Zodiac to return to base. Tonight will be a rendezvous of the whale research community.

Paddling back, I am alone. Robson Bight is dark with clouds, and without Maren it seems lonely and quiet. A rainbow, a half arc in the sky, stops suddenly over the strait. The cruise ships have gone by. A small sailboat still bobs about in the current. Seiners still waiting.

Quickly the night turns magical, and the grandness that we have not felt since the broad beaches of Cape Caution returns. In late evening the *Blue Fjord* arrives bringing researchers from other stations, the first time they have been together all summer. Someone strums a guitar, and salmon sizzles over the fire. Dave has brought the hydrophone amplifier from Eagle Eye. "I have speakers in my tent up on the cliff, and it runs all night so that if anyone comes by, they will just wake me up. I don't think I've missed anybody for years. When I go home to San Francisco for the winter, I play tapes of whale songs at night. I can't go to sleep without it. They sing my lullabies."

First, a growl. "The big burp of a black cod," Dave says, surfing the hydrophones around the strait. "Let's see if anyone is at the rubbing beach."

It is quiet.

"When they are rubbing, we can hear the pebbles falling off of their backs."

Then songs—high squeals and whistles, reverberating off the strait's walls. The sky is black and clear. A dark band splits the Milky Way, and Perseid meteors streak across the sky. I see one first as a reflection in the water; I glance upward to see it burn blue, then yellow before burning out. The water itself sparkles from bioluminescence. We see fish dart through it, tubes of light. One researcher remembers a night when the killer whales swam by, a whole pod, like brilliant green torpedoes.

"Hearing them is my favorite thing," Dave says, adjusting the volume. "There seems to be so much going on with their vocals. On a quiet night, when they can hear each other, they'll be spread out all over the strait, calling. And the calls are echoing off the walls. That's how the world had been for them before heavy boat traffic. Some of those whales out there might have been calves and remembered those really nice, quiet nights. And it seems like when they get this kind of night, they can do what must be in their genes from generations ago, having these long-distance, long-relaxing conversations, or whatever they are doing. I don't know what it all means, but I think it's the essence of who they are."

Tonight the tugs do not encroach, and we spend all evening between sparkling water and a meteor shower, listening to the great and cunning whales until at last they quiet, and the midnight sky smothers in fog.

AUGUST 12

As Maren and I paddle south, the Zodiac returns to Eagle Eye.

Transitions are rapid now but still consist of small additions: a second radio station, a drier crunch in the soil, the absence of slugs. For the next day, Johnstone Strait is the only thoroughfare between the mountainous walls of Vancouver Island and those of the mainland. Tremendous rivers gash the eastern shore of Vancouver Island, where the valleys now base logging operations, barren terraces, and orange trucks, a cacophony of machinery that lingers for several hours. Gradually, even the soundscape has begun to shift.

We find camp on an islet with a panoramic view of the

strait. From the high point, we can see far ahead to our paddle tomorrow, where we will cut away from Vancouver Island and follow the narrow, rushing channels of the Discovery Islands east to the mainland, away from the bigger towns and strip malls that punctuate Vancouver Island between Campbell River and Victoria. We will see that soon enough. It is a decision, like so many, that will determine the next weeks of paddling, sending us along the mainland, then back to Vancouver Island across the Strait of Georgia.

We worry about that long crossing of the Strait of Georgia, nearly the breadth of Frederick Sound, and the swerve seems a deliberate escape from the inevitable return to overdeveloped land. But there are many passages to Puget Sound, and we have simply chosen one, seeing how far we can get down the coast and still retain the sensation of the wilds. The tidal rapids ahead should keep us busy. With weeks to go, already we have spent our last night among a first-growth forest.

Near dusk, the familiar red-winged cruise ship appears, the one we saw plowing through Sumner Strait in Alaska, and seiners gather for an early opening. On the map, Johnstone Strait looks sinuous and protected, but such is the fantasy of maps. It is as vast and as treacherous as any passage we have yet seen and now funnels the prevailing northwesterlies to gale force against our sterns. We are tired and ready for the push home.

AUGUST 13

At first light the northwest wind blows, and fog banks obscure the strait. Our nameless camp—an island that bares to a peninsula at low tide—rises in a steep, humpbacked slope from its low southern edge to its precipitous northwestern face, a roche moutonnée. Its rising slope reveals the direction that the glaciers advanced, flowing northwest from the high mountain interior. As the ice scoured this bedrock, it abraded and smoothed the low up-glacier side, then broke and crumbled its down-glacier side into the steep face, an asymmetry so common to this coast that one falls into every glance.

Small Scotch pines, blueberry, and a snowlike lichen surround the tent. Last night I found an abalone shell tossed up—along with a wiener wrapper—more than ten feet above the water. From the stunted summit we have a stunning view north and south along Johnstone Strait. Seiners and gillnetters prepare for an opening tomorrow morning, and a crabber headed north last evening with pots stacked seven and ten high on deck, the bright iodine-quartz work lights blazing. Today high pressure is building, and when a ridge strengthens along this wind tunnel, it will blow at gale force from the northwest for days at a time.

Setting off, we manage to stay in the eddies and out of the wind, making good time along the shoals. Near Port Neville, an island with a single home under construction is completely logged except for a fringe and a lone tall tree. Then a young buck deer, its antlers fuzzy with velvet, runs suddenly onto the beach.

We stop at Port Neville to inquire about winds. From the water it appears just as a public dock, but arriving, an assembly of old log buildings front the water, the largest with a sign that reads PORT NEVILLE GENERAL STORE. On a house is a Canadian postal sign. A cheerful woman greets us. She is the granddaughter of the first settlers at Port Neville and keeps the post office her grandfather started in 1895. "You don't smoke, do you?" she asks. "Biggest threat out here would be fire." An Angora dwarf rabbit hops about the yard, and a frisky golden retriever snuffles my crotch.

There is a small-town friendliness amid this near-total isolation. Yacht people know her well and dock here regularly. She is the center of town. "You can stay here if you wish," she says. "When it blows like this in the morning, it usually blows for at least three days. You're welcome."

The offer is splendid, but our momentum is high, and camping so early could mean a fall. Trying to decide, we walk the grounds and peer into the old store. Inside are wooden boxes and outmoded radio gear. Out back, chickens and roosters stir the dust. The lawns are palatial, carved long ago from the forest.

At the dock a scruffy man wearing a ball cap that reads GRUMPY OLD MAN emerges from a Bayliner. When we ask about the winds, he leads us to a yachtsman who says he could put a tablecloth out today and do fine. The yachtsman and his wife live along the Sunshine Coast on their fine navy-blue craft. Despite this forecast and advice, we decide to continue along the shore. Although it is difficult for us to leave in such uncertain conditions, they are not paddlers, cannot travel where we can, cannot hide as easily. We are betting that things will be tolerable as we skirt the rocks. We reenter Johnstone Strait and quickly revert to negotiating waves and shorelines, leaving Port Neville regretfully, perhaps mistakenly, behind.

Soon the wind picks up, the fog rising and the clouds swirling, and we hug the mainland shore, more or less in the gale's lee. In the following seas we play hopscotch with a tug pulling a Davis raft of logs. First we overtake it, and then as we lunch it overtakes us, but we surpass it again in an hour. Its raft of wood is so massive that from near water level, it appears as an entire shoreline advancing at one or two knots.

As we corner into Sunderland Channel, the wind eases and waves decline. Basalt dikes slit the granite shores, and where the dikes have broken apart, small slot beaches of cobbles and boulders have formed. A fish farm breaks the waves for some time until they grow again in Topaze Harbour. We must hit slackwater at Whirlpool Rapids, so we continue paddling beneath the horned peaks of the mainland and islands that seem as high as they are wide.

Perfect timing. The tug rounds the bend at the same time as we do, and it seems as if we will share the ride through the rapids. The sweetness of cut wood wafts across the whitecaps. The current sucks us into the narrows, the sea suddenly running like a river.

The flow grips my bow—nudging me to one side, then to the other—slapping me awake. The tug has veered off, pulling its cargo into the hidey-hole of Forward Harbour, which is

filled like a parking lot with pleasure boats. The pilot shortens
the cable to the log raft, cuts the tight corner, and disappears.
I sit back, gliding quietly with the last of the current, wondering where to camp. Above us on the shore is a clear-cut with
blooming fireweed. Then rock. Then road. Then, suddenly,
the sound of the water changes to a rush, and the powerful
flood current surges toward us, and we must steer into the
eddies and begin the work of paddling. "If we had stopped
for another snack," Maren says, "we wouldn't have gotten
through."

At the end of Wellborne Channel, we camp on an abandoned logging dock of packed and graded cobbles, now eroding back to sea. Maren is elated because our bed is flat, and
we can air clothes on the wrecked rafters of a rooftop.

Into the night, the wind blows at thirty knots, waves
breaking against our small platform. Among the peaks of Vancouver Island, the visible sliver of Johnstone Strait is white
with mist. Maren has lit our candle lantern for the first time
in many weeks. Convenience seems like another life: sleeping
late, central heating, a permanent roof. So many abandoned
places out here—logging, homesteads, canneries, Native sites.
Each morning we, too, abandon a place, and each evening
we remake our temporal home, stretching nylon taut over its
aluminum skeleton, stomping a pathway between tent and
kitchen. The flickering light inside our tent is warm and wel-
coming. There is also a welcome aridity that we have not yet
known along the coast. The yachtsman at Port Neville pointed
south and said, "Down there, it's a different world." We are
a day away from summer.

AUGUST 14

Winds early, but no fog. Gusts stack the ebb current in Chancellor Channel into ranks of daunting whitecaps. From Queen
Charlotte Strait this all looked so easy. As I stare, a deHavilland Beaver roars around the point at tree level, sliding and

skidding against the wind. "We've been reported for trespassing." Maren says. When the pilot sees us, the wings quiver
and the plane rudders slightly to sea. People inside wave, and
the plane skims to a stop just down beach. "What should we
tell them? Where else could we have camped?" The plane is
green and white, owned by Timber West. A man with a back-
pack climbs ashore and gets into a pickup truck. Then the
plane roars away.

The western point of West Thurlow Island catches the
winds of Johnstone Strait and siphons them into Chancellor
Channel. As the ebb dies, the waves flatten, and we paddle.
In this swift passage, we can only paddle with the flood, and
so have six hours. Over the next two days we must face three
tidal rapids: Greene Point, Dent, and Yuculta, and timing will
be everything. Today we will run Greene Point with the flood,
positioning to race through Dent and Yuculta early tomorrow
at slack tide. They are much more tumultuous than Greene
Point, and not even the big boats will attempt them at
other times.

Small single-masted sailboats lie anchored in coves or beside beaches. Powerboats and large motor yachts, chromed at
the bow and stern, race by nearly every half hour. By the
time we reach Loughborough Inlet, the wind has died completely, the day warms, the wind cool but lacking the bite it
has carried since Alaska.

The wild opens and closes around each point, with each
turn of the head. Almost everywhere there are wrecked log
booms, clear-cuts, and cabins. All day we paddle toward a
distant peak that sags to one side like a nightcap. In Cordero
Channel we glide at nearly five knots without paddling. "This
should be fun," I say. Nearly every cobble beach has a black
bear. Froth boils over rocks. The current speeds as the water
is pinched toward Greene Point Rapids. A dark-blue sailboat
motors near in midchannel—the sailors we met in Port
Neville.

We hit Greene Point at maximum flood and, trying to
avoid going through the rapids, commit the error of crossing.
We wave at people on shore, but then hearing the thunder

of water, seeing the land smear past as we traverse the current, I realize that those waves are not greetings but warnings. We are being sucked toward the rocks of Erasmus Island. One man on shore has broken into a run. We face the current. Still losing ground, we paddle harder. It is like sprinting in a dream, where the faster I run, the slower I go. With no more than fifty yards to spare, we escape Erasmus and retreat into a kelp-ridden cove, panting. The rush is maddening and escalates our unease. We have no appetite, no thirst, focusing on currents. Almost against our will, we finally muster the courage to wrap around a cliff between two islands and into sluggish water. "Bad decision to cross there," I say, and for most of the day I replay a loop of being swept onto the rocks and losing everything to the current.

The afternoon is calm and sunny, and we fight eddies and eventually must pay for our mistake again, having to recross to Sonora Island to ride the waning flood. Several times I follow an eagle's shadow across the bulges and troughs of high rocks before it vanishes into the darkness of the forest. Eagles I never see.

Near high slack we paddle into Thurlow, a harbor full of yachts and tanned people backed by a quaint restaurant. We stop a couple trolling about in a skiff and ask them about the tides. He sneers, appraising us as he reels in a rod. She is disinterested. They wear the finest outdoor clothing and have a groomed terrier running about the flat-bottomed boat, but they cannot tell us when the tide changes at Dent and Yuculta. We apologize for our ragged look and paddle on.

Lodges have accumulated among the bays and coves of these tidal races like particles of sand. At Thurlow you can enjoy a meal and a few drinks while waiting for the tide to turn at Dent, Yuculta, or Greene Point. "A cove of slackers," Maren calls them. The tides at last are the great equalizer, and to see that these waters cause even the large boats to pause and obey the currents is powerful news. As slack tide nears, boats throttle from Thurlow. By the time we find camp, when we can again hear the current, the traffic ceases, and the night is absent of motors.

Warm winds by evening, a front approaching from northern Vancouver Island. A black fly bites my palm, welling a small pimple of blood. Again tonight we camp in an area cleared by a small logging operation and find cable, sprockets, pipe fittings, spark plugs, a rusted stove, torn sheets of corrugated aluminum scattered in the forest. My shorts are so salt encrusted that they stand on their own legs.

I read about Greene Point in *Sailing Directions*: "Caution. Low powered vessels and vessels towing, when eastbound through the rapids with the flood current, should take care not to be set on Erasmus Island." I flip to tomorrow's agenda—Dent and Yuculta Rapids—and keep this from Maren. It has shaken me enough, a waking nightmare that has followed me all day, and I need both of us to be confident for tomorrow. I have resolved to tell her when we pass Yuculta—when she discovers the passage about Greene Point on her own. "I knew we were being stupid," she says. "Tomorrow we are sticking to shore."

In the tent, we calculate and recalculate tomorrow morning to the minute. We will paddle against ebb in the eddies along Sonora Island and hit Dent Rapids during the last half hour of the ebb, then paddle the two miles between the rapids, hitting Yuculta as soon as possible afterward. If we mistime this, it will be a day waiting somewhere along the steep shores for another daylight chance to get through. Once inside Dent, the only exit is by tidal rapids: Dent to the west, Arran to the north, and Yuculta to the south—collectively known as the Yucultas. Dent floods at eleven knots, ebbs at eight. Arran floods at fourteen, ebbs at ten. Yuculta floods at ten, ebbs at eight. At Yuculta, we will bend south, like rounding a corner. From there, it is a direct line to Puget Sound.

The rapids are a barrier to the waters that lie south. Traveling from Johnstone Strait, you must encounter them. Every passage has rapids—Seymour Narrows along Vancouver Island, the various snaking channels among the Discovery Islands, the Yucultas—and running them is like breaking the sound barrier between the north coast and the south coast, the small isolated communities and the almost continuous shore of homes that undoubtedly awaits us.

At dark, a horrible groaning sound rises from the shoreline, low growling heaves—the sickening lurches of a vomiting bear.

AUGUST 15

Up at 6:00 and leaving by 8:00. We fight the ebb, paddling the eddies toward Dent Rapids. We are surprised that we progress at all against the swiftness. Trusty bull kelp slows the current, and we paddle inside the streaming leaves, often tangling in its knots. Just outside our barrier are huge overfalls, holes in the water. The tug and log tow we paddled with two days ago power against the current but are stopped dead by the flow.

When the kelp and protective irregularities of shore finally give out near Little Dent Island, we must wait. We are an hour early and must linger along the rock shelf until noon, mesmerized by the endlessly spooling water. The bull kelp fans and streams one way, then the other as small whirlpools spin from the main current and run ashore like miniature typhoons. A few gutsy captains chance the middle of the race, their big boats with American flags slipping past at frightful speeds, pitching and yawing and skidding sideways. It is a scene replayed from July 20, 1792, when the *Sutil* and the *Mexicana* of the Spanish expedition to the Northwest coast entered the Arran rapids:

> [T]he currents were violent, and the whirlpools frequent, and so strong that one, which the *Sutil* could not avoid, turned her around completely three times, at such a lively rate as to be surprising. The *Mexicana* was close to her but was more fortunate on this occasion. In spite of the danger in which the *Sutil* so unexpectedly found herself, a scene never before witnessed

by any of those present, it unavoidably caused great laughter, not only among those who were in danger, but among those who were momentarily expecting to be.

Less than a month before, Native canoes had towed Vancouver's small boats through.

Almost instantaneously, the ebb lessens, the gushing subsides, and it rains. "A change in the weather at the change in tides," Maren says. She pulls alongside and we give a rally handshake, a kiss. Then, gathering breath, we begin, sprinting along shore against the weakening ebb, praying to negotiate Yuculta Rapids before its thunder reawakens. The ebb and flood arrows on the chart whirl and curl and loop. *Sailing Directions* says: "Dent Rapids, between Little Dent and Sonora Islands, are swift and turbulent with dangerous overfalls and eddies. In Devil's Hole, violent eddies and whirlpools form between 2 hours after turn to flood and 1 hour before turn to ebb. Favour the Sonora Island shore of Dent Rapids." For now the water is calm, even listless, and unlike Greene Point, we follow the recommended course along Sonora.

During the four times a day when the water is quiet, the throb of motors consumes the air. From across the water diesel engines snort, boats we have seen in the past days poking from behind islands and bays to test the waters. In a matter of moments, the masses that have waited for slack water, perhaps overnight, peel out of Big Bay. The scene is like the formation of a parade, the grandiose floats falling into line, trolling cautiously in single file.

As we slip along shore, development thickens—lodges and resorts built on frail concrete pillars. The fishing is easy here because no fish can fight this tide, and the tide has created the need to loiter while waiting for slack. And so the resort communities have sprung up, contemporary fishing camps of sorts. Above us, the loafer soles, khaki shorts, and collared shirts meander on decks. "Slackers," Maren says again. "Today we are all slackers."

As we round the corner from Innes Passage, the water is

completely flat. Bull kelp hangs flaccid. It is slack. Success. Soon the parade of ships dwindles to a few distant boats speeding in from the south. Behind us, the tidal rush is already audible, and boats that did not get through either peel from the oncoming current and troll, throwing out salmon lines, or they motor away to explore other inlets for another six hours. We glide past two small homes with a boardwalk and a porch covered with cedar shakes. Just past them is a familiar sight, the first big-leaf maple.

As the water opens to the breadth of Calm Channel, a most extraordinary thing happens. Not far ahead, a mature bald eagle lands on a high branch. It cocks its head. Then it shudders, loosing a downy feather. The feather floats on the air, rising and dropping in the invisible currents. I maintain my course, and as it descends, it seems as if I am going to meet it. Then I am sure of it. And when it nears, I simply reach out my hand, as if grabbing the air itself, and pick the feather from the sky. I stare at it in disbelief. It is pure white, full of atmosphere, its fibers mingling with even my faintest breaths. Above, the eagle chatters and chirps, then circles into the forest.

"We will make it home," Maren says.

The rest of the day is placid among the high granite peaks. Everything is scratched, scored, and smoothed by ice. A king-fisher dives, then flits away. Mountain faces scrape through clouds. During an afternoon shower, a rainbow covers the sky. We have traveled into a new habitat zone, nearly another world.

The Rendezvous Islands are clustered with homes whose wood stoves curl smoke through the trees. Stairways and lawn chairs, decks, and latticework. A sign on a small island reads, FOR SALE 10 ACRES. But what we have noticed beyond these intermittent homes is a certain feel of the land, a familiarity with the vegetation, varieties we know from travels around Puget Sound and in the San Juan Islands. Clefts in the rock erupt with blond grasses; on a cliff, the peeling brick-red wood of a madrona, the first one we see. Without looking at the map, the land tells that we are crossing another border, and

over the past few days we have moved from traditional Kwakwaka'wakw territory to Coast Salish territory. We are near
the waters of home.

We circle the islands, unsure if the beach that we will
camp on is privately owned or not. Again we have no choice.

Rain pounds the tent fly for the first time in weeks. Days
are shorter, twilight more abrupt. Tonight we have a beautiful
point, mossy and soft. From this finger of land we watch the
sky darken, clouds forming and dissolving along the slopes of
Raza Island. I am amazed that a day can be filled with so
many emotions and events, that after so much time the winds
are at last warm into evening, and that Maren and I have
stayed the course. With the return of familiar forests, we picture familiar faces of the human landscape we know as our
home.

A Douglas fir stands behind our tent, thick barked and
straight, a welcome companion after so long an absence. Behind, old stumps rise from the forest floor like dormant volca-
noes, and the forest is strewn with erratic boulders. Leaning
against one while slipping off a boot, my fingers sink up to the
knuckles in moss, stopping against the damp and cold stone.

AUGUST 16

Starting out, Maren and I paddle in opposite directions, then
glide together, laughing. "So much for planning."

The huge peaks up Toba Inlet drop to islands in the west.
Today, if all goes well, we will leave the mountains and enter
the expanse of the Strait of Georgia. Morning clouds snare in
the crevasses and valleys and peaks. Fat pleasure boats work
their way up the channel. There is noticeably less commercial
traffic, more pleasure traffic, many small speedboats, weekend craft.

Fog is clearing out as high pressure builds in the west. In
Lewis Channel, we rest by a stream flowing from a chute in
the forest. Rather than the usual teak color, the stream bub-

bles clear over green moss. Filling the water bags, Maren notices a tin marker and yellow surveyor's tape. Nailed to a droopy alder a sign reads:

BC GEOLOGICAL SURVEY BRANCH.
REGIONAL GEOCHEMICAL SURVEY.
SAMPLE #92K883126.

Through Lewis Channel, the mountains subside and the water warms. At one beach, razor sharp with oyster shells, we take a midday swim. The waters around Desolation Sound are the warmest on the northwest coast and in places can near eighty degrees. Oysters grow in profusion, and inlets are dotted with the strings of floats, oysters dangling from sunken twine. Sheltered by the mountains of Vancouver Island, this is the top of the Sunshine Coast, dry for a coastal rain forest, even arid. The climate draws boaters, recreationists, and the shoreline is again dotted with dwellings. On an unmarked beach, two walls of boulders that clearly were piled long ago protect a canoe pull. In a cove that is marked as a beach on the charts we discover a fish farm.

An old sailboat follows us into Refuge Cove with all sails up, like a frightened fish with its fins splayed, spiny and sharp. The Refuge Cove store rests on an old wooden barge supported by pilings. We make a call, using a credit-card phone, slicing plastic through a magnetic strip. The store stocks general provisions, deli meats, various books and magazines, decorative maps, plastic egg containers, fruits, vegetables. Outside, a small book exchange maintains a high concentration of paperbacks with silver- and gold-lettered covers. Two professors who quit the university scene bake muffins and desserts at the Muffin Shack—elegant sweets created by people in the know. Canopied by the music of a Verdi opera, we tear at fresh bread and guzzle orange juice.

As we depart to look for an undetermined camp, I am enamored with a magnificent sailboat, the *Cecilie*. "Nice!" I shout to the bearded man working on deck. He is patently surprised to see kayakers and steps to the railing. In answering his disabling question, "Where are you going?" we spill the beans. He says he hiked the Appalachian Trail some twenty years ago and met many wonderful people. Without hesitation, he invites us to spend the night on board.

"I'm Jim," he says, pulling me up the ladder. We realize we first saw him at the telephone booth, when we heard him say, "I'll be back in three weeks." He is the founder of an environmental biotechnology company, and the ship is immaculate, a fifty-six-footer, once another company president's yacht.

After a spare dinner of potatoes flecked with parsley, he sings and plays guitar. Then we go on deck to enjoy the night air. He talks about traveling alone, of single handing the boat at sea, of gunkholing along the coast, of his girlfriend who will meet him here tomorrow. He marvels at how far we have paddled. So do I. We stand on deck in silence for a while beneath the stars.

"You know," he says, looking to the faint light in the southern sky, "you're in the suburbs now."

Emmonds Beach

AUGUST 17

We breakfast on egg-backed bacon muffins ($2.75 each) from the burger shack, the cook angrily peeling potatoes beneath a swelling Puccini aria. Locals—boat mechanics and plumbers—squat on steps talking to a close-cropped twenty-year-old about joining the military. A man drinking lattes argues against it. "Look," he says, uncloaking a hollowed abdomen. "Look at what it can do to you."

Jim is doing laundry, awaiting the floatplane that will bring his girlfriend. He tells us of a possible apartment in Seattle, gives us his number, then bids us farewell. "Oh yes," Maren says. "The apartment thing."

Desolation Sound is a boat highway that continues along the Malaspina Peninsula and Copeland Islands. Sailboats motor on this perfect sailing day. The land is brittle, summer dry, and the water splashes warm on our hands. As the current picks up with the wind, we slip around Kinghorn Island, leaving behind the blue peaks topped with cloud. It is the last we will see of the close, high land. From here the shores soften. The Coast Range drifts farther inland, and we follow the footprint of the Cordilleran Ice Sheet, which flattened the coastal lowlands along the Strait of Georgia and down through Puget Sound. Distant summits of Vancouver Island show to the west; ahead, the sandy glacial deposits of Hernando and Savary Islands.

The waves are more wake than wind, created by the abundant motor yachts. Many of the powered craft are faster here, smaller, sporty boats molded for those tethered to a weekend. But many of the powerboats are obese, chugging more *through* the water than *across* it, bows plowing under the water. Their steep wake assures somewhat adventurous paddling, but it has dumbed the water into predictable ranks that only lift the bow and send it slapping to the water again. The boats seem so large to us, so loud. Every crest and trough measures the volume of water being pushed aside for pomp and pleasure.

Power lines swoop over the channel, crackle the air, and climb the hill. Glacial striations are everywhere, as are speedboats and speed. People are amazed that we've paddled so far and are more likely to say, "What a great getaway" than the "Better be careful, it can get snotty out there" of farther north. These new responses at first cause us to laugh, but we are beginning to see that we are at the fringes of a different kind of coast, a different mentality, one that began shortly after we rounded the Yucultas. These comments that equate our journey with recreation and escape possess the undercurrent that people are vaguely displeased with where they are, generally irked with how things are going. It seems that to them, what we are doing, what we are seeing, is somehow very separate, even irrelevant, to *their* daily lives.

As we slip along the cliffs laden with homes, eyes peer from the forest—the eyes of vacationers and summer dwellers, the vacant glare of windows among the trees, estates camouflaged like marten. Many of the boats have tinted windows and carry an attitude of celebrities, an isolation, a withdrawal and aloofness. After the elements have splayed us open for so long, the weather and waves having cracked and leathered and humiliated our skin, these tinted windows gleam with a misplaced confidence, that with the power of their engines and the bulk of their craft, they somehow can control the sea.

Bliss Landing has a perfect beach, groomed like a sand trap. Canadian flags snap red and white against the blue day. Inside the Copeland Islands Marine Park, more graffiti, the pictographs of our day. One reads QUEEN in white spray paint; another, SHIRLEY. They are the names of tugs that used to tie up here. Ahead, Maren is whistling. In the distance we see the sailboat that followed us from Refuge Cove. It moves so elegantly at the whim of cunning and wind, the first sailboat we have seen that has no motor, the only larger craft that may share our sense of the elements.

Past the town of Lund—and more homes with flying wind-socks—we worry about where and how to make camp. Lund is either the beginning or end of the road, depending on your perspective, and for the first time in more than a week we see cars, old vans with dish mags, orange trucks, camper vans, camper pickups. Between here and Vancouver, the coastal road is only broken by two ferry rides. When we stop for a break near Hurtado Point, wake from a long-past yacht smacks ashore, bashing our kayaks among the rocks.

On the outskirts of Powell River, every cove or beach cradles a dwelling, and we prepare to knock on doors for permission to camp. After nearly stopping once, we round a lobe of polished rock and face a splendid pebble beach. Maren walks to the top of the grassy berm and talks to a woman who steps from a cabin. She points toward an older woman starting a pickup and says, "Gotta ask Len or Norma if you can stay."

Seeing Maren running toward the truck, Norma lowers the window. After some nodding and pointing around the grounds, Maren gives a thumb's up. Relief. I join the truck. "Hello," she says. "Welcome to Emmonds Beach. Have you seen the piglets?" They are snorting at us through a wooden crate a few feet away. "Just make yourself at home. Put your tent anywhere on the grass. We have a mixed-vegetables gar-den, organic." She laughs. "We also grow weeds."

We camp fronting the strait on the wonderfully level ground near the hooped greenhouses and rows of red-leaf lettuce. "We are fortunate," Maren says. "Can you believe we almost stopped a mile back?"

Crickets and grasshoppers. Dry country. On the edge of the berm stands a flourishing maple, its thick branches braiding upward from the trunk like octopus arms. All evening children infiltrate its lower reaches like squirrels, swinging on swings, squealing, chasing rolling balls. Visitors enter Len and Norma's house, and it is apparent that these people mean something to this place, that we have found a steadfastness here.

The parade of boats continues off the rock through early evening. Stars fade in the shimmering light above Powell River, and fireworks explode from Sea Fair in noiseless pops of color. Our dark nights have ended. A din of classic rock and the bursts from a poor drummer who tries to keep up with a record float across the beach, the paradiddles off tempo with the flash of navigation lights on Vancouver Island. Fluorescent ferries sneak across the Strait of Georgia. A night wind builds, rustling the soft maple. The clatter of dishes in a sink.

In the night we bolt awake. Sniffs and snorts penetrate the dark. The crunch of gravel. "Bears!" Maren whispers. Large forms lumber near the tent. Grunts. Something breaks into a run. As I fumble for the bear spray, there is a bellowing. "Cows," Maren says, collapsing back into her sleeping bag. "It's the cows." They spread across the berm, grazing, pieces of cloud and moon strolling past. In a steady, powerful stream, a cow empties its bladder by the tent. I lie back down but remain awake for some time, unable to shake the visions of udders by porchlight, the strange lunar sheen of a cow's pelt against the widening sea.

AUGUST 18

In the morning Len strolls to the tent, a Buck knife bouncing on his hip, and invites us for breakfast. It is flat calm, but the forecast predicts the westerly will back to the southeast later

today. Cow manure litters the campsite in mounds of hay-
filled cakes.

After a breakfast of fried green tomatoes, Len gives us a
driving tour of the property, showing off his new roads.
"Alder areas are good for gardening," he says as we bump
along. "Fir areas are rockier, good for road building.

"Regulations keep us running, too," he says, halting the
truck before a gate. "The cows that came through your camp
last night are here because regulations say that to keep the
property in the farm category, we have to have animals grazing on all the land, even though this farm is a vegetable garden. We also had to fence the whole property to keep the
cows in. A regulation. Regulations are the biggest drawbacks
I have. They make us abandon work on the garden, the weed-
ing, and rebuilding the greenhouse that collapsed under the
winter snows."

As we drive among the fields and pastures he cleared by
hand, he tells of his place. "My uncle came up in 1914 and
homesteaded one mile from here. In 1936, during the Depression, when I was nine years old, my father and my mother
brought me here. And we got this land in 1938. And in 1939
a fire came through and burned everything we had started,
all the trees and everything. And we wondered whether it
was worth keeping. But there was nowhere else to go, so we
held on to it. Got the things together to build another cabin.
We were starting from nothing."

Since his father bought the original thirty-three acres, Len
has bought thirty-three more; whenever a piece was for sale,
he and Norma purchased it. "People say I should put a hotel
out here. A tennis court. Nobody has the vision that we
have—wanting to preserve the whole thing." He repeats this,
in variations, as we ride. The soil is rocky, and the truck kicks
up a good dust. Returning to the house, Len tells of the many
projects under way on the property—prospects for an artesian
well, repiping water, and always the gardening and road building. "I spend my life creating possibilities," he says.

In the kitchen, Norma cuts rot from some unsalable tomatoes, preparing salsa. Customers knock, wanting to purchase

sweet corn, and they leave in several minutes with a full trunk. Len and Norma are self-made people, accustomed to doing things themselves. Norma works the vegetable gardens while Len helps and focuses on the heavier work of lifting equipment and laying pipe.

When they drive us to Lund for dinner, everyone seems to wave and call, "Hello, Mr. and Mrs. Emmonds." It is easy to see that they are esteemed people. Over "Lund Done" fish and chips, Len and Norma talk more of summer crops than of weather and how people who want the easy life are descending all around them. When they first moved here, they lived in a tent, eventually encasing it in log walls, which remain as the walls of a cabin behind their newer home. They are informed and articulate. "The city!" Len says, sipping his draft. "The city produces nothing but trash."

AUGUST 19

It is wonderful to be on a farm!

Again the day dawns with Len's invitation to breakfast. He knows we will not paddle today. The strong southwesterly slings waves against the beach. Norma has brought two cartons of fresh eggs from the hen house, and we feast on French toast and fried eggs, enjoying a morning of conversation.

"We met picking brush, gathering greenery for florists, on Texada Island about twenty miles down," Len says, smiling as he revisits the memory. "A logging camp moved in, and that's when I first saw Norma. We had always gone hunting together, clam digging. Never been on a date or anything. Just got to know each other. Her father was afraid we would get romantically involved, and I guess we did. So I was told to leave.

"I went back just to pick up my power saw six or so weeks later. Norma and I had hardly communicated since then, so I thought it was over. I wasn't even going to talk to her. But I had to go into somebody's house to find my saw. Just that day, Norma had told this person about her situation, and they got Norma to come over. So we left the island. Her parents happened to be in Vancouver."

"And when my parents returned home and discovered I wasn't there," Norma laughs, "the neighbors said, 'Oh, they left in a speedboat heading to Vancouver.'"

"The fastest boat I ever saw!" Len chuckles. "It took us all day to get from there to here with a three-quarter horse inboard. It was rather nerve-racking because we knew that if they came after us, he would have had a gun, I'm sure. On the way we saw twelve sharks, the most I've ever seen. Some were going right under the boat. We wondered what was going on. Three days later we got married. We had to get a lawyer because she was nineteen, and the legal age was twenty-one. They called her an infant spinster."

Norma cracks a grin and pats his lap. "Your infant spinster."

"Eighteen years later," Len says, "we went back to that same place on Texada, expecting to see my cabin gone. But it was there, and we walked in, and it was the same way I left it. That's how remote the area was. The target that I used to throw my knife at was still on the door. My yew-wood nails in a tobacco can. An old bill from Dayton's store with my name on it. My old boots. It was all still there. That's where I met Norma, where nobody ever went.

"We went there in September. Before Christmas a guy moved into the cabin. And the following year, the cabin burned down."

Len is visibly saddened by this recollection, and we break for morning chores. After lunch they go back to talking and remembering: home canning, the last storm that took out the electricity.

"One of the neat places over on Texada was up the beach from our cabin," Norma says. "Where they built the hydro. It was a nice, clear area. We had a jump for the horse. And that was really a shame to go back and see where they put the power line, right through one of the nicest spots on the island."

"In that area," Len says, "and one or two on Cortez and Hernando, there were beaches that had huge fir trees. You never needed a tent under those trees. The tree beaches . . . every one of them has been ruined."

Len pauses, then continues, "The amount that used to be here . . . if that disappeared overnight or in a month, you'd recognize it. But it's happened so slowly. Not really so slowly. Fifty years. This time of year there would be so many ducks out there that if the noise bothered you, you could hardly sleep. About halfway to that buoy out there you would think it was land because of the seaweed."

"People would take the cowhides onto the beach to be cleaned," Norma says. "Instead of scraping, they would put some rocks on them and the crabs would just clean them off."

"The whole cowhide would be just black with crabs," Len adds. "Now there are none. You couldn't find a one."

A smooth lobe of rock shields the house from the west, and a shoal of similar form bares as the tide recedes. "This used to be a rubbing beach," Len says. "But the killer whales don't swim by anymore. Not for a while now. There was one time when the killer whales were going by six or a dozen or twenty pods. They were scattered maybe a quarter or a half mile apart, all in the whole area and as far as you could see, and I didn't know how long they had been passing before I saw them. You could see them all the time. They just moved down the coast.

"I used to fish with the Indians over at Misty Reef. They were from Sliammon. They said there were times when they would be three days over at Harwood Island; couldn't get back because of the killer whales. These were the old guys. They would all row into the kelp and stay there when killer whales were near. Maybe the killer whales, before the white man started killing them, would have attacked the Indians. Or in the number that were passing that day, maybe they would have wrecked a canoe."

Gradually the conversation drifts to organic farming, and Norma tells of experiences with a program that helped urban youth from other parts of Canada learn alternative lifestyles: farming, raising animals, self-sufficiency.

"Why is teaching self-sufficiency important to you?" Maren asks.

"Because I figured that we're going to have to be more self-sufficient with so many people out of work and so many young kids. There is always some land somewhere that could grow a garden. And welfare is going to be cut off one of these days. People will be looking for food."

"And they won't know how to do it," Len says. "They haven't a clue. They think plants are so forgiving. They're not."

He pauses. "The ability to work, to do handwork, is vanishing. Everybody wants a machine to do everything. A book that we get most information from is a book written in 1908—that was when they used horse-drawn equipment and hand labor. And that explains virtually everything. It says 'A quick man can plant five thousand cabbages.' Can you imagine anyone doing that today?"

Norma chuckles and smiles at Len. "You have to be a quick man, remember."

We all have a good laugh at this. And finally, when the hilarity at last dies, I ask what endures here.

"Virtually nothing," Len says abruptly.

"They are still digging clams," Norma says. "But there are fewer beaches with clams on them."

"They are getting prawns," says Len. "But I would say that the harvest is good because the codfish aren't there to eat the prawns. Nobody ever used to fish prawns at all. Eighty-five seiners came up here one day and wiped out the herring. Destroyed the run forever."

Disgusted, Len looks out across the water, wincing before speaking again.

"I was a hunter and a fisher and a trapper. I think that's the best education you can possibly have. You learn to wait. You find where the animals run. You have to foresee where the animal is going to put his foot and put that trap precisely where an animal is going to step. It requires a lot of consideration. You go to a stream and look at it. Just sit there on a rock for I don't know how long. Time meant nothing in those days. I was always thinking, How can I do it without disturbing things? because if you disturb things, you disturb the animals. And I'd walk away from it. A day later I would come back—or maybe on the way from setting lines or other traps—and I'd look at a place again and try to figure out what to do. Where to put this little thing that something had to step on."

Norma studies him, and Len again smiles as he talks, rekindled by the sheer magic of those earlier days.

During an afternoon rain shower, Len and I pick corn and walk to a pond where he has seen Pacific giant salamanders, but we see none. I cut four zucchini from Norma's vegetable garden. She washes lettuce in a steel sink, shaking water loose in two quick twitches, and piles it on the counter next to an order of broccoli, lettuce, beans, and squash. Then, in the shade of a spacious umbrella, we eat corn from a silvery steel bowl.

The evening explodes in a thunderstorm, then opens to a starry night. The lingering clouds above Campbell River and Comox and Powell River glow like nebulae. Jet fighters lift from Comox, silent, the steady flames of afterburners rising quickly to the south and circling. It is as though we are seeing the cirrus of an approaching front, the limits of a larger system in these first bright layers of population.

The candle in the tent quivers with a change of wind. Len and Norma have created an outpost of good community living, a place on the edge, which we have met with the growing extravagance of the southern coast. Reflecting on Len and Norma's words, I see that advice so often originates in the cities: radio, television, products, medicines, books, records, news. . . .

Tonight I remember my father taking me to see Jupiter in the backyard of our suburban home. I can remember looking through the haze of urban lights, how frustrated he was about the neighbors putting up a security streetlamp that erased the southern sky. To him it was a sign of paranoia at the expense of the night. I believe he became a man of faith because he saw how closed humanity can be, how afraid people are of risks, of breaking convention, of stepping from the crowd. I feel, although he has never said this, he believes that through living a life of faith, he can give to humanity the courage to open horizons rather than close them, to sustain a civilization on Earth, the planet that has given him such an uncommon awe. An awe that through seeing the moons of Jupiter in a backyard telescope, he has gifted to me.

Crossing Strait of Georgia

AUGUST 20

We part with Len and Norma in the early slanting sun. They stand and wave on the beach for a while, then walk away. It is like seeing an era slip behind, receding slowly like the ice sheets must have once gradually retreated from view. And we turn to the plat of Powell River—gray against the hill, with fallout from the mill raining on the neighborhoods, melding with the cloud banks above. "South Texada will be the last wild land you see," Len said. He told us the legend that Texada Island rose from the sea, which is why it has no bear or cougar. And, someday, he said, Texada will sink back again. But we hear nothing more about it.

AUGUST 21

For two days we work our way south, skipping from the sandy shores of Harwood Island to the tiered mines and steep rocks of long Texada, past the gouges of cement companies billowing quarry dust into the air. The beach where Len and

Norma met has generally been obliterated by a hydroelectric relay station and a log-loading operation. But in front of the towers and altered land is a fragment of crescent of beach, and we want to tell them that it is not all lost.

Texada seems wild but developed, a strange middle ground. Last night, near Gilles Bay, we camped on a public beach squealing with children and mufflerless trucks blaring King Harvest. Then this morning we paddled into headwinds, past an outcrop of pillow lava, assorted homes and cabins, and along the high dry rock of southern Texada. Bare of buildings and beachless, amid the rest of the growing populace, the end of Texada is wonderfully remote, descending more than two hundred meters in a quarter mile, dropping sheer into the sea. We leave Texada's western shore and cross to Jedediah Island, to the only legal camp we can find in the middle of the Strait of Georgia, at a provincial park.

The park is so new that it greets us with mixed messages: NO TRESPASSING. NO FIRES and WELCOME TO JEDEDIAH ISLAND. We pitch camp on a clearing between the signs, above a shallow, muddy bay with private oyster beds. For the past three camps we have been on either private property or designated parkland. Tomorrow, as we head to Nanaimo, we will camp in another park. "We are in the park belt," Maren says, and our days are oriented to these destinations, the small points where we can spend the nights. Stops are less frequent. Night by night, our upcoast lifestyle erodes. The tides, however, never calm. Fronts still sweep the sky.

At dusk we walk the two worn ruts across the island to Home Bay, site of the island's old homestead. When the Palmer family left the land to the province, they set the farm animals free. One horse and all the sheep, goats, and cows died in the winter, and resident minks ate the chickens and geese. The lone survivor of the transfer to public land, a widowed horse, dines alone in a broad field.

We are in the middle of the Strait of Georgia and initiate the ritual of calculating the morning's crossing. Lines and boundaries marked CABLE AREA lattice the chart. Near the compass rose, a circular area is marked DISUSED EXPLOSIVES.

A bundle of cables trail from Vancouver Island over Texada to the mainland. A gas line crosses Malaspina Strait. Two rhomboid areas named WF and WG are tagged: SEE WARNING/ VOIR AVERTISSEMENT. The strait is big again, like Frederick Sound, mischievous, notorious, and to us, little of this civility really means a thing. We are creatures of the tides. From Lasqueti, the crossing to Vancouver Island is some six miles. If we can make it tomorrow, we will be nearly home.

AUGUST 22

Radio: *Security: Military activity warning area Whiskey Gulf. Area Whiskey Gulf will be active today from zero eight zero zero Pacific Daylight Time until one six zero zero Pacific Daylight Time with surface and subsurface nonexplosive torpedo firings. Area Whiskey Gulf is considered to be extremely hazardous during operations, and all vessels are to remain well clear.*

Leaving Jedediah Island, we glide beneath a granite cliff fissured like a cortex. New homes are going in on Lasqueti. Powerboats are tucked into Lasqueti Bay.

Rounding the very southern tip of Lasqueti, we discover the point is for sale, a sign on a tiny rocky beach. Then the horizon opens, and off this southernmost land we pause in a motorless quiet. We gaze south to a rising fog bank and westward toward the haze that is Vancouver Island. Our first destination, the Ballenas Island light station, flashes ahead. There is no shipping traffic, a light and variable northwest wind wrinkles the sea, and a high-pressure system building over central Vancouver Island parts the sky, extending its clear domain north and south.

From here, Vancouver Island appears dusky, and even nearby islands are touched with unclarity, still fogged in humidity from yesterday's low-pressure trough. Clouds smear like watercolors. Vultures circle. Cormorants stand gawking with wings spread, looking like old gentlemen meeting on a street corner. From this angle I see no homes. It is our moment of silence. Our prayer. Near the other side, torpedoes.

As we pull from shore, a large wooden ship rounds the head of Lasqueti. Silhouetted, white sails stark against the eastern light, its hull possesses the same lines of the cedar canoe. This ship carries the romance of all sailing ships, the complete lure of going to sea.

Vancouver Island burns from the haze of this moist August day, its mountain crags still cupping snow in their shadows. Winds hold at light and variable, and we keep on course easily. Near the Ballenas rocks, a submarine's conning tower cuts through waves like a black steel dorsal fin, then disappears. Area Whiskey Gulf is the "WG" stamped on our chart, and we will pass within a quarter mile of its northern boundary. I frighten myself, imagining a submarine surfacing beneath us, the midnight-colored steel rushing from the deep. Recalling the killer whales, I fear things rising from below. It is a primal fear, the same fear that propelled *Jaws* to success. And on this chart, WG is a symbol for that fear—the contemporary engraving for that long absent one, the coiling sea monster.

In the middle of the strait, we are beneath a great bowl of blue. The sky has cleared, and far to the south is a familiar snowy cone. "Yahooo!" shouts Maren. "Hello, Mount Baker!" And we stop, pointing the kayaks toward the volcano like compass needles. Around the kayak the tides swirl, the surface glimmers, and our paddles—now nicked and worn even by the water itself—stir it all to life. It is no different than Alaska, the lunar body still tugging at Earth. But now the pull is a distant beacon of a known place.

After a breather at Ballenas Island, we embark on the last leg, crossing the short span to Vancouver Island. There is a uniformity to its trees. Nearly the whole island is a garden except the highest peaks. The closer we get, the more the island takes on a manicured feel. Clear-cuts just north of Nanaimo are replanted, while those nearer town and farther south hold magnificent homes with views of the strait and the sawtooth skyline of the mainland.

Then the whole shoreline becomes either rock or development. Two big cruisers plow through before us but no cruise ships. The water has been invitingly vacant. Tomorrow, a Friday, will be different. At least the submarines have remained well clear.

The beaches have been improved with borders of rocks and boardwalks to the water, and new subdivisions sit atop the sandstone cliffs, which slowly erode to beaches below. It all seems gargantuan and unnecessary, yet we, too, have been a part of this all along. Without this, Maren's beautiful songs would have been impossible. *This* made our kayaks, our radio transmissions. . . . More wide-eyed windows peer across the Strait of Georgia to the Coast Mountains, to the glaciers hanging in the highest plateaus, the relics waiting to descend once again.

Three large ferries slide in and out of Nanaimo, blasting their horns. Roads roar like speedways. Day and night are both warm, even hot, and we hardly expect rain. Even the low-pressure system that moved through yesterday brought only a countable number of raindrops.

Entering Nanaimo, a taut, shirtless kayaker with headphones and a tattoo on his left pectoral makes us part of his evening paddle. "Nanaimo is a beautiful place," Maren says. "The sandstone is sculpture."

"Ha! It's a scumhole if you live here. You don't want to go down that side of Newcastle. It's too industrial." Then, changing a CD, he fumbles and drops the portable player, and it sinks from sight. "Fuck! What's a fucking three hundred bucks!" And he paddles away.

We make camp just outside downtown Nanaimo on Newcastle Island Provincial Park, unloading on an apron of sandstone. Tides have honeycombed the island's shores into webs and globes of rock. Ashore await grassy glades, large trees, and campers. The open ground is pleasing, luxurious, and we stroll about the acreage, past park buildings and people on benches, in unobstructed bliss, giddy with our untangled strides.

Today we pierced the zone of easy access: an abundance of everything. Just a few paddling days north, communities sewn in by precipitous slopes or a beach's smallish curve had a tougher time obtaining supplies. Here, the city sprawls as the land allows, and Nanaimo drops from a few glimmering towers to a field of single-family homes. We will likely receive no more salmon fresh from a boat, or if we do, the gift will be the byproduct of a vacation package.

Garbage, which we have been saving and carrying from town to town, is now simple to dispose of in a trash can near the tent. As Maren gathers the week's trash, I shout, "Freeze!" And she looks up as two joggers stride past on the cinder track. "We haven't seen any of those yet."

"I can't imagine running after a day of paddling," she says, lifting the lid and dropping the small parcel of three days' waste. "Exercise *is* our life."

Our five-foot cable secures the kayaks to a thirtysomething western hemlock. Vancouver flickers across the strait. A laughing pack of teens in baggy pants strolls by. Soon after dark a ranger rattles to a stop on a lawn tractor. "Eight dollars, please. Which campsite?"

"Oh," I say, groping for cash. "Number eight."

Nanaimo to Stuart Island

AUGUST 24

We spend two clear, blustery days dustbowl camping on New-castle. The summer drought has coated everything with a fine film of earth. We luxuriate on the warm grass, sit under trees, and resupply in Nanaimo via the small paddlewheel ferry. We spend the time among the tall buildings and peopled fields as one would spend time at an Everest base camp, acclimating to a new environment. During one trip to town, the chummy paddlewheel captain tries to sell me health food products: "Maintenance, man. Maintenance."

In the post office I meet Niki from Namu. And we stand there, speechless.

Families of raccoons prowl the park grounds, growling packs of glowing eyes in trees, on trails at dusk. The first night one grabbed our lunch bag and dragged it off, until Maren stomped after it, shouting, finally chasing it away. "At least we are out of bear country," she says. We never once had a problem.

While Maren is in town, an old quarry worker strides into camp. "Have any work?" he asks, dropping the sledge from his shoulder. "I work sandstone."

"You can drive in these tent stakes," I say. "The ground is pretty hard this time of year. How long you been looking for work, anyways?"

"Oh, quite some time, sir. The sandstone is particularly high grade here on Newcastle. Coal, too. In fact, Newcastle was named in 1853 by the officers of the Hudson's Bay Company for the coal city of Newcastle upon Tyne, Northumberland, England. And like I was sayin', the sandstone here's so pure that it was used to make the pillars of the San Francisco Mint. Single columns, tall like timber. Sixty feet of pure Newcastle sandstone."

"What work did you do?"

"Whatever work there was, sir. In the coal days, we called mining 'chipping the roof of Hell.' But you know, there were more than miners on Newcastle. First there was the Salish Indians, then Spanish explorers in 1791 to 1792, the English coal miner from 1853 to 1903, then me, the quarry man from 1864 to 1932, then the Japanese fish plant workers from 1910 to 1932."

"And now me, a camper insulting your long and distinguished career by asking you to pound in a few tent stakes."

At this he finally breaks character and introduces himself as a living-history ranger. "You want something contemporary?" he says. "Ever read *Dead Reckoning*? It's about Native and West Coast fisheries. We have ourselves a time bomb ticking out there. We're going to take it all. And I really don't know what we're going to do. Policy seems so lagging and ineffective. And how can you manage the sea? It's tough enough to manage this park at peak season.

"Well," he says, raising the sledge to his shoulder, "gotta be on my way. Gotta find work today." And he strolls into the woods, whistling.

At nightfall, rabbits come hopping through the shadows.

AUGUST 25

Morning is full of bird calls. In the early light, I walk the Newcastle sandstones. Shadows reach among the stratified canyons, the swirled layers, the pits and pocks. I kneel, and particles rub off on my hands and knees. Not once have I felt truly insignificant on this journey. Every movement has had a consequence. Inadvertently, I have crushed barnacles, scattered birds, flushed seals from rocks, sent crabs scuttling into the shadows, and startled fish that dive and swerve to avoid our path, thinking us predator rather than mere traveler. I part algae with my bow, and the bow wave itself, however slight, reverberates downward and outward, sensed by untold creatures. Grasses are flattened by footprints and tentpads. Fragile moss crumbles or is torn loose like a toupee flung off by a gust of wind. Across the shore, limpets quarry the soft stone, leaving smooth craterlike impressions. Gulls stride among the outer slabs carrying sea stars, holding them proudly, then gulping the tense arms in three swallows.

Scored by fractures and fissures of erosion, this landscape of the ocean depths has risen to a landscape of the arid surface, the bedrock of Nanaimo, a city built on a seabed. For the next days as we begin our homeward leg, we will paddle through the Gulf Islands, of which Newcastle is a northern member. As a group, they are linear and thin, running northwest to southeast like a scratch, and they show most graphically the flow of ice that raked this country. Tectonics pressed and folded these sedimentary layers into strata of sandstones, conglomerates, shales, and coal seams that constitute most of Vancouver Island's eastern coast. This cemented beach on Newcastle is the first of many ahead.

The mainland peaks are hazy, and except for the white ferries bound for oblivion in fog, there is little hint that the city of Vancouver exists. The moon is waxing toward the last full of our journey, and its glow will ease the absence of stars.

Breaking seas on the way to Gabriola Island remind us that we are still far from home. This is our first day to paddle in shorts and T-shirts. The spray is cold on my arms and across my back. Sunblock leaks into my mouth. Along Gabriola, we slip beneath the lovely sandstone cliffs globed into hives and cathedraled into slender pipes and scrollwork. Pelagic cormorants build their nests in hollows among the guano-streaked sandstone. Orange and black lichens trail the seeping water. Above the galleries, the rock is darker and flaked, topped with grass, madrona, spruce, shore pine, and garry oak. As the rock curves to face the windy southwest, the cormorant nests decrease.

Near False Narrows, the level-headed alternative to surging Dodd Narrows, barges of wood pulp line the shore across from a mill. Where logs are tied into a raft, we wait for slack. Perhaps a tree we have seen along the way is buried somewhere in the mountains of pulp that surround the mill. Small logs, perhaps only a quarter the size of logs farther north, compose the raft. What kind of trees were these? They are cracked and weathered, trees cut at an earlier time or salvaged from a beach. Above us, glorious log homes with high windows top the sandstone cliff.

We sail through False Narrows, its sandstone slabs lining the shallows, and as the current slows, Sunfish sailboats tack in front of the cottages. People load coolers from a weekend at the island place, preparing to return to another home. A Nanaimo Realty sign hangs yellow and translucent in the sun. Gradually, the seas quiet among the islands, and the bluster of the strait eases to a slight tailwind, pushing us along with the tide.

At Pirates Cove Provincial Park in the DeCourcy Islands, we stop at a small beach. Children run among the picnic sites, and colorful tents are set along the bank. Once this was known as Gospel Cove, where Brother XII and the Aquarian Foundation had established a colony. Brother XII (actually Edward Wilson) had a knack for luring the educated and affluent to help him create a "Fortress for the Future," which they did in 1928 at Cedar-by-the-Sea. But discord festered early, culminating in colonists suing Brother XII to retrieve their lost fortunes. By then, he and his cohort, Madame Zee, had disappeared for good. A sign found near Brother XII's

Mystery House read: THIS SECTION IS RESERVED FOR INNER WORK, AND MUST REMAIN UNDISTURBED. PLEASE DO NOT PASS THIS POINT.

In quiet water we follow the heart of Trincomali Channel. From this distance the massive sandstone cliffs of Valdes Island read like a wall of hieroglyphics, chipped and blocked into textured images, phrases, and sentences that run on for miles. Beyond a cormorant colony on a miniscule guano-white rock, we find an islet hardly bigger and unload gear onto ledges pebbled like cement. Scouting a tent site, Maren meets others who are camped here, but we do not talk with them. They stay to themselves. "We're kayaking to get *away* from people," they say.

The islet grows its flowers close to ground, and stakes penetrate no farther than an inch in the shallow red soil. Crickets sing in toasted grass. A first gibbous moon peeks through the clouds, and again the clouds take on the guise of islands. Maren sees them, too: Prevost and Saturna.

The tide spills through Porlier Pass, the narrows between Valdes and Galiano Islands. It is a window to the wind-tossed strait, to the sodium glow of greater Vancouver. We fall asleep on this small shield of stone among the currents, illuminated by the sheen of a distant city and a distant moon.

AUGUST 26

Current lines stream away from Porlier like a V of geese. A northwesterly blemishes the Strait of Georgia, but inside the islands it is again quiet and calm. Boats idle near the stew of Porlier, waiting for slack water. We will stay the morning to wait for the midday ebb, as two more hours here seem a wise use of a beautiful day and this gorgeous place.

The islet is intimate, no bigger than an infield, its amber grass matted into soft footpaths that meander among the junipers and madronas, tracing the natural troughs of rock, leading everywhere to pads of softness and shade. This will most likely be our last full day in Canada. Two months since Pearse Canal and Prince Rupert.

The islet lies somewhere between summer and city homes, between the mainland and Vancouver Island, well within the vacation belt. Boats speed past but never nose ashore. I lie among the grasses, beside some shoots of Scotch broom, a hearty European shrub that has invaded these dry woodlands of Vancouver Island and the Sunshine Coast. In 1850 Scottish immigrant Captain Walter Colquhoun Grant planted broom in Sooke on southern Vancouver Island, using seeds he had obtained from the British consul in Hawaii. Only three seeds germinated, but the plants thrived, and today every broom in this region is a descendent of those first three successful ancestors.

But broom is just one of the many plants that have altered the environment here. Many, such as holly, are garden escapees, while others were introduced, either purposely or accidentally. Himalayan blackberry now infests disturbed areas, and spartina cord grass, which consumes intertidal zones in Washington, was transported here when its seeds were inadvertently scattered near wharfs. It is not a new lesson that cultural changes bring about biological changes, but it is an enduring one. As we have seen farther north, it is easy to discover where people live or have lived simply from the vegetation patterns. This translates to contemporary logging and farming, as well. A tree stump is as much a culturally modified tree as a cedar that Native peoples used for planking wood centuries ago. Clear-cuts are filled with CMTs. I lie here for some time until the roar of Porlier fades; then I pull myself from the trench, grabbing a madrona's boney limb.

But the theme still turns. If these invaders can thrive, perhaps they should be allowed to. When I talk of environmental preservation, I must first step into time and decide what period of life, which environment, to preserve. Then there are questions of why. This coastal forest has been evolving since the latest glacial retreat, changing among dominant covers of alder and shore pine, hemlock and spruce, and most recently yellow and red cedar, which arrived only five thousand years ago to many parts of the coast, sweeping northward—like much of today's human population influx from California.

As the flood slackens, we cross to Saltspring, largest of the Gulf Islands, waiting first for the *Sojourn* to power by, its captain atop the flying bridge looking far ahead with the same westerly squint that statues in America often depict. And again the homes. Often there are two empty chairs outdoors. A flower arrangement. A windsock. A sculpture of seagulls. These are palatial homes, extended on pilings and equipped with their own breakwaters. One pier says NO TRESPASSING. PRIVATE PROPERTY. KEEP OFF. Another: OYSTERS AND CLAMS PRIVATELY OWNED. TAKING OR DESTROYING IS HIGHLY PROHIBITED. Far ahead looms the gray bulge of Mount Constitution on Orcas Island. The United States. We have climbed that mountain before.

As we paddle by these houses, we recall how Tenakee Springs looked abandoned from the water, yet how inside it was well kept and friendly. These homes face the water, purposely oriented for panoramas—signs of a culture trying to see beyond itself. There is no main street running behind and most often no physical community in sight. From the sea, the homes appear isolated and withdrawn. Their owners must be tired of looking at people and seek the companionship of water, instead.

The push toward camp is arduous in the twilight. Again, it is an islet, the only public land within a day's range. We arrive at dusk and must carry gear up a crumbling embankment to a tent-sized clearing as the sun chokes in cloud. Within a half hour the moon rises orange. All night, ferries ply the crook of Active Pass, blowing horns as required by law. Some ships breathe a major chord; others, a minor. After a time, we can nearly identify the tubby craft by their calls, as distinctive as whales.

AUGUST 27

Slugs all over the tent last night, and this morning four snot along my kayak and map case. The climate has moistened again, and the tent's nylon has lost its Nanaimo crispness.

Radio: *Today's ultraviolet index for the south coast is near five point nine. This value is in the moderate range with average time to sunburn around thirty minutes. Index indicates the ultraviolet intensity in full sunlight at midday. For personal weather consultation call 1-900-565-4555. Charges will apply. . . . East Vancouver Island: Today, cloudy with sunny periods, cooler. Highs twenty-three to twenty-seven. For tonight, becoming mainly cloudy, low of thirteen. For Wednesday cloudy with sunny periods, a chance of a shower, highs near twenty-three. Chance of precipitation: ten percent today, twenty percent tonight, forty percent on Wednesday.*

It is a woman's voice, schooled in broadcasting. She recites the statistics in cool, seductive tones. You can hear the spittle in her voice as if she is whispering in your ear, telling you, "There will be high pressure building in the south today." Then comes the casual offer of personal weather consultation, the 900 number. "Charges will apply."

The American weather announcer speaks in a more matter-of-fact tone: *South Coast synopsis: Significant changes in the weather pattern along the coast will take place over the next few days. The strong ridge of high pressure that has been providing sunny, hot weather for most regions is now moving east. Cooler marine air has begun to invade the south coast, with some areas reporting low cloud and fog this morning, especially on the outer coast.*

"The end of summer," Maren laments, piling on layers of clothes.

Tony had told us about this seasonal transition on the *Segue.* As we paddle, a wind has sent the summer east, and we are again bundled in long underwear and Gore-Tex.

All morning I am frustrated. "We are aliens," I tell Maren. People we now meet seem to have little understanding of our experience, whereas farther north, even those who did not paddle knew more about the elements. They had to. "Now that we're near the cities, we know if it will sprinkle in the morning or be sunny by noon!"

"You're self-destructing. . . ."

When I click off the radio, I return my trust to the waves, absorbed into the reality of paddling that will hold until we scrape ashore in the tidal flats of the Nisqually Delta in southern Puget Sound. And I shut up.

A minor chord blares, and a white ferry noses from Active Pass. We wait. At last, when there are no horns, we race across Swanson Channel. As we near South Pender Island, a major chord blasts—the big ferry. For a time it steams directly at us; then, adjusting its course as it rounds Prevost Island, it veers west. Turboprops whine low on their half-hourly hops between Victoria and Vancouver. On North Pender Island the porches, flag poles, and scant wooden stairsteps down to the water continue and multiply.

Halfway down the west side of North Pender, a bald eagle, our first in days, has captured a duckling and flies with its soft prey dangling, swaying with each beat of the powerful wings.

Wind chimes tinkle, as if people here need to be reminded of the shriek of wind. The farther south we travel, the more images, carvings, and trinkets depict wildlife. Eagle silhouettes are nailed to doors, and cast-iron gulls alight on decks.

The tide has turned against us, so we stay close to the cliff. Down Haro Strait, Canada falls into the southern murk, and the United States climbs again on the south. To us the masses appear nearly identical: two low, sloping islands.

We stop at Bedwell Harbor, where Spanish explorers anchored in 1791, and enjoy a spinach salad and a shower, renting towels from the innkeeper, dropping a few extra bucks into the coin box to keep the water hot. When the tide is nearly high, Maren and I paddle a short distance along South Pender, shake hands, and begin. Somewhere ahead amid the restless currents of Boundary Pass there is an international border.

Soon after we depart, a tanker plows northward, rounds Turn Point, and hugs the American shore. Its sudden appearance startles us, a looming hulk of gray steel. Like the cruise ships, freighters power through the water deceptively fast, able to outrun even some of the recreational boats. We wait for a time, then pull again from shore. It is slack tide, and every channel in the San Juans, every channel of the entire coast, is nearing a calm, each slowing, pausing, then reversing at its signature rate and time.

Offshore a line of chop lingers, then smoothes. Jitters again. Digging into the water, we maintain heightened watches for boat traffic, unexpected currents, the uncertain state of winds. Although we have paddled for more than a thousand miles, these remain unknowns. We have learned about the past. We can extrapolate the present. And so often in kayaking and in making a crossing, a desire to know the future intensifies. What will the weather do? The waters? Will the beach marked on the chart be landable? As much as it is possible, we strain to glimpse into time ahead. Make a prediction.

Somewhere in midchannel we cross the invisible border that zags sharply south along Haro Strait, then west in the Strait of Juan de Fuca. We are never sure quite where it is. Although the chart shows it as a band of plus signs, the water is seamless.

At last we near Stuart Island's grassy cliffs and layers of rock tilted abruptly vertical. Aiming to camp in the state park, we land where an immaculate dory, the *Li'l Titanic*, flies an American flag as if there to greet us. We unload, stacking the bear canisters on shore, then the tent, the chart cases, the flares. . . . Looking up, we find people on boats looking away. Others stare, asking questions.

Amid the occupied sites we find a leafy camp next to a family, and all evening parents hush children who refuse to sleep in the night air. Above the continuous glugging of bilge pumps, a southeast wind races through the trees, delivering wafts of perfume from nearby yachts. The San Juan Islands. In the outhouse I glance into the hole—an aerial view of a mound of toilet paper, heaps of it piled like a dirtied volcano. Maren sees it, too.

"Back in the USA," she says.

SOUNDSCAPES

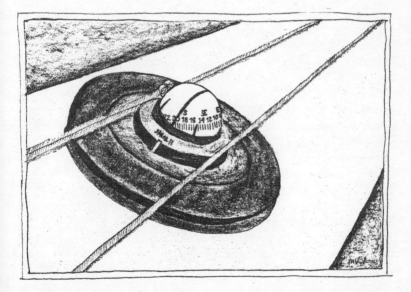

Stuart Island to Swinomish

A morning of eddies and mixing currents. As the spring tide
pours across the ragged seafloor off Johns Island, we paddle
into the cloud banks toward Flattop. Small riptides taint the
water, and whirlpools dot the chart. The kayak pivots, swinging north, then south as it edges the slick boils that overlie
crags and knobs where the currents well up and race. The
waters are unwieldy and erratic as we are carried first toward
the open of Boundary Pass, then into San Juan Channel, the
islands sweeping north, then south until, spinning and correcting, we are bobbing off Flattop. A sign warns: NATIONAL WILD-
LIFE REFUGE. STAY 200 YARDS AWAY. The islet is about the size
of those we have camped on for two nights now, and Maren
is quick to note the point. In a painful way, our range is
diminishing, and like the wildlife, we converge on the few
places reserved for our paddling ways. In the past weeks, the
life we knew farther north is now endangered.

Soon we are off with the flood for a quick ride to Jones
Island State Park. Landing on the northern cove, we are in
the midst of a blowdown that occurred in 1990. Deer strut
about looking for handouts, and bees circuit among the

mighty downed trunks. As Maren traverses the island to survey the southern camp, a family from a powerboat walks the dock to shore, staying for about a minute before screaming, "Bees! Bees!" The dad, long shorts to his knees, waddles behind, rolling his eyes. And then they are gone.

Maren returns, having claimed a campsite by placing her hat on a picnic table, and we paddle to the southern shore, setting up near the two-man crew of the *Li'l Titanic*. Yesterday they were caught, roped to a buoy, in the tide rips of mid-Boundary Pass. "We had to be towed in by a damn powerboat!" one of the men says. "Jeez, they just gunned it. We were taking on water!"

After dinner, when it is dark, I light a candle, place it on shore near camp, and slip the kayak into the water. This is something I have wanted to do all summer long: paddle beneath the full moon. Other moons have somehow been elusive, but tonight, the sky is golden. Through a thin vapor, the moonlight refracts. A moondog. The water is completely quiet—a glossy ink.

The bow wave of my kayak and swirls from my paddle sparkle with light. At first I think it is moonlight, but as I paddle in and out of the glittering pockets, I realize it is bioluminescence. The water teems with plankton, Noctiluca— "night light." When I stir them with atmosphere, a chemical reaction between oxygen and their organic compound luciferin emits a flash of light, a cold light, green and gray.

When I glide through a pool of Noctiluca and the water again darkens, I see the reflected sky—clouds and a rippled moon. Calls echo across the water. Chirping crickets. Bursts of laughter. The occasional red, white, and green blink of navigation. Homes blazing with light perforate the far shores. A few sailboats lie quietly at anchor. I drift with the current, not paddling, whispering prayers of thanksgiving, twirling in the tide.

From the darkness come puffs of air, at first intermittent, then encircling me. The breaths of porpoises. Then I can see the breaths as they catch the Noctiluca, hurling it skyward in plumes of luminous mist rising and falling all around. A distant tail slap lights the water. Dark fins streak the surface. Once I see the whole form of a porpoise, glowing as it torpedoes beneath my hull. Gradually they move on or I drift away, and the water again glazes to a mirror of sky.

From a quarter mile away our beach is white with moonshine, my faint candle shining yellow into the whole night; one candlepower, home. I recall past full moons—the moon at Hoonah, the moon of the Stikine, of Dixon Entrance, of Cape Caution. How far we have paddled! If we were to travel this passage again, it would never be the same. The whole impression of places would change with the tides, we would make different decisions and at different points, and the passage would be before us and all new again. For a time I follow the slurp of paddles, the glowing swirls spinning behind like galaxies. On this journey, for a final night perhaps, the moon has blotted out the glowing dome of southern sky that is Seattle.

AUGUST 29

We leave Jones before the powerboaters and ride the swift ebb eastward between Orcas and Shaw Islands, celebrating the familiar sights of the Washington State Ferry terminal on Orcas. We have journeyed here many times for weekends with parents and friends. This day it is a splendid landmark, and were we traveling by more conventional means, we would be in Seattle by lunchtime.

All afternoon we dodge speedboats and ferries. I buy a Cadbury from the nuns on Shaw Island. We stop at the bird sanctuary at Spencer Spit State Park. Maren remembers when the San Juans felt so cozy—when once they were our urban escape. I say the tides are still wild, and she agrees. Cable-crossing signs are ubiquitous along every shore, the entire island group now teleconnected.

In Thatcher Pass, two eagles battle in flight, one stealing the other's prey and knocking the empty-taloned bird into the water.

Unable to swim, the eagle flounders, at last lifting its wings and rowing ashore. Then seeing us, it flies high and away.

Camp on James Island is thankfully quiet, and we follow the orange moon rising over Guemes Channel, where more than two centuries before, Captain Cook, beneath his towering masts, first met the Coast Salish who paddled dugout canoes. Tomorrow, if the weather is good, we will cross Rosario Strait, the last open water before the realm of continuous roadways.

AUGUST 30

A stormy morning with driving rains. After squalls, the wind calms before blowing again, and in one of these lulls near slack, we paddle into Rosario. The currents here are as impulsive as any we have seen, funneling and spiraling among the various San Juan passes. Cars, apparent from midchannel, flash like distant fish. Strangely again, it has calmed though curtains of rain drench the Strait of Juan de Fuca to the south. We scan for ship traffic. All is clear.

Off Fidalgo Head the current sweeps us north in a confusion of standing waves, and we must power against it to turn inside Burroughs Island, where we skirt landscaped lawns of cobbles and salals and boulders. The houses are built on cliffs of glacial deposits, mudstone that smears underfoot and home to hundreds of bank swallows. Drainage pipes flop down from the bluff tops. Used tires form a breakwater. Behind Burroughs Island is a dark rock bolted with light ripples—the familiar pattern we first saw in Misty Fiords. Then an ornate wooden home. Then the same rock patterns again and again.

Then *whoosh!* A black back, a fin—a whale off Edith Point, the only unhoused parcel of earth. The whale surfaces twice more before diving deep. When we nose to the beach, the land is signed: JOHN GEARY SHORELINE PRESERVE. PRIVATE PROPERTY. NO FIRES. PLEASE HELP PROTECT THE SHOREBIRD HABITAT. THE SAN JUAN PRESERVATION TRUST. For us it is a respite, a beach with the familiar drift logs and old trees—not first

growth but larger than most. It seemed as if the whale knew
that this was its place also, this small but quiet shore. Then
the houses start again, plus a small marina. A big heron stands
in the shallows, shawled in long feathers.

A mile north of Deception Pass, luxury homes top the
cliff, one apparently designed after Monticello. The rock soon
eclipses these aeries, however, and slipping beneath, among
the open waters to the west and the low swell sucking at the
rock, we gather the lost feeling of complete out-thereness that
has subsided with all the development. Suddenly we are in
an envelope of lapping waves and wind, and a spell that had
been cast near Refuge Cove breaks. We believe in the coast
again, that these places still exist, that we will see more of
them, that people here, too, live within the breath of wild.
For this mile, we are lost somewhere in the maze of islands,
somewhere upcoast, somewhere we call a wilderness.

We tent on a mowed lawn near an open-sided log-and-
stone pavilion built by the CCC in the 1930s. Instead of bear
scat, we negotiate dog scat as we travel to and from the water
pump. This marine-trail campsite caters exclusively to paddlers, and we are its only occupants. Vacationing children
walk the beach, stepping among the rocks as if they are stepping among poisonous snakes. Maren phones Ray and Dorraine, friends she first met nearly a decade ago when writing
her master's thesis about the Swinomish Tribal Community.
They will meet us there tomorrow. When I turn off my headlamp, a glow continues though the moon is hardly risen.

AUGUST 31

The final day of August. Last night I spent six minutes ($1.25)
on a hot shower, and today I feel presentable to friends.

Chopping and pounding fills the morning campground as if
it were a factory. Against the procession of Subaru wagons, men
in muscle shirts loiter beneath enormous striped tarps. Mini-
bikes. Jet Skis. From the water spigot, a tall grassy trail follows

the overflow stream nearly fifteen yards to our tent. "Can you believe this is camping?" Maren says. Powerboats skim through Deception Pass at max current. People marvel at gulls.

We head into Deception Pass, and jet fighters—A-6s that went to the Gulf War—thunder from the Whidbey Island air base, then rocket overhead. Always noise. Yesterday at times we could not hear the water, and it struck us how much we depend on its sound for our knowledge of waves, subtle changes in currents, and tide rips, the way it breaks upon the shore. Overhead spans the Deception Pass Bridge that made Whidbey less of an island. Most powerfully, though, is the known water. We have paddled here before, to Skagit and Hope Islands and among the estuary of the Skagit River. And we have friends on the other side of the island ahead. Good friends, at last.

In the dredged route to Swinomish Channel, boats motor near, and we shoulder this two-lane watery road. Somehow we have forgotten that the seafloor is manufactured here, that the bottom rises abruptly to shallows no deeper than two feet. Just as we cross this line, the wake from a passing boat suddenly steepens and breaks from behind as big as ocean surf. I teeter, the crests skimming along the top of my deck, and Maren, who has gone farther into the shallows is nearly capsized—the closest she has come the entire journey.

Swinomish Channel looks different: the cliffs and rock we have missed from the highway, the old pilings from cannery and logging days, the underside of the arched spans of Rainbow Bridge—which we have driven over many times—gateway to La Conner and Swinomish.

Then we see the faces of Ray, Dorraine, Carrie, Ken, and Jim on a sweep of sandy beach. When Maren and I make our way to shore, we all hug and smile, and our friends laugh at our sopping legs and spray skirts. After we talk with a local reporter who has tagged along, Jim wraps a stole around his shoulders and holds two cedar boughs tied in red ribbon to the sky and sings. His song is hymnlike and beautiful and dances with the afternoon breeze. As he sings, he blesses us and our kayaks with the cedar boughs, dusting them through the air, twirling, sweeping, fanning cedar. We are here among friends who have become dear friends simply by being on this beach on this shining day.

We unload and head into Ray and Dorraine's home. In the evening, we enter the sweat lodge.

In the blackness the water pours, hissing over glowing rocks. Ever so slightly, the cold air sucks from my body before the steam descends, rolling down my shoulders, my hunched-over back, a searing wind burning my nostrils. A warm front moving over me, through me, over the ocean, the hills and mountains and across the water. A bank of vapor swirling and curling and clinging to leaves and twigs, the dark undersides of boulders, blades of grasses, enveloping all and giving all drink. Hiss and heat and dripping sweat and calling our ancestors to be with us, a council with the all of life. Red fire and crackling cedar, the rush of oxygen-hungry flame. Hiss. The wind. High peaks and watery troughs, the drifting, the breaking waves, the distant shores coming to focus, the bank of gray and murk, the far rock now living with trees. Hiss. The searing winds descending my head, my neck, my back, a wind breath—the breath, as Ray has said, of God.

An image: Hands. Reaching. They are my hands, so small against a mysterious and solitary stone that seems to have rolled from nowhere. My first touch with the all of time.

With each of the four rounds, the evening advances, and at the close the first stars are appearing. Bright Jupiter, Cassiopeia, the great wild of the universe evident once more in these distant pinpricks of light. I touch the cedar shakes and look at the glistening faces of friends gazing skyward. We drink from a garden hose, our bodies steaming, small clouds condensing and rising from us, around us, and into the cool night. Then hot soup and bread and sleep in deep cotton sheets.

SEPTEMBER 1

September, a transitional month, the seasons changing once again. I study a wall-sized Washington state map in Ray's home office. The land is partitioned in boxy patches of color: national parks, red; national forests, green; wilderness areas, green with dark borders; Indian reservations, brown; highways, bright red; urban areas, ochre; and the rest, which is private land, off-white. A single editorial decision perhaps separates the state into groups of people, places of trees, places of city, places of privacy. It is very difficult to see one world when we look at our maps.

Ray and I talk a lot today, across the table along the six-foot map on which we have traced our route. "Did you feel differently at different places on the journey?" he asks.

"Many places," I say. "The central British Columbia coast—once we paddled through there, we *were* different. We didn't need to know what was coming next. We knew we would endure."

"Hmm," he says, making a connection. "There is an idea in the teachings: People who like big drum powwows congregate around and go to big drum powwows. So do the spirits go to where they feel comfortable: the undeveloped lands, where it was like in the days of the hunts, the old fishing grounds. It's interesting to me that you had those feelings there. And greater that you are aware of them."

In the evening, Dorraine gives us a medicine bag and a braid of sweet grass wrapped red-cotton cloth. She says it is a gift of unity, marking the beginning of who we are to become. It is a reminder of the responsibility we now have with our increased teachings and experiences.

As we repack the drybags, preparing for the morning departure, Ray says, "The elders tell us that if you say you will be somewhere, be there, for your spirit has already prepared you to go and may already be there. If you do not go, then you are not whole, your spirit may be missing, and something bad can happen."

So we send our spirits to Nisqually Delta and gather the bits of us that linger in places along the way. This is how a home is assembled—by the complete presence of places been.

Swinomish to Seattle

SEPTEMBER 2

As Maren and I load the kayaks, Ray, Dorraine, and Carrie ease into their canoe. As soon as they are afloat, the current grabs hold, and tall Ray takes a mighty stroke from the stern. The canoe wobbles, and several gallons of water spill over the gunnel. Continuing to drift toward some pilings, Ray's next stroke dumps them into the cold bath. All three bob up whoofing and laughing. "Leave it to the Indians to sink the canoe," Ray says, sloshing ashore.

We paddle from Swinomish Channel and along the pebbled shores of Whidbey and Camano Islands, the fresh cedar boughs bound in red ribbon streaming from our kayaks, the wind breathing their sweetness back to the cockpit. It is Labor Day, and despite the boat traffic and the cliff-top homes, the shoreline is new, as unfamiliar as anywhere we have been.

The Skagit River delta is shallow and flat and recalls the Stikine delta, having two islands—Goat and Ika—and plains of shoreline grass. Both Whidbey and Camano are heaps of glacial till, high cliffs studded with loose cobbles and pebbles that erode and fall to the shore, reminiscent of Malcolm and Cormorant Islands. The cliffs ascend steeply for about a hundred feet, then flatten, sprouting madrona. And we see what we have not seen before: Nearly all of Puget Sound is a splendid beach.

As the summer's last boaters slight Whidbey Island with the frequency of cars on a freeway, the old stone walls of a fish trap lap above the wake. A haze of cloud crops and frames glimpses of Mount Rainier—the snow-crevassed base, the glacial dome. All day we paddle toward it like salmon heading toward the Nisqually River, where Rainier's silty meltwaters meet Puget Sound.

A heron launches from the shore, screeching, slowly tucking its craning neck. With each beat of wings its body ripples, its flight uneven as it rides waves of air. On a Camano Island beach we pull ashore to use an outhouse. A couple walking their dog strolls past. "Where did you come from?" the man asks, smirking, eyeing the loaded kayaks, "Glacier Bay?" We look at each other and laugh, and when we tell him it is true, he steps a few paces back, mildly embarrassed, then advances with renewed interest, asking about training and equipment.

"By now," Maren says, "we have years of experience." They stroll down the beach and wave with both arms as we paddle by.

We camp at Camano Island State Park and again have the luxury of a marine-trail campsite. HUMAN-POWERED BEACHABLE WATERCRAFT—CAMPING ONLY, reads the sign. The site is tucked away at the corner of the beach, away from the parking lot.

The evening weather announcer declares that an autumn-like weather system will affect Puget Sound for the next week, and raindrops fall large and loudly against the tent. In the last moments of sunlight, rays ignite the flowering grasses against the sky of rain. The burst lasts but minutes, and then it is dark.

SEPTEMBER 3

Quiet rain and cool.

The city of Everett is shrouded until clouds lift to reveal

its steaming mill. As we cross to Whidbey, the holiday boaters have gone, and we are left among the cries of gulls. Puget Sound is lonely today. Whidbey is in a deluge. Large modern homes built mostly on the sand spits line the shores, and a mud slide has devastated part of a hill, leaving the new cliff-top homes within feet of the edge. These homeowners should take notice: graffiti is not painted on Whidbey's shores, but gouged with a fingernail.

Still, the coast is diverse, unexpected, and unknown despite our previous travels here. We stare at the beach, the cliffs, and the trees, looking for patterns that we need to determine landing and camp, how far the tent stakes will penetrate the soils, how well they will hold. Then we hear a sound we haven't heard for weeks: a tug. The engine's drone, the methodical hammering of its pistons, is guttural and steady, so unlike the buzzing of recreational craft, with their surges of power and unsteady throttles in weekenders' hands. The tug plods through the water toward Admiralty Inlet, the Strait of Juan de Fuca, and the open Pacific.

In January 1855, directly across Possession Sound from here, the Suquamish and Duwamish Chief Seattle signed his name with an "X" to the Treaty of Point Elliott, which relinquished Native land title of much of the Puget Sound region, making way for pioneer settlement. Although Seattle was a baptized Catholic and never fought against the settlers, in light of the treaty, it seems a dubious honor—if one at all—to give the city that grew on this land, that soon displaced the chief and his people, his name.

In an earlier speech—delivered in December of 1854 at a reception for Governor Isaac Stevens, commissioner of Indian Affairs for Washington Territory, that announced treaty negotiations—Chief Seattle had said, "Every part of this country is sacred to my people." Seattle was speaking of his homeland, a concept the settlers and Governor Stevens did not understand in terms of this region. To the settlers, this was new country, open opportunity.

Now the land around us is parceled, either kept or unkept from fence to fence. As Jim Mackovjak had said way back in

Gustavus, everybody has a plan for the land. We notice the fences now more than ever as we follow the shore, climbing to headland and falling again to beach, the way land lifts from the sea, the way it is smoothed or broken.

With the fences comes a freedom that has been taken. We enter the dense city wondering where we are to sleep. As kayakers, the boundaries, the regulations that we understand as citizens, are all but erased. The places to land, the sheltered shores still exist as they have for millennia. But the culture has encroached upon the shores, closed them down to this type of seeing. Then memory goes spinning on its peculiar way, and Maren and I talk often of the beautiful northern beaches, the remote rocks, the bears that stepped from the forests, and remember the nearly countless camps, the high waves, with much the same fondness that Len Emmonds recalled his trapping days.

After this long journey, I now understand what has happened, the extent of our work, the reach of our cities. Yet among it all, the tides still rush, and we still can paddle. There is still enough wild to continue. And our velocity, the velocity of the paddle, is one that endures, as it always has, in places as everyday as the human stride.

"I just don't know why people need so much," Maren finally says. "We should sell everything we put in storage. You with me?"

But, in fact, this proposition is difficult. All too soon we will return to society. It is a transition that will be much more difficult and take much longer than we had imagined months ago. Looking at these shores, I confront the self I created to fit this place, someone I now barely know. Maren and I have found a happiness on the water, a meaning between us, a home together along this long and varied coast. In an age where interactivity so often describes the virtual world of computers, as the American experience becomes more and more a vicarious experience, we have lived in real time, in a tangible world, open to its nuances, insight, and meaning, and now we must face the headwind of modern life.

When we cross to the mainland, we cross to a continuous

railroad, a sheer wall with muddy water draining from pipes. Occasionally a relic beach juts seaward from the railroad grade—the only beaches left along much of this shore.

By evening, the only place to camp is a day-use park where no camping is allowed. A Burlington Northern freight train roars overhead as we unload through a stone walkway beneath the tracks.

Thankfully, the park ranger has taken us in and fed us pizza.

SEPTEMBER 4

We load by the mouth of a stream that empties beneath the train trestle. Today we will make downtown Seattle.

As we slip the kayaks into the water, a jogger joins us. "How'd you persuade your wife to do this?" he asks, marking time.

Maren bristles.

"My wife won't even go camping. She needs two-hundred-dollar-a-night hotel rooms."

He talks of always wanting to get away, to adventure. He clutches dumbbells wrapped in neoprene, zestless, waiting for a response. Fumbling for words, we finally say that someday he will surely get away to travel. As we paddle, he waves and for a short distance runs along shore by our side before striding inland.

We parallel the railroad grade for most of the day. Slowly the houses compress into tight gridded streets. Each view property has the vacant stare of a workday afternoon. Only the rich are home, lounging in yards or manipulating geraniums. Anvil thunderheads build across the sound, truncating the Olympic foothills.

At Shilshole Marina, a forest of masts that stand like a grove of trees, we paddle into the ship canal toward downtown. Sea lions lounging on a green buoy bark at us. In the locks we tie up next to a crab boat from Juneau. The *Victoria*

Ann from Petersburg. The *Annie Sue* from Seattle. We are all vessels of the Passage, coastal travelers in microcosm. Above, tourists video and point at our kayaks. And when the massive steel doors open, they open to the city.

We paddle through the shipyards, beneath known bridges, past enormous bows, welders, the hiss of speeding tires. We pass boats: *Boom Child*, *Star Rover*, *Nasdaq Calls*. Traffic roars all around. At last narrow Fremont cut, a strait slice made by the Army Corps of Engineers to connect the seawater with fresh, opens to brackish Lake Union and the city center.

Lake Union. The city surrounds us; low jets and freeways always sound like distant rapids. It is freakish, a novelty, as a glacier is a novelty, something that one would visit and then soon depart.

When we dock at our friend Judy's houseboat on the eastern shore, she is playing Hovhaness's "Mysterious Mountain" and "God Created Great Whales."

"Hello! Hello!" she calls, elated to be part of our journey. She has heaping platefuls of stir-fry ready and tells us that she just returned from a silent retreat. So had we, we say laughing. And more good friends meet us for a toast. We are pleased to be among these known faces, grateful for the waterfront hospitality, the companionship of town. When they leave, it is raining, and on deck, Maren and I slip into the hot tub.

Crossing Puget Sound

SEPTEMBER 5

A Macintosh chimes, and I bolt awake. Windy this a.m., even in the boathouse area. Plants are swinging, and cats are meowing early.

Off by 10:15. Blustery winds from the south kick up Lake Union, and we skim beneath the spans of bridges and arches, through the locks and back to open Puget Sound as if we have escaped a small room.

Near Discovery Lighthouse, at the metro sewage treatment plant, we look for a bathroom before crossing Puget Sound. Amid a landscaping project are two outhouses and a man mulching newly planted trees. He is the same man whose portrait is on the side of a large truck. As we ask about the outhouse, he wonders where we've paddled from. We tell him and he brightens. "I used to be a gillnetter near Kodiak! Boy, you've seen a lot. Wow! All I've been doing is blowing bark." It is pleasing to hear his fishing memories, and we talk with him about the coast, about various islands and coves, and when we are paddling again, we are happy that we have met this big man who blows bark.

Despite the city, Puget Sound is a crossing no different

than any other, and in midsound, sudden gusts chop the water and hurl bullets of rain into our faces. The going is slow, then not at all. In the shipping lane, we scan for traffic, for freighters departing Port of Seattle. None. When I look back, the city emerges from the bluffs like the snout of a glacier that has shrunken into its hollow. On the magnificent scale of Elliott Bay, downtown Seattle seems a village.

Black clouds stream down like the tendrils of jellyfish. The wind paws across the water, finally backing with enough angle so that we can power forward. Ahead, the "Commuter Islands"—Bainbridge and, tomorrow, Vashon. We pick up glare off distant windows. A ship approaches, a jet floats over the city. Then the city is far enough away to be silent, transforming into a singular shimmering mass.

On Bainbridge Island we rest, hidden beneath shoreline trees; then we paddle to Blake Island State Park in a rough water that we have not seen since Kelp Head. My kayak loses stability. Water sloshes inside, flooding to my knees. I pump it out, but it refills quickly in the heave. I am taking on water somewhere and must pump out the kayak twice more before Maren discovers that my spray skirt knot has loosened, causing the seal to leak profusely. She reties it, and we limp to Blake near dusk.

I search for a phone to make arrangements for a pickup at Nisqually Delta. At Tillicum Village, a north-coast-style longhouse that holds nightly salmon feasts and Native dancing shows, a guy smoking outside says, "There's no phone here, fella. Hope it wasn't urgent. Gotta go dance now." He flicks the cigarette butt and enters the longhouse.

Forty-five degrees Farenheit tonight with a dew-point spread less than five. Breath condenses. From camp, we overlook the sound. Seattle glimmers, calving ferries across water. Deer stroll our beach. Always jets. The sodium-vapor glow creates a Martian atmosphere, and the Space Needle's blinking disk appears ready for liftoff. Seattle seems such a small place for such a large city.

Blake Island to Nisqually Delta

SEPTEMBER 6

Radio: *The following sound is transmission of digital data that permits anyone to receive printed weather information including the hearing impaired and public safety officials.* *SHHRRREEEEEEEEEEEEEEEEE . . .*

From Blake Island we paddle south through Colvos Passage, a short day highlighted by frequent stops to gather blackberries that flourish along shore. Hills eclipsed the city center in less than an hour. Seattle is now a memory. Tomorrow, Tacoma. The Narrows Bridge. Standing atop the picnic table for good radio reception, I arrange a ride to meet us at Nisqually Delta in two days, Sunday, at 3 P.M. when the tide is high. Then I sit and stare at the candle. We are preparing for the end of a lifestyle. A journey completed. A time, strangely, where mourning is equal to joy. All night cars snarl through the parking circle, then peel away.

SEPTEMBER 7

This morning brings the sliver of a moon and a broken vestibule pole. Our final full day. The water off Point Defiance is blue and filmy with gasoline, and fishermen are trolling. When the water clears, there are instantly more sea stars. High above, two eagles soar. New construction is everywhere—houses, hammers, saws, and new wood. All morning we approach the twin towers of the Tacoma Narrows Bridge.

Tacoma is a glance through Dalco Passage, a port choked with mills that smoke as if the whole city is ablaze. A sooty yellow stratum of sulfur dioxide floats above the city—the Tacoma Aroma. On the water, oil coats our kayaks at the waterline, and our bow waves refract rainbows. Stumps with plank marks from the old logging days still litter the woods.

At the narrows the current increases, and we sail under the Tacoma Narrows Bridge—the Galloping Gertie that shook apart in gale winds of 1940. It was my favorite film in high-school physics, that bridge rolling like an ocean. Large madronas cling by a few roots, and others lie on the beaches below.

At one o'clock, the wind starts abruptly, and the crossing to McNeil Island is arduous but uneventful. Our momentum is slowing. McNeil is a prison, the island a penitentiary. On shore a deer carcass lies in the tide, bloated, haloed by flies. The prison is a pale yellow and dreary. Razor wire coils the fences. Signs read: STAY CLEAR 100 YARDS. As we slip past, a ferry that shuttles to and from the prison waits at the dock, and two small children press their faces against the window, staring at us. The prison is a low-pressure center, drawing everything down. We have little energy. We are tired of wind.

On this final night, the only camp, at last, is illegal. We pitch the tent behind a NO CAMPING sign on a tiny island, but we have no choice. Even this day has its logic. We wait like burglars in the trees for a ranger to patrol or issue fines. Two boys row ashore and announce it is OK for us to camp. They are Boy Scouts and often camp here and help keep up the island because no rangers stop by anymore. All evening, though, people in the nearby homes watch us. Someone yells something about the island, but we do not understand.

We spend time recounting our energy, in disbelief. At last we are seven and a half miles from being finished. Tomorrow, when we round Anderson Island, the land ahead will wrap around, and there will be no more salt water. Although Puget Sound fans out into inlets to the south and west and descends a few miles farther south to Olympia, the Nisqually Delta is a more fitting end. Like so many places we have been, it is a meeting place, where cultures have long lived, mingled, and clashed and where fresh and salt water mix, the meltwater of the Nisqually Glacier on Mount Rainier flowing in silty currents as the Nisqually River. The continuity is as surprising as it is meaningful, that throughout the countless passages, along what appears to be a fragmented and broken coast, we have discovered the intersections, a confluence of lives and landforms, and it seems that this is what the Inside Passage has long been: a tapestry of homes and homelands interwoven with this grand inland sea.

The places we lived, the string of campsites, have each become known, ephemeral homes where we dreamed of where we had been and tried to push ahead. Each camp carried an emotional component, distinct and essential to our journey, and even now we can recall any one of them with clarity and powerful feeling. If we are a lost people today, as so many complain, it is perhaps because we have lost this capacity to be at home with the land and our lives as we live them. A true home is not claimed through mere tenure but through a depth of living. We have lived fully within almost every place on our journey, between its dawn and dusk, along its slope of land, encountering the way waves curl across the rocks at various stages of tide, its parcel of forest, and learned how it all shapes our lives. Now these places assemble themselves as a region, and we begin to see the larger home we have found on this coast. Although we do not have a cultural legacy of ten thousand or more years living here, we have paddled these shores as many once did, and we now know the coast in ways they once did, in ways that all people once knew their homelands—through its weathers and waters and work.

Patio lights blaze across the water. Seals, our constant companions, circle the island, and a lone sea lion barks from a green buoy. The screech of herons. These elements—the creatures, the tides, the winds—used to be *the* elements; they enwrapped life only a few generations ago, before the abundance of modern convenience. In those days an end to a journey such as ours would simply be a continuation of the life we have come to know as paddlers in a slightly different form. Now it seems we must break from this routine almost entirely. That we may benefit little from the knowledge of high or low tide, of cloud types, of sea state in this city by the sound. Our time on the water is nearly over. Tomorrow at high tide, at 3:00 P.M.: another world.

SEPTEMBER 8

Radio: *The weak weather disturbance moving overhead this morning will bring mostly cloudy skies and a chance of light rain or drizzle to western Washington. High pressure will be slow to move in over western Washington Sunday afternoon, with some improvement by early evening.*

Our final morning. I say this several times to myself, but it does not sink in. *Our final morning.* Just as on our first on Sebree Island in Glacier Bay, the sky is full of low, undulating clouds. Again the great weather powers are jousting, the Aleutian Low returning, the North Pacific High retreating. The seasons again in flux.

We shove off and curl inside the island, heading east. "We are done!" Maren shouts. "Done! Did it! Done!"

"You wonder why it is difficult for the salmon to come back; it's difficult enough even for two kayakers to come back," I say.

"We're done! DONE!" And she sings. The sun breaks through clouds, and Maren is asking for a kiss. The sea lion barks from the buoy again, echoing all around. We pass the razor wire of McNeil the watchtower. The walls are closing in, and we talk often of what will come next and how to pay for things. Ahead, the shoreline and its houses are blotted out in a gray squall. The wind is warm, and shafts of sun move along the water, columns of light from a distant star. A low chop splashes across the bow.

At the base of Mount Rainier, the snouts of glaciers rise into the clouds. Always the ice! A drizzle washes salt from our kayaks and from our jackets and hats. A cleansing. The seawater, too, has a fresh layer from the many rivers flowing into the south sound. There is a grandness this morning; the whole sound has been unveiled. Bridges I have driven over I now view from below. I see the soft and vulnerable rock eroding into beautiful beaches, gathered, graded, and washed by tides. For a moment, Maren and I stop paddling. There are no motors. Waves rush the beach. Wind. Bird cries. All morning we glide through pockets of these primal soundscapes as if they are barriers of time itself.

Around Anderson Island, there it is. The Nisqually! The place we have pictured for five months. The land drops in a low green of shrub and grass, and at last we have run out of salt water. It is the last pristine estuary in Puget Sound, protected as a wildlife refuge. "After this, it's where we belong," I say.

After fighting a final headwind that nearly ceases our forward motion, we lunch with a group of kayakers on a tour. And once more we tell our story. Many are beginning paddlers but want to purchase kayaks, and they ask about performance and capacity and rudders. Instead, we tell them of the storm on Dixon Entrance or of the Yucultas. They are thrilled to meet us on this last day. When they ask where are we headed, we simply point.

After lunch, Maren and I follow them into the Nisqually's glacial milk, only to lose them among the grasses. The Nisqually braids into a maze of channels, and we find one that leads to the main river. Clouds race above the high blond grass, and drifting, I float into a pocket and hear the wind as clearly as I could at the Muir Glacier.

This place also holds many histories. In 1833 the Hudson's Bay Company established Fort Nisqually in the Nisqually homeland here. Soon the endeavor expanded and became the Puget Sound Agricultural Company, employing workers from the Nisqually and several neighboring tribes as well as Native Hawaiians, who arrived on Hudson's Bay vessels. For nearly three decades, farm products from the Nisqually Delta enriched ports and people from northern California to southeast Alaska.

Along the delta's western shore, under a tree that still stands, the Medicine Creek Treaty was signed in December 1854 by the tribes of southern Puget Sound. Like the Treaty of Point Elliott of the following month, it ceded Indian title to the land. This afternoon, the spongy delta is full of birdsong, a refuge, much as the place we began: Sit' Eeti Gei, the bay that belongs to where the glacier used to be.

We paddle upriver for a while, then lapse and float. Cars and campers flash past on I-5. Then powerboats. Nisqually men are fishing from a small skiff, placing gillnets from midchannel to the outside curves, where the fish will be drawn. Another skiff, working in tandem, empties a net. In it flops a huge salmon. The fisherman holds it up and smiles. We, too, are home. Slowly the kayaks spin in the current, the silty flow streaming against us, pushing us back, and when we look up, there is nowhere but north.

We paddle in the shallows toward the boat ramp, where we are to meet our ride. A small crab boat putters by, and the flotilla of kayakers we met at lunch are unloading ahead of us, a screen. Then across the water sound drums and voices and songs. Old songs. The Nisqually people are here to greet us and raise their arms. Ray must have called them from Swinomish. An ensemble of friends has gathered. Maren and I raft together, clasping hands and hoisting our paddles high. In the tradition of the canoeing nations, we ask permission to come ashore. And when it is granted, Maren smiles at me. "I think we owe some prayers," she says, and we fall silent as the beautiful singing mixes with the afternoon breezes, the blustery noons, the still nights, the rushing tides. Then, striding across the water, for a final time, we nose ashore.

The singing is loud and joyful, and the people are standing there in a wall of smiles. "We welcome all of your people to our land," says a Nisqually elder. "We have prepared a meal for you at our home and welcome you and all of your people to the celebration. We have towels and showers for you—and anything else that you might need. You have traveled a long distance, and the people of the Nisqually give you welcome to our land and to our waters."

Then we all go to the feast and dig into bowls of chicken and macaroni and salad and fruit and gulp down lemonade and soda. Then come speeches and toasts and gifts and thanksgiving. We gather for a group photograph, then slowly disband into the deepening night.

With Ted, Lisa, and Mark, the friends who drove us to the ferry on that early April morning, we speed north to Seattle, the two-lane roads growing to four, then to six, then to eight. Past Tacoma. Past Sea-Tac. The talk is fast and elated, and then strangely quiet. At our exit, Ted flips the turn signal, and we whir onto the ramp and work through the city, past two green lights, and onto a dark and familiar street.

We unload the kayaks and the heaps of blue and yellow bags into the garage. And we stare at it, then walk away. Somewhere the tide is beginning to rise. And for a moment, there is no sound. Nothing at all.

ACKNOWLEDGMENTS

There is a belief that one can be an independent traveler in the wilds. No greater misunderstanding exists. The same holds true for writing a book—a score of supporting members always stands outside the solitary chamber. More than at any period of my adult life, I have depended upon others.

Above all, I must first thank Maren Van Nostrand, my wife and paddling partner. We have found a unity among these shores that few people ever know, a home with each other. Without you, this journey, this writing, would have been vapor. By your vision, steadfastness, encouragements, toleration, strength, and sacrifices, you have shown me the true nature of a selfless love. There is no greater gift.

Ted and Lisa Steudel inspired our journey by one of their own. Without your encouragement and mentorship as we prepared and then paddled, this adventure never would have left shore. To you we owe a season of sunsets.

Our steadfast friend Lona Badget, who has traveled this coast, served as our logistics coordinator, managing our affairs, fielding phone calls, and mailing food boxes at every request. Lona also introduced me to the Bashō quotation, that is the epigraph to this book. You were our downlink to civility, a superb counselor, a true friend.

We are most grateful to longtime friends Don and Joyce Leak for opening your home, making way for loads of paddling gear and our weary selves both before and after the journey. We gained much strength and stability during those days together.

We cherish Ray, Dorraine, Carrie, Ken, Jim, Father Pat, and our many friends in the Swinomish Tribal Community for the hearty welcomes we receive with each visit. Joseph and Verna Kalama and the Nisqually people, you have gained a place in our hearts. For your drums and voices and reception at the Nisqually Delta, we thank you. And for all of the Native peoples along the coast, for opening your homelands and hearts so that we could learn of your ways, your legacies, your enduring spirit. You have taught us many lessons.

A host of friends deserve all the wildflowers we can gather: Chris Pyle and Jill Sacket cared for our two cats during our absence. Chris Keenan nurtured our forest of plants with her green thumb. We entrusted our musical instruments to the creative talents of Art and Serene Petersen. Unfailing friends Kelly Huffman, Lyn Gatz, and Joanne Grebinoski, saw that we needed to shed for this trip, and cleared their basement for our belongings. And Roger Thorson and Ann Amberg at the Carnation Tree Farm stored our cars and made a place for us once we returned from this grand adventure.

Abundant thanks go out to all of the people who had the courage to appear within these pages. Without you—your efforts, your words, your direction—this journey and this book would not have been possible.

Before we headed north, outdoor equipment companies enabled the journey with technical advice and indestructible equipment: Garcia Machine: bear canisters; Snap Dragon Designs: spray skirts and pogies; Northwest Design Works/Werner Paddles: paddles; Cascade Designs: drybags, Therm-a Rests, seat cushions; Kokatat: paddling jackets; Mountain Safety Research (MSR): water filter; Outdoor Research: stuff sacks.

Cam and Matt Broze at Mariner Kayaks spent many hours talking with us about kayak design and safety. Their sheer enthusiasm sent us headlong into ocean paddling. They know the kayak and the coast like few others. Instructors Ted and Merle at Northwest Outdoor Center honed our roll and rescue techniques and spent innumerable hours discussing equipment. We are grateful to have had the help of Dave Egan, who believed in this journey from the first.

I must uplift those who cheered us from afar—our parents: Robert and Sondra, Catharine and David; grandparents: Thelma Search, King Herr, and Margaret Herr; sisters and brothers: Heidi and Kevin, Laura and Pete, Catharine and Peggy. Many thanks to Jennifer New and Andrew Epstein, who sent us off with a grand celebration. And to Brian Milford for your many encouraging phone messages along the way.

A ball of sun to the people we met along the way, many of whom appear within the pages and some who do not. Bill Paleck, superintendent at North Cascades National Park, helped arrange initial contact with Randy King and the NPS staff of Glacier Bay. Lori, Helena, and Vic—your friendship on the ferry eased our fears and welcomed us to the north. David Job and Marinke van Gelder opened their home and hearts in Juneau. Warm thanks to Peter Wright and Kayaks Express for the lift to Glacier Bay. To Bill Brown for a marvelous talk about wilderness on the dock at Bartlett Cove, and Mike Jackson, who shared an evening of wisdom in Kake. Tom, Ben, and Stephanie filled an evening with food and song in Hoonah, and Jim Stoll shared his knowledge of the coast. In Angoon Marc and Sandra welcomed us with a lunch of hot soup and hearty conversation. Heidi Lewis opened her home in Ketchikan while we dried and rested, and Geoff Gross and company at Southeast Exposure in Ketchikan stored our kayaks during our days in town.

Chris, Seana, Rene, and Sherrill—our days at Ivory Island were profoundly beautiful.

Jody Holmes, Nick Beatty, Barb Lando, and Stephen Ziff, your friendship and insights continue to enrich us. Doug and Francie Dailer at Meadowdale County Park, you had the courage to pluck two salty people from the shores of Puget Sound and show them true hospitality. Mike Dziobak, Laura Law, and Mike Hannigan—here's to the evenings shared on those beautiful beaches.

After the journey, the adventure of writing commenced, and many joined the expedition here. U.S. Forest Service geologist Jim Baichtal read many portions of this book, making invaluable suggestions and confirmations concerning elements of natural history. John Neary provided information on Admiralty Island, and Charles Smythe, repatriation anthropologist at the Smithsonian Institute, and John Autry of the U.S. Forest Service, informed me on issues of archaeology and culture. Continuing our friendship from the ferry, Lori Trummer supplied much-needed information on Alaska geology. Darcy, Sue, Lorna, Lael, and Kate at the Carnation Library maintained my battery of research materials far beyond the call. Many thanks to Phil Barress, Richard Morhous, and Bob Zeigler for your ongoing encouragements.

I also benefited from the expertise of the staffs of the following museums: Wrangell Museum and Shakes House in Wrangell, Tongass Historical Society Museum in Ketchikan, Totem Heritage Center in Ketchikan, the Museum of Northern British Columbia in Prince Rupert, and the Burke Museum in Seattle. Any errors that remain are my own.

I uplift the many authors listed in the bibliography whose knowledgeable words and durable research have helped guide me down the literary coast and to the works of other contemporary thinkers of people and place. I have learned much from your words and am greatly indebted.

Ann Naumann provided an acute critical eye and ear at early stages of writing, and Kim Brown provided unabated encouragement throughout. I have the fortune to know Paul Frichtl, Eric Lucas, Charles Smyth, Dee Smith, Skot O'Mahony, Margaret Elson, and Carol Walter as devoted colleagues and friends. You have helped me more than you know. Todd Powell fielded many of my emotions and questions, and through your enthusiastic comments about the manuscript, you and Stacy helped sustain me through a Northwest winter.

Far before this book's beginning, Curtis Harnack, Sterling Lord, and Adrian Zackheim gave me the invaluable time, attention, and encouragement that a writer needs. During that snowy trip to New York, you enabled me to make the commitment.

And finally, I must express utmost gratitude to my agent, Jennifer Hengen, and to my editor, Hamilton Cain, who believed in this project before there was a journey to write about. You have been with me for the duration and helped me realize this dream.

NOTES

EPIGRAPH

p. vii   Matsuo Bashō, *Oku-no-hosomichi*, or *Back Roads to Far Towns*, trans. by Cid Corman and Kamaike Susumu (New York: Grossman Publishers, 1968), p. 15.

PROLOGUE

p. 3   **"From north to south along the passage":**
The cultural groups listed here are those that traditionally live along the Inside Passage, not the entire Northwest coast. The many other Northwest coastal peoples, such as the Nuu-chah-nulth on the west coast of Vancouver Island, are omitted for this reason only.

I wish to emphasize that many smaller nations compose these larger linguistic and cultural groupings, and the borders among them are only approximations and drawn most often by anthropologists. In my experience, Northwest Native peoples most often refer to their particular nation, rather than the larger linguistic group, when telling where they are from.

p. 3   **"the second most linguistically diverse area":**
Wayne Suttles, ed. *Northwest Coast*, Volume 7, *Handbook of North American Indians* (Washington D.C.: Smithsonian Institution Press, 1990), p. 30.

TO GLACIER BAY

p. 13   **"Pleasant Island, named in 1879 by W. H. Dall":**
Donald J. Orth, *Dictionary of Alaska Place Names* (Washington, D.C.: U.S. Government Printing Office, 1967).

IN GLACIER BAY

p. 18   **"Changes came rapidly to these waters.":**
Dave Bohn, *Glacier Bay: The Land and the Silence* (New York: Sierra Club/Ballantine Books, 1967), pp. 36–50, esp, pp. 48–50. Ted C. Hinckley, "The Inside Passage: A Popular Gilded Age Tour" (*Pacific Northwest Quarterly*, 56, No. 2, 1965), pp. 67–74.

p. 18   **"The Tlingit of the Tcukanadi clan":**
Nora M. Dauenhauer and Richard Dauenhauer, *Haa Shuká, Our Ancestors: Tlingit Oral Narratives* (Seattle: University of Washington Press, 1987). Susie James's rendition of the Glacier Bay story is on pp. 244–259; Amy Marvin's rendition, pp. 260–291.

p. 22   **"Not long after Muir's first visits":**
Theodore Catton, *Land Reborn: A History of Administration and Visitor Use in Glacier Bay National Park and Preserve* (Seattle: National Park Service, Government Printing Office, 1995), pp. 33–66.

p. 28   **"On nature shows":**
For a thorough dissection and commentary on how televised nature affects our perception of nature and natural events, see: Charles Siebert, "The Artifice of the Natural—How TV's nature shows make all the earth a stage" (*Harper's*, February 1993), pp. 43–51.

IN HOONAH

p. 58   **"bubble feeding":**
Bubble feeding, more accurately known as bubble-net feeding, gets its name from the shield or "net" of bubbles that humpback whales blow to congregate their prey. With their prey "trapped" and confused within this vortex of bubbles, the whales pursue the center of the bubble net, gulping prey and finally exploding through the surface. Dr. Charles Jurasz of Juneau first described this feeding habit.

p. 59   **"Glacier Bay National Park" and "monument":**
Glacier Bay was first preserved as Glacier Bay National Monument in 1925. In 1939 its area was increased to protect brown bear habitat. The current name, Glacier Bay National Park and Preserve, was given in 1980 to recognize another land acquisition and its new designations.

p. 59   **"Huna people":**
This spelling of "Huna" refers to the Tlingit people centered around Icy Strait and Glacier Bay, people of the Xunaa Ḵwáan, and is different than "Hoonah people," which refers to those who merely live in the town of Hoonah.

HOONAH TO TENAKEE SPRINGS

p. 68   **"killer whales carving a channel":**
Kenny Grant shared this information.

p. 68   **"Sit-a-da-kay or Ice Bay":**

John Muir, *Travels in Alaska* (Boston and New York: Houghton Mifflin Company, 1915), p. 143.

CROSSING CHATHAM STRAIT

p. 78   **"In Tlingit country":**
Katherine L. Arndt, Russell H. Sackett, and James A. Ketz, *A Cultural Resource Overview of the Tongass National Forest, Alaska. Part 1: Overview* (Fairbanks: GDM, 1987), pp. 90–91.

p. 80   **"The Chatham Strait fault":**
Cathy Connor and Daniel O'Haire, *Roadside Geology of Alaska* (Missoula, Mont.: Mountain Press Publishing, 1988), pp. 47–49.

IN ANGOON

p. 85   **"Killer Whale House . . . traditional chief's title is Guctahín . . . dorsal fin":**
Frederica De Laguna, *The Story of a Tlingit Community: A Problem in the Relationship between Archaeological, Ethnological, and Historical Methods* (Washington, D.C.: Bureau of American Ethnology, Bulletin 172, 1960), p. 189.

ANGOON TO TYEE

p. 88   **"Seaweeds, mussels, and clams were gathered":**
Ibid, pp. 28–31. This work is a definitive source for Tlingit culture in the Angoon area.
Frederica De Laguna, ed. *The Tlingit Indians*, by George T. Emmons (Seattle: University of Washington Press, 1990), pp. 140–158.
Philip Drucker, *Indians of the Northwest Coast* (Garden City, N.Y.: The Natural History Press, Garden City, 1963), pp. 9–45.

p. 88   **"on October 22, 1882":**
Frederica De Laguna, *The Story of a Tlingit Community: A Problem in the Relationship between Archaeological, Ethnological, and Historical Methods* (Washington, D.C.: Bureau of American Ethnology, Bulletin 172, 1960), pp. 158–176. A superb delineation of precursers to the Angoon destruction; includes several versions of the story from both sides.

p. 90   **"But the great ice":**
My understanding of the complexities of coastal geology, glaciers, and the peopling of the coast has come from many sources. Most helpful were:
Jim Baichtal, Greg Streveler, Terence Fifield, "The Geologic, Glacial, and Cultural History of Southern Southeast," *Alaska Geographic*, **24,** No. 1, pp. 6–31, 1997.
E. James Dixon, *Quest for the Origins of the First Americans* (Albuquerque: University of New Mexico Press, 1993).
Greg Streveler, Richard Carstensen, and Gretchen Bishop, *A Naturalist's Look at Southeast Alaska* (Juneau: The Alaska Discovery Foundation, 1993). This book provides an accessible overview of geologic and environmental processes.
Katherine L. Arndt, Russell H. Sackett, and James A. Ketz, *A Cultural Resource Overview of the Tongass National Forest, Alaska. Part 1: Overview* (Fairbanks: GDM, 1987), pp. 81–84.
For lucid descriptions of southeast Alaska's tangled and complex geology, I often consulted Cathy Connor and Daniel O'Haire's *Roadside Geology of Alaska* (Missoula, Mont.: Mountain Press Publishing, 1988), pp. 1–19.

p. 91   **"coming from the interior":**
As the above sources, these speak particularly to the peopling of the coast.
Frederica De Laguna, ed. *The Tlingit Indians,* by George T. Emmons (Seattle: University of Washington Press, 1990), pp. 8–10, 25–27.
Wayne Suttles, ed. *Northwest Coast,* Volume 7, *Handbook of North American Indians* (Washington D.C.: Smithsonian Institution Press, 1990), pp. 205–206.
Robert A. Henning, Marty Loken, and Barbara Olds, eds. "The Stikine River," *Alaska Geographic*, **6,** No. 4, p. 79, 1979.

Frederica De Laguna, *The Story of a Tlingit Community: A Problem in the Relationship Between Archaeological, Ethnological, and Historical Methods* (Washington, D.C.: Bureau of American Ethnology, Bulletin 172, 1960), pp. 130–132.

p. 92   **Stories of The Flood:**
Ibid, pp. 130—131.

p. 92   **"some finds are turning up":**
Timothy H. Heaton, Sandra L. Talbot, and Gerald F. Shields, "An Ice Age Refugium for Large Mammals in the Alexander Archipelago, Southeastern Alaska," *Quaternary Research*, 1996, **46,** pp. 186–192.

CROSSING FREDERICK SOUND

p. 96   **"They spoke of it repeatedly":**
John Muir, *Travels in Alaska* (Boston and New York: Houghton Mifflin Company, 1915), p. 128.

p. 96   **"Its vastness divides":**
Katherine L. Arndt, Russell H. Sackett, and James A. Ketz, *A Cultural Resource Overview of the Tongass National Forest, Alaska. Part 1: Overview* (Fairbanks: GDM, 1987), p. 91.

KAKE TO WRANGELL

p. 122   **"The Tlingit know the Stikine as 'the great river' ":**
Robert A. Henning, Marty Loken, and Barbara Olds, eds. "The Stikine River." *Alaska Geographic*, **6,** No. 4, 1979.

IN WRANGELL

p. 128   **"Wrangell-to-Glacier Bay canoe route":**
For a map of Muir and Young's canoe routes, see Samuel Hall

Young, *Alaska Days with John Muir* (New York: F. H. Revell, 1915).

WRANGELL TO MEYERS CHUCK

p. 133 **"same pole John Muir sketched":**
Edward L. Keithahn, *Monuments in Cedar: The Authentic Story of the Totem Pole* (Seattle: Superior Publishing, 1963), p. 38.

p. 137 **"With such a high metabolic rate":**
Rita O'Clair, Robert H. Armstrong, and Richard Carstensen, *The Nature of Southeast Alaska: A Guide to Plants, Animals, and Habitats* (Bothell, Washington: Alaska Northwest Books, 1992), pp. 129–130.

IN MEYERS CHUCK

p. 142 **"I saw the moon spinning swiftly through her quarters":**
H. G. Wells, "The Time Machine" in *The War of the Worlds, The Time Machine, and Selected Short Stories.* (New York: The Platt and Munk Co., 1963), p. 270.

KETCHIKAN TO PORTLAND INLET

p. 152 **"In the 1930s the original poles":**
Viola E. Garfield and Linn A. Forrest, *The Wolf and the Raven* (Seattle: University of Washington Press, 1948), p. 8.

p. 152 **"the great poles were little known in earlier times":**
Much is written about totem poles, and these sources were most helpful in understanding its tradition, artistry, and context:
Edward L. Keithahn, *Monuments in Cedar: The Authentic Story of the Totem Pole* (Seattle: Superior Publishing, 1963), Chapter 3: "The Antiquity of the Totem Pole," pp. 35–49, especially pp. 43–45.

Viola E. Garfield and Linn A. Forrest, *The Wolf and the Raven* (Seattle: University of Washington Press, 1948), introduction, pp. 1–12.

Wayne Suttles, ed. *Northwest Coast.* Volume 7, *Handbook of North American Indians* (Washington D.C.: Smithsonian Institution Press, 1990), p. 132.

p. 153 **"Native lore and wisdom":**
Tony Angell, *Ravens, Crows, Magpies, and Jays* (Seattle: University of Washington Press, 1978).

p. 167 **"whose predecessor was taken from this beach":**
The definitive source for this event is Viola E. Garfield, *The Seattle Totem Pole* (Seattle and London: University of Washington Press, 1980).

Also, Edward L. Keithahn, *Monuments in Cedar: The Authentic Story of the Totem Pole* (Seattle: Superior Publishing, 1963), p. 40.

CROSSING PORTLAND INLET

p. 173 **"Pleistocene glaciers could have played a role":**
Richard A. Rogers, Larry D. Martin, and T. Dale Nicklas, "Ice-Age Geography and the Distribution of Native North American Languages" (*Journal of Biogeography*, **17**, 1990), pp. 131–143.

p. 173 **"there are five major linguistic families":**
Wayne Suttles, ed. *Northwest Coast*, Volume 7, *Handbook of North American Indians* (Washington, D.C.: Smithsonian Institution Press, 1990), pp 30–51.

p. 173 **"their original homeland":**
See sources from "But the great ice," and "coming from the interior," in the chapter "Angoon to Point Gardner."

PORTLAND INLET TO PRINCE RUPERT

p. 177 **"In 1857 William Duncan":**
Philip Drucker, *Indians of the Northwest Coast.* (Garden City,

N.Y.: The Natural History Press, 1963), pp. 199–204.
Wayne Suttles, ed. *Northwest Coast*, Volume 7, *Handbook of North American Indians* (Washington, D.C.: Smithsonian Institution Press, 1990), pp. 294–295.

PORCHER ISLAND TO CAMPANIA ISLAND

p. 194 **"red tide":**
Red tide is a phenomenon caused by microscopic alga, a dinoflagellate. When these organisms, which produce a toxin, multiply rapidly, or "bloom," they often turn the water a reddish hue. Paralytic shellfish poisoning (PSP) is a potentially lethal affliction which can affect people who consume clams, mussels, and fish contaminated by red tide.

LAREDO CHANNEL TO IVORY ISLAND

p. 207 **"a map that shows the original extent of old-growth forest":**
The Rain Forests of Home: An Atlas of People and Place. Part 1: Natural Forests and Native Languages of the Coastal Temperate Rain Forest (Portland, Oregon: Ecotrust, Pacific GIS, and Conservation International, 1995).
The Sierra Club of British Columbia has produced a similar map, *Canada's Rainforest—Worth Saving* (1997), which shows with great detail the forest status of the British Columbia Coast.

IVORY ISLAND TO BELLA BELLA

p. 223 **"many Northwest tribes have landed here after canoeing the old paddle route":**
For a beautifully documented account of the canoe resurgence among the Northwest coastal tribes, see:

David Neel, *The Great Canoes: Reviving a Northwest Coast Tradition*, afterword by Tom Heidlebaugh. (Vancover: Douglas & McIntyre, 1995).

p. 231 **"Kaiete is a hereditary chief's name":**
Frank Brown shared this information.

CROSSING FISHER CHANNEL

p. 236 **"an exhausted Alexander Mackenzie":**
Barry Gough, *First Across the Continent: Sir Alexander Mackenzie*. (Norman, Okla.: University of Oklahoma Press, 1997), pp. 148–149.

PORT HARDY TO ALDER BAY

p. 266 **"anthropologist Franz Boas":**
Wayne Suttles, ed. *Northwest Coast*, Volume 7, *Handbook of North American Indians* (Washington, D.C.: Smithsonian Institution Press, 1990), pp. 75–76, p. 79.

p. 266 **"In the Land of the War Canoes":**
Edward S. Curtis, *In the Land of the War Canoes*. (New York: Milestone Film and Video, 1992). *In the Land of the War Canoes* is a video recording made from the only surviving print of Curtis's original 1914 film, *In the Land of the Head-Hunters*, which was restored in 1972 by the University of Washington with a score of music and chants recorded by the Kwakiutl. Today, the work is most widely known as *In the Land of the War Canoes*.

p. 266 **"it was George Hunt's mother who commissioned a large totem pole":**
Bill Holm and George Irving Quimby, *Edward S. Curtis in the Land of the War Canoes: A Pioneer Cinematographer in the Pacific Northwest* (Seattle: University of Washington Press, 1980), p. 40.

p. 270 **"the potlatch collection":**
Douglas Cole, *Captured Heritage: The Scramble for Northwest*

Coast Artifacts. (Seattle: University of Washington Press, 1985), pp. 249–254.

ALDER BAY TO REFUGE COVE

p. 279 **"legacy of orca research in Johnstone Strait":**
John K. B. Ford, Graeme M. Ellis, Kenneth C. Balcomb, *Killer Whales: The Natural History and Geneaology of Orcinus orca in British Columbia and Washington State* (Vancouver: UBC Press, 1994).

p. 290 **"a scene replayed from July 20, 1792":**
Extract of the diaries of Galiano and Valdés, from the voyage of the *Sutil* and the *Mexicana* in Henry R. Wagner's *Spanish Explorations in the Strait of Juan de Fuca* (Santa Ana, Calif.: Fine Arts Press, 1933), p. 219.

NANAIMO TO STUART ISLAND

p. 318 **"Scotch broom":**
Jim Pojar and Andy MacKinnon, eds, *Plants of the Pacific Northwest Coast, Washington, Oregon, British Columbia & Alaska* (Vancouver: Lone Pine, 1994), p. 83.

p. 318 **"I must first step into time":**
For more thinking on wilderness management and cultural ideas concerning preservation, see:
Dan Flores, "Making the West Whole Again: A Historical Perspective on Restoration" in *Reclaiming the Native Home of Hope: Community, Ecology and the American West*, Robert B. Keiter, ed. (Salt Lake City: The University of Utah Press, 1998), pp. 58–68.
Daniel Botkin, *Discordant Harmonies: A New Ecology for the 21st Century* (New York: Oxford University Press, 1990).

STUART ISLAND TO SWINOMISH

p. 329 **"thesis about the Swinomish Tribal Community":**
Maren Van Nostrand, *Planning for Cultural Continuity: Community Participation, Applied Anthropology, and Resource Management in the Swinomish Tribal Community* (Seattle: University of Washington Graduate School, 1993).

SWINOMISH TO SEATTLE

p. 335 **"In an earlier speech":**
For a thorough delineation on the three versions of Chief Seattle's Speech, see Rudolf Kaiser's "Chief Seattle's Speech(es): American Origins and European Reception" in *Recovering the Word: Essays on Native American Literature*, Brian Swann and Arnold Krupat, eds. (Berkeley: University of California Press, 1987), pp. 497–536.

Many scholars and authors whose works are listed in the bibliography have devoted their lives and talents to the exploration and study of the Northwest coast and its people. Their work has given insight to many portions of our journey and to the writing of this book. I am most thankful to have encountered their words and wisdoms.

Angell, Tony. *Ravens, Crows, Magpies, and Jays.* (Seattle: University of Washington Press, 1989).

Arndt, Katherine L., Russell H. Sackett, and James A. Ketz. *A Cultural Resource Overview of the Tongass National Forest, Alaska, Part 1: Overview.* (Fairbanks: GDM, 1987).

Baichtal, Jim, Greg Streveler, Terence Fifield. "The Geologic, Glacial, and Cultural History of Southern Southeast." *Alaska Geographic,* **24,** No. 1, 6–31.

Bashō, Matsuo. *Oku-no-hosomichi,* or *Back Roads to Far Towns,* trans. by Cid Corman and Kamaike Susumu. (New York: Grossman Publishers, 1968).

Berry, Wendell. *The Unsettling of America: Culture and Agriculture.* Second edition. (San Francisco: Sierra Club Books, 1986).

Berton, Pierre. "The Strange Case of The Brother XII," in *My Country*. (Toronto: McClelland and Stewart, 1976).

Bohn, Dave. *Glacier Bay: The Land and the Silence*. (New York: Sierra Club/Ballantine Books, 1967).

Botkin, Daniel. *Discordant Harmonies: A New Ecology for the 21st Century* (New York: Oxford University Press, 1990).

Catton, Theodore. *Land Reborn: A History of Administration and Visitor Use in Glacier Bay National Park and Preserve*. (Anchorage: National Park Service, 1995).

Cole, Douglas. *Captured Heritage: The Scramble for Northwest Coast Artifacts*. (Seattle: University of Washington Press, 1985).

Connor, Cathy, and Daniel O'Haire. *Roadside Geology of Alaska*. (Missoula, Mont.: Mountain Press Publishing, 1988).

Cronon, William, ed. *Uncommon Ground: Toward Reinventing Nature*. (New York: W. W. Norton, 1995).

Curtis, Edward S. *In the Land of the War Canoes*. (New York: Milestone Film and Video, 1992).

Dauenhauer, Nora M., and Richard Dauenhauer. *Haa Shuká, Our Ancestors: Tlingit Oral Narratives*. (Seattle: University of Washington Press, 1987).

Dauenhauer, Nora M., and Richard Dauenhauer, eds. *Haa Kusteeyí, Our Culture: Tlingit Life Stories*. (Seattle: University of Washington Press, Juneau: Sealaska Heritage Foundation, 1994).

De Laguna, Frederica. *The Story of a Tlingit Community: A Problem in the Relationship Between Archaeological, Ethnological, and Historical Methods*. (Washington, D.C.: Bureau of American Ethnology, Bulletin 172, 1960).

Dixon, E. James, *Quest for the Origins of the First Americans*. (Albuquerque: University of New Mexico Press, 1993).

Dowd, John. *Sea Kayaking: A Manual for Long-distance Touring*. (Vancouver: Douglas & McIntyre, Seattle: University of Washington Press, 1988).

Drucker, Philip. *Indians of the Northwest Coast*, (Garden City, N.Y.: The Natural History Press, 1963).

DuFresne, Jim. *Glacier Bay National Park: A Backcountry*

Guide to the Glaciers and Beyond. (Seattle: The Mountaineers, 1987).

Emmons, George T. *The Tlingit Indians,* Frederica De Laguna, ed. (Seattle: University of Washington Press, 1990).

Flores, Dan. "Making the West Whole Again: A Historical Perspective on Restoration" in *Reclaiming the Native Home of Hope: Community, Ecology and the American West,* Robert B. Keiter, ed. (Salt Lake City: The University of Utah Press, 1998).

Ford, John K. B., Graeme M. Ellis, and Kenneth C. Balcomb. *Killer Whales: The Natural History and Geneaology of Orcinus orca in British Columbia and Washington State.* (Vancouver: UBC Press, 1994).

Garfield, Viola E., and Linn A. Forrest. *The Wolf and the Raven,* (Seattle: University of Washington Press, 1948).

Garfield, Viola E. *The Seattle Totem Pole.* (Seattle: University of Washington Press, 1980).

Gehrels, George E., and Henry C. Berg. *Geologic Map of Southeastern Alaska.* (Denver: U.S. Geological Survey, 1992).

Gough, Barry. *First Across the Continent: Sir Alexander Mackenzie.* (Norman, Okla.: University of Oklahoma Press, 1997).

Heaton, Timothy H., Sandra L. Talbot, and Gerald F. Shields. "An Ice Age Refugium for Large Mammals in the Alexander Archipelago, Southeastern Alaska." *Quaternary Research,* **46,** 186–192, 1996.

Henning, Robert A., Marty Loken, and Barbara Olds, eds. "The Stikine River." *Alaska Geographic.* **6,** No. 4, 1979.

Hinckley, Ted C. "The Inside Passage: A Popular Gilded Age Tour." *Pacific Northwest Quarterly,* **56,** No. 2, 67–74, 1965.

Holm, Bill, and George Irving Quimby. *Edward S. Curtis in the Land of the War Canoes: A Pioneer Cinematographer in the Pacific Northwest.* (Seattle: University of Washington Press, 1980).

Kaiser, Rudolf. "Chief Seattle's Speech(es): American Origins and European Reception," in *Recovering the Word: Essays on Native American Literature.* Brian Swann and Arnold Krupat, eds. (Berkeley: University of California Press, 1987.)

Keithahn, Edward L. *Monuments in Cedar: The Authentic Story of the Totem Pole.* (Seattle: Superior Publishing, 1963).

Krause, Aurel. *The Tlingit Indians: Results of a Trip to the Northwest Coast of America and the Bering Straits.* Translated by Erna Gunther. (Seattle: University of Washington Press, 1956).

Kruckeberg, Arthur R. *The Natural History of Puget Sound Country.* (Seattle: University of Washington Press, 1991).

Kurtz, Rick S. *Glacier Bay National Park and Preserve Historic Resources Study.* (Seattle: Government Printing Office, 1995).

Mander, Jerry. *In the Absence of the Sacred.* (San Francisco: Sierra Club Books, 1991).

Muir, John. *Travels in Alaska.* (Boston: Houghton Mifflin, 1915).

Muller, J. E., and J. A. Jeletsky. *Geology of the Upper Cretaceous Nanaimo Group, Vancouver Island and the Gulf Islands.* (Ottawa: Department of Energy, Mining, and Resources, 1970).

Nash, Roderick. *Wilderness and the American Mind.* (New Haven: Yale Univesity Press, 1982).

Neel, David. *The Great Canoes: Reviving a Northwest Coast Tradition.* Afterword by Tom Heidlebaugh. (Vancouver: Douglas & McIntyre, 1995).

O'Clair, Rita, Robert H. Armstrong, and Richard Carstensen. *The Nature of Southeast Alaska: A Guide to Plants, Animals, and Habitats.* (Bothell, Washington: Alaska Northwest Books, 1992).

Orth, Donald J. *Dictionary of Alaska Place Names.* (Washington, D.C.: U.S. Government Printing Office, 1967).

Pojar, Jim, and Andy MacKinnon, eds. *Plants of the Pacific Northwest Coast, Washington, Oregon, British Columbia & Alaska.* (Vancouver: Lone Pine, 1994).

Rain Forests of Home: An Atlas of People and Place. Part 1: Natural Forests and Native Languages of the Coastal Temperate Rain Forest. (Portland, Oregon: Ecotrust, Pacific GIS, and Conservation International, 1995).

Rogers, Richard A., Larry D. Martin, and T. Dale Nicklas.

"Ice-Age Geography and the Distrubtion of Native North American Languages." *Journal of Biogeography*, **17**, 131–143, 1990.

Siebert, Charles. "The Artifice of the Natural—How TV's nature shows make all the earth a stage." *Harper's*, February 1993, pp. 43–51.

Smythe, Charles W. *A Study of Five Southeast Alaska Communities, Appendix A: History of Occupation and Use.* (Anchorage: Institute of Social and Economic Research, University of Alaska Anchorage, 1994).

Snowden, Mary Ann. *Island Paddling—A Paddler's Guide to the Gulf Islands & Barkley Sound.* (Victoria, B.C.: Orca Book Publishers, 1990).

Stewart, Hilary. *Looking at Indian Art of the Northwest Coast.* (Seattle: University of Washington Press, 1979).

Stewart, Hilary. *Cedar* (Vancouver: Douglas & McIntyre, 1984).

Streveler, Greg, Richard Carstensen, and Gretchen Bishop. *A Naturalist's Look at Southeast Alaska.* (Juneau: The Alaska Discovery Foundation, 1993).

Suttles, Wayne. *Coast Salish Essays.* (Seattle: University of Washington Press, Vancouver: Talonbooks, 1987).

Suttles, Wayne, ed. 1990. *Northwest Coast.* Volume 7, *Handbook of North American Indians.* (Washington, D.C.: Smithsonian Institution Press, 1990).

Upton, Joe. *The Coastal Companion, A Guide for the Alaska-Bound Traveler.* (Seattle: Coastal Publishing, 1995).

Van Nostrand, Maren, *Planning for Cultural Continuity: Community Participation, Applied Anthropology, and Resource Management in the Swinomish Tribal Community.* (Seattle: University of Washington Graduate School, 1993).

Vancouver, George. *A Voyage of Discovery to the North Pacific Ocean and Round the World 1791–1795,* W. Kaye Lamb, ed. (London: Hakluyt Society, 1984).

Wagner, Henry R. *Spanish Explorations in the Strait of Juan de Fuca.* (Santa Ana, Calif.: Fine Arts Press, 1933).

Walbran, Captain John T. *British Columbia Coast Names*

1592–1906, Their Origin and History. Ottawa: Government Printing Bureau, 1909).

Washburne, Randel. *The Coastal Kayaker's Manual: A Complete Guide to Skills, Gear, and Sea Sense.* (Old Saybrook, Conn.: Globe Pequot Press, 1993).

Washburn, Wilcomb E., ed. *History of Indian-White Relations.* Volume 4, *Handbook of North American Indians.* (Washington, D.C.: Smithsonian Institution Press, 1988).

Wells, H. G. "The Time Machine" in *The War of the Worlds, The Time Machine, and Selected Short Stories.* (New York: The Platt and Munk Co., 1963).

White, Richard. *It's Your Misfortune and None of My Own: A New History of the American West.* (Norman, Okla.: University of Oklahoma Press, 1991).

Wyatt, Victoria. *Images from the Inside Passage: An Alaskan Portrait by Winter & Pond.* (Seattle: University of Washington Press, 1989).

Young, Samuel Hall. *Alaska Days with John Muir.* (New York: F. H. Revell Company, 1915).